AUTISTIC PHENOMENA
AND UNREPRESENTED STATES

AUTISTIC PHENOMENA AND UNREPRESENTED STATES
Explorations in the Emergence of Self

Edited by

Howard B. Levine and Jani Santamaría

First published in 2023 by
Phoenix Publishing House Ltd
62 Bucknell Road
Bicester
Oxfordshire OX26 2DS

Copyright © 2023 to Howard B. Levine and Jani Santamaría for the edited collection, and to the individual authors for their contributions.

The rights of the contributors to be identified as the authors of this work have been asserted in accordance with §§ 77 and 78 of the Copyright Design and Patents Act 1988.

All rights reserved. No part of this publication may be reproduced, stored in a retrieval system, or transmitted, in any form or by any means, electronic, mechanical, photocopying, recording, or otherwise, without the prior written permission of the publisher.

British Library Cataloguing in Publication Data

A C.I.P. for this book is available from the British Library

ISBN-13: 978-1-80013-126-2

Typeset by Medlar Publishing Solutions Pvt Ltd, India

www.firingthemind.com

This book marks the first English language publication to originate from the seminars sponsored by the newly created Antonio Santamaría Foundation in Mexico City, Mexico. Antonio Santamaría Fernández was a passionate and devoted pioneer and leader of psychoanalysis and psychoanalytic education in Mexico and Latin America. It is in his memory and spirit that we dedicate this volume.

Jani Santamaría and Howard B. Levine

Contents

About the editors and contributors   ix

Foreword   xiii
Jani Santamaría

CHAPTER ONE
Making the unthinkable thinkable: vitalisation, reclamation,
containment, and representation   1
Howard B. Levine (USA)

CHAPTER TWO
Finding the wavelength: tools in communication
with children with autism   21
Anne Alvarez (UK)

CHAPTER THREE
"Making a person": clinical considerations regarding the
interpretation of anxieties in the analyses of children
on the autisto-psychotic spectrum   39
Joshua Durban (Israel)

CHAPTER FOUR
The birth of emotional experience under the sea: a clinical case   67
Jani Santamaría (Mexico)

CHAPTER FIVE
The third topography: a topography of the bond,
a perinatal topography   89
Sylvain Missonnier and Bernard Golse (France)

CHAPTER SIX
Infantile autism: a pathology of otherness   115
Didier Houzel (France)

CHAPTER SEVEN
Multi two-dimensional: on autistic thinking   129
Marganit Ofer (Israel)

CHAPTER EIGHT
From screaming to dreaming: notes on anxiety
and its transformation   151
Jeffrey L. Eaton (USA)

CHAPTER NINE
A "felt-self": aspects of symbolising through psychotherapy   167
Jeffrey L. Eaton (USA)

CHAPTER TEN
The mute voice: autistic enclaves and transgenerational
transmission   189
Suzanne Maiello (Italy)

CHAPTER ELEVEN
From nothing to being? Technical considerations
for dealing with unrepresented states   219
Bernd Nissen (Germany)

Index   235

About the editors and contributors

Anne Alvarez is a consultant child and adolescent psychotherapist, retired co-convener of the Autism Service, Tavistock Clinic, London, and a leading author and innovator in the treatment of autistic and developmentally disturbed children. She is the author of *Live Company: Psychotherapy with Autistic, Borderline, Deprived and Abused Children* (Routledge) and *The Thinking Heart: Three Levels of Psychoanalytic Therapy with Disturbed Children* (Routledge), and co-editor, along with Susan Reid, of *Autism and Personality: Findings from the Tavistock Autism Workshop* (Routledge). In 2002, her work was celebrated and extended in the book, *Being Alive: Building on the Work of Anne Alvarez* (Routledge) edited by Judith Edwards.

Joshua Durban is a training and supervising child and adult psychoanalyst at the Israeli Psychoanalytic Society and Institute, Jerusalem and Tel Aviv (IPA) where he also teaches. He is on the faculty of the Sackler School of Medicine, Tel-Aviv University, The Psychotherapy Program, Post-Graduate Kleinian Studies. He is a member of the IPA inter-committee for the prevention of child abuse. He has a private practice in Tel-Aviv and specialises in the psychoanalysis of ASD and psychotic children, adolescents, and adults.

Jeffrey L. Eaton is a graduate and faculty member of the Northwestern Psychoanalytic Society and Institute in Seattle, WA. He is author of *A Fruitful Harvest: Essays after Bion* and several chapters in edited collections devoted to the understanding and treatment of autism and primitive mental states. He was awarded the tenth Frances Tustin Memorial Lecture Prize in 2006.

Bernard Golse is a paediatrician, child psychiatrist and psychoanalyst (Member of the French Psychoanalytical Association), and Professor Emeritus of Child and Adolescent Psychiatry at the University of Paris. In 1994, along with Serge Lebovici, he founded the French-speaking group of studies and researches in the field of infant mental health, a group officially affiliated to the WAIMH (World Association Infant Mental Health). He is President of the Pikler Lóczy-France Association since 2007 and a founding member and President since 2014 of the European Association of Child and Adolescent Psychopathology (AEPEA). In 2021, he founded and became Scientific Director of the Institut Contemporain de l'Enfance dedicated to teaching, training, and research in the field of childhood. In 2016, he received the Serge Lebovici Award from the WAIMH.

Didier Houzel is Honorary Professor of Child and Adolescent Psychiatry at the University of Caen (France). He is a Full Member of the French Psychoanalytic Association and chief editor of the *Journal de la psychanalyse de l'enfant*. His work is primarily concerned with child psychoanalysis and more specifically the analysis of children with autism and psychosis. In 2002, he was awarded the Frances Tustin Memorial Prize.

Howard B. Levine, is a member of APSA, PINE, the Contemporary Freudian Society, on the faculty of NYU Post-Doc's Contemporary Freudian Track, on the editorial board of the *IJP* and *Psychoanalytic Inquiry*, editor-in-chief of the Routledge Wilfred Bion Studies Book Series, and in private practice in Brookline, Massachusetts. He is the author of *Transformations de l'Irreprésentable* (Ithaque, 2019) and

Affect, Representation and Language: Between the Silence and the Cry (Routledge, 2022), and editor of *The Post-Bionian Field Theory of Antonino Ferro* (Routledge, 2022). His co-edited books include *Unrepresented States and the Construction of Meaning* (Karnac, 2013); *On Freud's Screen Memories* (Karnac, 2014); *The Wilfred Bion Tradition* (Karnac, 2016); *Bion in Brazil.* (Karnac, 2017); *André Green Revisited: Representation and the Work of the Negative* (Karnac, 2018), and *Covidian Life* (2021, Phoenix).

Suzanne Maiello is a member of IAAP and ACP, founder member and past President of AIPPI (Italian Association of Psychoanalytic Child Psychotherapy), teacher and supervisor of the AIPPI Tavistock model postgraduate training programme, faculty member of the MA programme in Psychoanalytic Observational Studies, University of Essex, and member of the International Symposium on Psychoanalytical Research on Autism (INSPIRA). She lectures and supervises in Europe and worldwide and is the author of over a hundred publications in psychoanalytic journals as well as co-author of books on prenatal proto-mental development, primitive mental states, early trauma, breakdown of psychic development, and autistic states. She writes in Italian, English, French, and German. She was the recipient of the first edition of the Frances Tustin Memorial Prize.

Sylvain Missonnier is Professor of Clinical Psychology of Perinatality at the University of Paris. Psychoanalyst of the Psychoanalytical Society of Paris (IPA). President of the Virtual Seine West Institute (IVSO). Director of the collection "The Life of the Child" at Eres edition and "Living Psychoanalysis" at In Press Edition. Website : www.rap5.org.

Bernd Nissen is a psychoanalyst in private practice in Berlin, and a member, and training and supervising analyst, of the DPV/IPV. He has published many articles in various journals in several different languages with a particular interest in and emphasis upon hypochondriacal and autistoid disorders and unrepresented states, and their implications for psychoanalytic theory and technique. He has edited and co-edited several books and is co-editor of the German *Jahrbuch der Psychoanalyse* (Yearbook of Psychoanalysis).

Marganit Ofer is a training and supervising child and adult psychoanalyst at the Israeli Psychoanalytic Society and Institute (IPA), where she also teaches. She chaired the child training track and now co-chairs (with Joshua Durban) the three-year programme for early developmental pathologies. She works in private practice in Givatayim and specialises in the analyses of autistic and psychotic infants, children, adolescents, and adults.

Jani Santamaría is a training analyst and supervisor of children and adolescents at the Mexican Psychoanalytic Association (APM); Latin American Board Member of the International Psychoanalytical Association (IPA) 2019–2021, 2021–2023; Director of the A. Santamaría Psicoanálisis México A. C. Educational Association; Chair of the International Bion Conference Mexico City, 2022; Chair of the Latin-American Winnicott Congress, Mexico City, 2017; Former director of community and culture for FEPAL (2016–2018); and a Member of the International Advisory Committee: Routledge Bion Studies Book Series. Member of the International Committee of Spanish Language Psychoanalysts. She has a private practice in child and adult psychoanalysis in Mexico City and has authored many national and international articles, book chapters, and reviews.

FOREWORD

Antonio Santamaría and the foundation in his name

Jani Santamaría

6 July 2013 was the date history chose for Antonio Santamaría Fernández to pay tribute to Mother Earth by returning to it at the age of eighty-three. On that day, he handed over his sacred heart and set out on his journey to the underworld.[1] His vitality was not at all affected by his disease—cancer. He faced agony and cancer with the integrity and strength that had always characterised him. Death was certainly not part of his plans.

It is difficult to summarise in a few pages the rich life of an outstanding analyst like my father. I will certainly not be able to encompass all that he is and was, but I will do my best to talk about his personal and professional life.

---

[1] In the sacred book *Popol Vuh* of the Mayan culture, it is written that life is endless. Death was not a final destination. Man had a sacred heart made up of soul components that travelled through the spaces of the cosmos. At the time of death, some of these soul components would be destroyed with the body, some returned on All Souls' Day, and others travelled to the underworld together with the physical body, where they were cleansed of all transgression and personal history, and were reinserted in a different element or individual to begin a new life. Ximénez, F. (S. XVIII). *Popol Vuh*, translation from Quiché to Spanish. Mexico.

He was born on 17 January 1930. He lost his mother when he was six and his father died six months later. This double tragedy repeated itself several decades later when in 1996 my older brother, the first-born, died in an aeroplane accident, followed by my mother one month later—her heart could not bear the loss and shattered. Life sometimes insists on defeating us with one punch after another, but my father's spirit, tempered by the heat of the crucible of psychoanalysis, was forged to assimilate and elaborate these tragedies.

He was born in Ciudad Altamirano, in the state of Guerrero. We are told that at five he could already read Latin; he read everything he could get his hands on at that age. He was the eldest of three children—and only boy. One of his sisters was three years younger than him and the other five years younger. They lived with their cousins and their paternal grandmother who became their guardian after the passing of their parents. The town priests wanted to adopt him but the family did not allow it. His paternal family owned a lot of land there and that enriched his life, along with the historical Mexican figures who visited his grandmother's house frequently. He conquered them with the extensive knowledge that he was accumulating. This intellectual curiosity and intense yearning to learn led to him being sent to another city to live with a paternal aunt who was a teacher for the entire region where he grew up—to study primary, middle, and high school in a boarding school. Reading (culture) was vital for him; as Sor Juana Inés de la Cruz would say, "I do not study to write, even less to teach … but just to see if by studying I ignore less."[2]

He shone, both with intelligence and erudition, at such a young age, and he conquered the town mayor after reciting several poems he had learned by heart when he was only eleven. The gift of a photographic memory and intellectual precociousness opened doors and windows to scholarships, awards, prizes. It was the beginning of a prolific academic career which brought him to Mexico City to study medicine, graduating from the National Autonomous University of Mexico (UNAM). After that he showed qualities of a lively university student and walked a path of ethics that became a standard of life. His residency was in psychiatry

---

[2] Santamaría, A. (1981). El Sueño Primero Sueño de Sor Juana Inés de la Cruz. In: *Cuadernos de Psicoanálisis, XIV* (1-2-3-4): 230–248. Mexico: APM.

at the Military Hospital. He met Erich Fromm there, who was about to move to Cuernavaca, in the state of Morelos. Fromm offered to analyse my father, but my father declined and they became good friends. He was analyzed by Ramón Parres, one of the pioneers of the Mexican Psychoanalytic Association—also Frida Kahlo's analyst. Dr Parres studied psychoanalysis in New York and was analysed by Sandor Rado.

These intellectual qualities were enhanced with other values like the love for his family. He married my mother, who also studied medicine, and had five children with whom he shared projects, trips, and congresses. He also had many friends, enjoyed practising sport, art, music, and tequila. The philosophy of sustaining life with love and work was deeply rooted in him.

We grew up in an atmosphere of *hope in change* that my father conveyed every day at home, as my mother created the right environment for the great pioneers of Latin American psychoanalysis to sit at the table and enjoy Mexican dishes that she prepared, like a chef.

He continued his training as a didactic psychoanalyst and actively participated in institutional life. He was President and Institute Director of the Association (APM). In 2002, he obtained a doctorate in psychotherapy from Universidad Intercontinental (UIC). He was the first Chair of the International Psychoanalytical Association (IPA) Standing Committee on Myths. I will also mention, from his extensive résumé, a nomination he received in 2010 from the American Institute of Biographers as one of the hundred most brilliant minds of the twenty-first century.

He actively contributed as Vice-President of COPAL (Coordinating Council of the Psychoanalytic Organizations of Latin America) in its transition to what is known today as FEPAL (Latin American Psychoanalytic Federation) in December of 1980, in Río de Janeiro, Brazil. He received numerous awards and worked relentlessly on creating the psychoanalytic banner that unified this federation.

My father was nurtured by his love for the pre-Hispanic peoples. He was very close to the history of Mexico from a very young age, and built a social network in every academic space he ever found. He travelled the world, and proudly claimed the infinite wealth of the land where we were born. He would give lectures, fought for causes, or delivered papers (always off the top of his head), then would always come back to his family, to enjoy his daily life. Close to my mother, proud to be

Mexican, committed to his work, he revived old traditions, like going with his students to visit the Pyramids of Teotihuacan and visiting many academic venues teaching psychoanalysis inside and outside the classroom.

I could go on writing about all the national and international positions he held, but I think it necessary to share what Antonio Santamaría represents in the psychoanalytic world.

As a professor

He always conveyed a firm conviction about the unconscious world. Likewise, his poetic ability and creative style facilitated his teaching tasks, which he carried out with great enthusiasm. He was devoted to psychoanalysis, passionate about culture and learning, and much loved and sought after as a supervisor and teacher.

He is the author of numerous articles published in Latin American journals. Having an unusually sharp photographic memory allowed him to give thousands of papers which he memorised—he wrote down very few of them. Some of his work was even published thanks to students recording his conferences. Many colleagues learned with him about the magnitude of Freud, the interpretation of dreams, his description of the legacy and psychology of the Mexican people standing in front of the Pyramid of the Sun, the songs in the myths. Without doubt, those who knew him hold him dear to their heart, remembering his love for psychoanalysis and for Mexico. He was a great social fighter and inspired many with his strength.

As a father

My father showed me a different world than the regular, day-to-day one. From when I was a little girl, he took me to many corners of the country to show with great purpose the infinite wealth of the Mexican land where I was born. With him I discovered the greatness of Teotihuacan, the song of the mockingbird, the legacy of integrity, and, of course, the passion for and commitment to psychoanalysis. He taught me that everybody is born with a mission, and the only way of being thankful for the gift of life is to fight for it with integrity. I am more and more convinced that he gave me the wings that keep me flying. Sometimes I imagine him in heaven, drinking Mexican *cafe de olla*, eating a delicious *mole pan dulce* with my mother, supporting the dreams of those who fight for freedom and for a better world.

As a grandfather

When my son José Luis,[3] was ten years old, he wrote a poem about a tree called Antonio in tribute to his grandfather:

> Grandpa, so many ideas blossomed, and a family thrived
> You had years and years of experience; more years of experience, than your age
> You are a tree, because your trunk is hard, and no one can bring you down
> Your roots, like your heart, will be forever under the ground, beating every minute
> The rain will keep you fresh
> Your shade will sooth the pain, your branches will embrace love
> The birds will build nests on your leaves while they need to grow, until the time comes to go
> Thank you, for teaching us how to fly

As a colleague

Integrity, friendliness, rigour, and reflection are some of the traits that made Antonio Santamaría a very respected and beloved figure across the world. He was a pioneer and leading voice of psychoanalysis in Mexico and Latin America. He influenced many generations of analysts and many even named him "the sower of dreams" because he planted seeds of knowledge in as many institutions and cities as he could. These seeds flourished and became peers who today apply many of his academic traditions. He helped in the founding and development of many societies and associations in my country.

---

[3] Hinojosa, J. L. (Julio, 2015). Poem "Los Abuelitos." In: *Revista Psicoanalítica Ania*, 8. Sociedad Psicoanalítica de Sonora. Sonora, Mexico: Ed. Obregón.

He was a pioneer in studying and transmitting Heinz Kohut's work, but also studied in depth all psychoanalytic schools of thought. He had a great didactic capacity to combine, integrate, and apply them in clinical and social fields alike.

One of his most important legacies is his teaching about dreams, notably the study of dreams in ancient Mexico.[4] He looked for ideas in different sources, and thanks to his vast knowledge, he dialogued with experts in other fields because he was convinced that exchanging ideas fertilised and enriched the space of dreams and dreaming. He is an important reference in the field of myths and dreams.[5]

Another ever so present concern he had was the mental state in which analysts work. He wrote two important articles regarding this: one in the year 2000, *El mito personal en la contratransferencia* (The personal myth in countertransference)[6] where he proposed the thesis that as well as the "personal myth" of Kris which spreads in the transference, the "personal myth" of the analyst also operates reciprocally in his countertransference and in his co-transference; the other, *La psique del analista, de la observación a la explicación empáticas* (The analyst's psyche, from empathetic observation to explanation)[7] was published in 1993. In it he highlighted the importance of working at different levels of listening. The purpose was to contribute to the improvement of psychoanalytical clinical work.

He was committed to his country and his politics. He wrote various articles on historical figures. In his work titled *Usos y Abusos del poder en la Formación Psicoanalítica* (Uses and abuses of power in psychoanalytic training)[8] presented in 1984, he raised questions about power

---

[4] Santamaría, A., & Duarte M. (2002). Los sueños en el México Antiguo a la luz del psicoanálisis. In: *La Interpretación de los sueños. Un siglo después* (Vives y Latirgue Comp.). Mexico: Plaza y Valdéz.

[5] Santamaría, A. (1995). Los mitos, los sueños y la realidad en el psicoanálisis. *Cuadernos de Psicoanalisis, 28(3–4)*: 225. Mexico: APM.

[6] Santamaría, A. (2001). El mito personal en la contratransferencia. In: *Cuadernos de Psicoanálisis, 34(1–2)* (January–June). Mexico: APM.

[7] Santamaría, A. (May, 1993). La psique del analista: De la observación a la explicación empáticas. Keynote speech given at the Annual Scientific Meeting of the Mexican Psychoanalytic Association.

[8] Santamaría, A. (1984–1985). El uso y el abuso del poder en la formación psicoanalitica. Cuadernos de Psicoanalisis. México: Mexican Psychoanalytic Association.

in psychoanalysis and/or psychoanalysts in power. His phrase "we must give more life to analysis and not more analysis to life" is a testimony of an analyst committed to Eros and with respect for the candidate. A book soon to be published will include work written by Claudio Eizirik, Otto Kernberg, Charles Hanly, former IPA Presidents, and César Botella, among others. Horacio Etchegoyen,[9] the first South American President of the IPA (1993–1997), described my father in the following way:

> Antonio Santamaría was—and still is—one of the most prominent and loved psychoanalysts in Latin America. From his native Mexico, he influenced our psychoanalytic culture. Friendly, generous, and sincere, he was one of the most powerful psychoanalysts in Latin America. We became good friends in meetings and congresses. His passing was painful for all of us and a profound loss for psychoanalysis.

The editors of this volume believe that the best way to pay tribute to him is to take up his torch and keep the fire of curiosity and devotion alight. Following this effort, Howard Levine and I have established a foundation in his name with a group of colleagues.

The Antonio Santamaría Foundation was created as a non-profit free-standing, independent psychoanalytic educational foundation, in his memory to honour and continue his love of psychoanalytic learning, his dedication to the continuing education of practising clinicians, and his commitment to the future of psychoanalysis. Our goal is to create international opportunities for psychoanalytic study, learning, and discussion in an open, free-thinking milieu, outside of the context of organised psychoanalytic institutions and training centres. To that end, we have begun to offer seminars, conferences, and other learning and study opportunities with internationally prominent psychoanalysts, who are among the leading clinical and theoretical contributors to our field. This book is the product of one of our conferences: Autism, México 2020.

We invite you to visit our website (www.asfpsychoanalysis.org—info@asfpsychoanalysis.org) and we hope that you will join us in what we believe will be an exciting and worthwhile adventure!

---

[9] Etchegoyen, H. (2013). Mi amigo Antonio Santamaría. Article to be published.

CHAPTER ONE

Making the unthinkable thinkable: vitalisation, reclamation, containment, and representation

Howard B. Levine

I

The genius inherent in Freud's initial formulation of psychoanalysis was his discovery that the manifest content of everyday discourse and experience was a potential indicator of unconscious meanings related to significant psychic conflicts. These hidden meanings were pre-existing (i.e., already represented by more or less fully formed, potentially verbalisable ideas in the mind), could reveal themselves through slips of the tongue, jokes, and dreams—the latter anointed as "The Royal Road to the Unconscious"—and, most important of all, they determined and explained what otherwise seemed to be "irrational" neurotic symptoms. In essence, to those who could begin to hear and discern these meanings, the symptoms of neurosis offered a continual, disguised, symbolic discourse about unacceptable or problematic desires, fantasies, fears, and childhood trauma, the psychic conflicts they produced, and the defensive responses that they elicited. The aim of treatment was summarised in the expression: "Making the unconscious conscious".

The assumption that there was intention, motivation, and significant, already formed hidden and unconscious sense and meaning that could be discovered, intuited, or hypothesised about in hysterical symptoms, obsessive thoughts, compulsive acts, and paranoid suspicions justified Freud's categorising these disturbances as "neuro-psychoses of defence" and lay at the heart of his first topography (the so-called "Topographic Theory"). The latter is a theory about specific ideational elements (wishes, desires, perceptions, fears, and fantasies) that are saturated in regard to meaning, capable of being more or less fully described in words, have potential symbolic value, and can appear strung together in the patient's discourse to form chains of signifying associations. It is a theory that has proven—and continues—to be of enormous value in guiding the understanding and classical treatment of neurosis and the neurotic sectors of the mind. (I am using the term "neurosis" here to imply representation and a higher level of psychic structural organisation in which unconscious conflict between internal objects, part or whole (which are represented entities), is a significant factor.)[1]

However, Freud's deepening clinical experience—with narcissism, trauma, unconscious guilt, negative therapeutic reactions, and the various phenomena that he would categorise as lying "beyond the pleasure principle" (Freud, 1920)—led him to hypothesise the Death Instinct and propose his second topography, the so-called Structural Theory (Freud, 1923). While the North American ego psychologists emphasised the implications of the latter for defence analysis and adaptation in the treatment of neuroses, Andre Green (2005), among others, explored its implications for the understanding and treatment of those conditions, mental states, and diagnoses that lay beyond neurosis, at or beyond the limits of what was once deemed to be classically analysable. In particular, Green noted that Freud's theoretical shift marked a change from a theory centred upon psychic contents (ideational *representations*) to a theory about the movements needed to tame the unstructured, not yet represented aspects of *the drive*—that is, emotion, impulse, and somatic discharge—within the psychic apparatus.[2] Thus, the aim of analytic treatment shifted to: "Where Id was, there Ego shall be", with

---

[1] For further discussion, see Levine, Reed, and Scarfone (2013).
[2] For further discussion of Green's work, see Reed and Levine (2018).

the important proviso that the drive now was not only a problem *for* the ego, but a problem *within* the ego.

As psychoanalysis has progressed into the twenty-first century, the capacity to create psychic representations has increasingly been seen not as a given, but as a developmental achievement. Its absence, weakness, or failure can leave one at the mercy of "psychic voids" (Green 2005) and "unrepresented states" (Levine, Reed, & Scarfone, 2013). These formulations challenge "the fundamental credo of psychoanalysis that psychological states are full of meaning" (Alvarez, 2019, p. 867) and imply that in many important instances, *meaning is something that is absent, potential, or emergent—yet to be created*—rather than uncovered or discovered.

Unrepresented states and psychic voids not only reflect excitations of somatic origin (e.g., drives), but also reflect the initial registrations of perception,[3] especially in regard to events of the preverbal period and the sequelae of massive psychic trauma. They are assumed to categorise, and sometimes underlie and contribute to, the psychogenic and/or experiential manifestations that are encountered in patients diagnosed with autism and Autistic Spectrum Disorders (ASD) and who present with autistic nuclei and autistic defensive organisations in otherwise non-autistic character structures. Unrepresented states are also implicated and encountered in other, non-autistic, non-neurotic conditions, such as psychosomatic disorders, addictions, perversions, and primitive character disorders. The affects that unrepresented states produce or are associated with are often those of terror, emptiness, annihilation, and despair. As Alvarez (2019) has noted, to speak of "the unrepresented" offers a potentially new paradigm that "involves the inclusion of psychoanalytic inquiry and attention to the existence of empty meaningless states, and then to the question of their treatment" (p. 878).

---

[3] In his theory of alpha function and container/contained, Bion (1962b, 1970) described how the initial registrations of the events of external reality produce *raw facts without meaning* and give rise to emotional phenomena (beta elements) that are unsuitable in their initial manifestation to form thoughts, can be used to think with or to be thought about. Both the raw facts of perception and their attendant beta-element emotions must be transformed (Bion, 1965) by dreamwork (alpha function) in order to acquire "sense" and personal meaning.

Given the organisation of the psyche—with psychotic—that is, unstructured—as well as neurotic parts of the mind; unintegrated as well as integrated areas; unrepresented areas of more or less "force without meaning" as well as represented states consisting of specific ideas imbued with affect—we should expect to find both an unstructured and a dynamic unconscious in all patients. This implies that, to some degree, unrepresented and unintegrated states are universal and will exist and be encountered in all of us. Consequently, the opportunities and challenges presented by the understanding and treatment of autism and ASD, where the unrepresented and its consequences (e.g., defensive organisations employed to protect against annihilation anxiety and catastrophic dread) can be encountered, may offer us metaphors and clues that may be relevant to aspects of the treatment of all patients, no matter what their dominant diagnoses may be.

II

The idea that raw existential Experience begins with a pre-psychic or proto-psychic registration that does not yet qualify as being a psychic representation in Freud's sense of the term assumes that both drive movements and the products of perception begin as somatic registrations or sensations that must then be transformed in order to become representations and be made psychic. (Think here of Bion's (1962b) description of alpha function transforming beta elements to alpha elements in the construction of the mental apparatus and the containment of thoughts.) The results of that transformation, which, in relation to the drives, includes the more familiar concept of what Freud called "drive derivatives", will appear in one's mind and/or experience as either—or some combination of—affect, impulse to action, somatic discharge, or representation. The latter, representation, is the potentially most adaptive and "successful" end product of transformation and provides a form of containment, and often reduction to tolerable levels for what otherwise would be potentially disruptive excess excitation. (Think here of Freud's (1920) theories of trauma (= disruption of psychic regulatory processes) and sublimation, where the unruly and peremptory, potentially disruptive force and energy of the drive is harnessed, channelled, and transformed into an artistic or otherwise culturally valuable creation.)

The work of both Bion and Winnicott has been among the most useful in describing the essential role of the earliest objects in the developmental facilitation of psychic growth and the strengthening of the infant and developing child's capacity for autonomous transformational/regulatory capacities. As contemporary psychoanalysis has been absorbing the contributions of these two seminal authors to help work through the clinical significance of Freud's second topography, we have increasingly found ourselves considering the implications, results, and need to remediate the effects of psychic *deficits* as well as conflicts. These have been understood as some combination of the failure of a necessary environmental provision on the part of the primary (maternal) object and/or a constitutional inability of the infant to make use of what for another child would be a "good enough" bit of mothering.

Put another way, our attention has been turned to all that is pre- or proto-psychic; all that is emergent or still potential in development, unsaturated in regard to ideation and meaning, not yet fully formed and that requires dialogical and intersubjective containment and transformation in order to be "metabolised" and expressed. Here, the implications of Winnicott's famous dictum that "there is no such thing as an infant"[4] and Bion's theory of thinking (1962a), description of alpha function and container/contained (1962b), and his insistence that the development of the mind is a two-person creation are most relevant.

One consequence of this change in theory is that analysts have increasingly come to recognise the importance of understanding, formulating, and learning to clinically catalyse the processes through which the self is vitalised, representations are formed, and psychic regulatory processes are strengthened and created. As they have done so, they have embarked upon a change in emphasis—although *not* a move completely away from—the analysis of contents, that is, ideas and representations, a predominant focus upon the recovery of repressed childhood memories, the healing of splits, and the uncovering and discovering of hidden feelings, thoughts, phantasies, and desires. We now find ourselves increasingly concerned with the problem of how to help catalyse and accomplish an analytic work that helps strengthen and

---

[4] Discussion at a Scientific Meeting of the British Psycho-analytical Society, circa 1940. Referenced in Winnicott (1960, p. 39, footnote 1).

sometimes even helps create for the first time, the development and/ or strengthening of psychic capacities and processes that underlie and ensure the instruments for thinking, dreaming, emotional regulation, and object relating.[5]

The latter statement applies to some extent to all patients, but becomes increasingly relevant as we address the less organised, more primitive or archaic, more traumatised aspects of the patient's mind and experience, especially in those patients whose difficulties lie "beyond neurosis" in the widening scope of psychoanalysis. One of its clearest iterations appears in Winnicott's later work—see, for example, his 1974 "Fear of breakdown" paper—where he emphasises that the analyst must unconsciously fail the patient—contribute to the production of an *actual* micro-trauma in the here and now—in the way in which the patient needs him to, so that an attenuated version of what once occurred prior to the formation of a constant and organised infantile self can then be experienced in the transference under the aegis of the patient's unconscious omnipotence and therefore "suffered" for the first time as personalised, subjective experience and worked through.

Analogous formulations are those of Pierre Marty (1980), one of the founders of the Paris Psychosomatic School, who insisted that non-hysterical somatic symptoms, unlike hysterical symptoms, were without psychic representation and initially absent of personal meaning. He viewed them as inherently opaque and asymbolic and suggested that they only acquired signification and unconscious "meaning" *après coup* in the course of an analytic treatment. Michel de M'Uzan (1984), another leading member of the Paris School, spoke of patients that he called "slaves of quantity", because their symptoms were economic overload phenomena that occurred without unconscious motivational intent or symbolic meaning. And Jean Laplanche (1987) implied that there was an unrepresented, non-specific, non-ideational component inherent in the untranslatable residue of unconsciously transmitted sexual desire that initiated the infant's psychosexuality in the "fundamental anthropological situation".

The point I wish to emphasise is that contemporary psychoanalysis has generated a number of theories of deficit (unrepresented states that

---

[5] For further discussion of these points, see Levine (2020, 2022a).

require transformation in the service of psychic development, regulation, and homeostasis) and assumed that deficits and voids can weaken and traumatise the psychic apparatus. These present clinicians with the challenge of how to deal with patients whose treatments do not conform to the expectations of classical analysis and may require modifications in theoretical understanding, listening stance, and analytic technique.

It is for these reasons that a close examination of the psychic functioning and analytic treatment of patients who present with the problems of autism, autistic spectrum disorder, and/or autistic enclaves, nuclei, and defences in otherwise non-autistic patients should prove useful to an even broader range of difficulties. This inevitably leads us to the work on psychogenic autism of Frances Tustin (1986, 1992, 1993) and the many authors she has influenced, whose work is featured in this volume.

III

I would like us to begin by considering not the aetiology of autistic states and pathology, which I assume will vary and may entail some combination of constitutional and environmental factors, but the existential problems faced by autistic patients and their analysts. What is the psychic capacity and experience of self and other like of an infant or child that we will come to diagnose as being autistic or having an ASD? What is their capacity to engage in more normal developmentally facilitating relationships and activities and make use of the resources that their environment may afford them?

Perhaps it is axiomatic to begin by noting the weakened sense of the subjective existence of other people and of one's own self in autistic and ASD patients and their impairments in vitality, object relating, symbolic capacity, language, and play. Alvarez (2012) reminds us that faint or disordered signs of relatedness or object seeking may nonetheless be present in autism and early developmental disturbances: "even autistic children look for something without knowing what they are looking for, but recognise it when they get it" (p. 134). She has further learned that if this faint searching is recognised and responded to, it may be amplified:

> Regardless of aetiology, ... a disorder of the capacity for social interaction may require and benefit from a treatment which

> functions via the process of social interaction itself. Such a relationship will need to take account of the nature and severity of the psychopathology and the particular developmental level at which the non-autistic part of the child is functioning.
>
> (Ibid., p. 167)

Another vital issue in these patients, one that lies at the root of all psychic development, is the question of how they deal with the inevitable emotions of frustration and pain. For the infant, "dealing" requires and "involves the capacity for shared experience, and for making contact through interaction with the mind of another. Through this contact one begins to sense the possibilities opened by such shared experience with a live-minded subject" (Eaton, 2011, p. 41). But for some infants, this capacity for shared experience cannot be taken for granted. The object may be, or may be felt to be, inaccessible or unreachable, traumatising rather than containing. There may be an actual failure of environmental provision on the part of the object or some constitutional inability of the infant to make use of what is being offered.

Whatever the case, the infant may begin to withdraw from object contact or may never emerge from an inherently encapsulated, auto-sensuous state, discouraging his or her objects and setting in motion a series of responses and failures in development that lead to an autistic presentation. How do we understand the latter? To what extent is it a self-protective defence (a psychic retreat) or a quasi-reflexive biological, homeostatic reaction? What, if anything, lies *behind* the auto-sensuous world of the autistic infant? Is it a bad object or nothing? A void? Does a "no object" lie behind a bad object? And is a "no object" an object or a void? Does an unrepresented or unintegrated part exist cordoned off behind the autistic part? (Alvarez, 2019).[6]

Autistic manoeuvres and defences are often resorted to in the face of catastrophic fears of annihilation due to endless falling, spilling, tearing apart, or tearing away. To what extent do these anxieties reflect organised (i.e., saturated, represented) unconscious phantasies? Or, are they the raw emotions aroused by the individual's approach to the "black holes" and "voids" of unrepresented and unintegrated states?

---

[6] See also Bion (1970) for discussions of the "no-object".

Power (2017) following Tustin summarises the problem as follows:

> the infant fated to become autistic is exposed *prematurely*[7] to recognition of the mother as a physically separate object and because this recognition is experienced as developmentally premature (from the standpoint of the infant's experience) it is felt as a violent rupture of the physical intactness of the infant itself, opening a hole through which the infant's existence can pour out never-endingly. Tustin's image for this process, again from the infant's perspective, was that the removal of the nipple tore off with it the infant's mouth. That is to say, the shock of prematurely recognising physical separateness (metaphorically, the removal of the nipple from the mouth and the physical space between infant and mother created by this action) is experienced by the infant *somato-psychically* (a physical tearing of the nascent self through which existence spills out). Part of the traumatic impact of this experience stems from what is *not* experienced—the infant fails to subjectively appropriate possession of an orifice with which it can, increasingly under its own control, regulate movements into and out of itself in congress with the object world.
>
> Without this sense of voluntary closing and opening, but with a sense of traumatic injury instead, psychic emergency measures ensue aimed at plugging this "black hole". It is the objects and actions clung to and repeated as emergency measures and attempts at repair that Tustin called "autistic objects" and "autistic shapes." Both terms denote *a turning toward sensory experience as a means of blocking the wound and providing a seal to protect the endangered self*. Along with attempting to plug the black hole, these sensory preoccupations psychically obliterate the awareness of separateness and in this way they substitute for object relatedness rather than promote it. Thus, unlike transitional objects, autistic objects and autistic shapes do not facilitate a path toward object relations, but instead block

---

[7] The extent to which this recognition is premature is determined by both constitutional hyper-reactivity and environmental factors.

or even erase this path. Said more simply, in Tustin's view the autistic object or shape substitutes for the object rather than fostering its gradual and tolerable recognition as separate, thus derailing the development of true object relatedness that would follow on from this evolving recognition. With respect to the object's absence, in these states faith in the object withers and hopes for its return vanish.

The process described by Tustin subverts the development of thought, representational capacities and symbolisation, because it short-circuits the ability to recognise and tolerate the absence of the object and the frustration that accompanies this absence. There is no representation of an absent other, not even an hallucinated other; and consequently no mental evolution toward a capacity for bearing absence via recourse to phantasy and thought. In Winnicott's terms, there is no transitional space within which objects can be found/created. As others have pointed out this short-circuiting of the processes for thinking leads to a flattened psychic spatiality, a spatiality that tends toward the two dimensional and away from the growth of an internal space in which phantasy and thought can gestate. There is an atrophy of identificatory processes such that adhesive pseudo-relatedness dominates and mimicry and various forms of adopting physical/sensory aspects of the other are prominent.

(pp. xxi–xxii)

In conjunction with this description, I would like to note a series of comments made by Alvarez about what she has found necessary and useful in the treatment of children with autism, ASD, and various forms of early childhood borderline states, childhood psychoses, and pervasive developmental disorders. As I have implied elsewhere (Levine, 2022a), I find her descriptions most relevant to thinking about certain incapacities and ego deficits of non-autistic adult patients. The common ground lies in the formulation of unrepresented states, inadequately developed regulatory capacities, and the need to find ways to understand and catalyse previously thwarted vitality affects and essential ego development and states of intense withdrawal and being "undrawn" (Alvarez, 2010).

IV

In one of her most quoted papers, Alvarez (2010) speaks about three conceptual levels of intervention: *explanation*, *description*, and *reclamation*. The first, which entails offering alternative meanings structured by the paradigm of "Why? Because!" is most suited to work with neurosis. The second level orients the patient and helps them attend to and name "what is" in their experience. Comments such as "You seem angry" or "That must have hurt!" name names, mark cause and effect occurrences around significant emotional experiences, especially within the setting of the analytic relationship, and help enlarge meanings via description or amplification. The third level is an intensified, *vitalising level of reclamation*—("Hey!")—that signals the alive presence of the object, calls patients into contact, and insists that something called "meaning" can and sometimes does exist in life and between people.

It is especially this third level that offers analysts and therapists interpretive options and considerations that go beyond the uncovering of hidden, pre-existent meanings. It also offers the rationale for viewing and using the analytic dialogue as a verbal, Winnicottian Squiggle Game in which the analyst's co-participation can play an intersubjective role in recruiting and upregulating a severely withdrawn or "undrawn" patient's emotional availability. It is this latter dimension of the analyst as partner-in-containment that is one of the conceptual foundations of Ferro's (2002) Field Theory.[8]

Autistic, ASD, borderline, psychotic, and other patients who are "beyond neurosis" have limited ego capacity and can be too overwhelmed by despair or persecutory fears to benefit from interpretations that seek to remove defences against painful truths. They may be both hopelessly and self-protectively *withdrawn* or tragically and/or traumatically *undrawn*. Speaking of these patients, Alvarez (2012) writes: "I learned that I needed to respond to, or even carry for them, their hopes and aspirations, and that such interventions need not encourage manic denial when thoughtfully applied" (p. 1). Put another way,

---

[8] For further descriptions of Ferro's work and its conceptual foundations, see Levine (2022b).

> long before certain patients process their hatred and find their capacity for love, they may have to develop the capacity to be interested in an object with some substantiality, life, or, in the case of perversion, strength and a capacity to excite in a non-perverse fashion.
>
> (Ibid., pp. 5–6)

With patients, who often dwell in states of dissociation, despairing apathy, or deviant excitement, "the question arises of whether feelings or meanings matter at all" (ibid., p. 7). Objects may be experienced as "uninteresting, unvalued (not devalued), useless and possibly mindless" (ibid., p. 10). Addressing these difficulties will require work "at the foundations of mental and relational life" (ibid., p. 12) in order to treat "patients in affectless states of autism, dissociation or apathy following chronic despair" (ibid., p. 12) and neglect, patients who cannot listen or feel. At its extreme, these patients may demonstrate "a chronic apathy about relating, which goes beyond despair. Nothing is expected" (ibid., p. 13). Such patients may best be described as "undrawn" rather than "withdrawn". In their treatment, they "First … need to be helped to be able to feel and to find meaning … Then, feelings can begin to be identified and explored; eventually, explanations, which bring in additional, alternative meanings, may be heard and taken in" (ibid., p. 11).

In some non-neurotic patients, "so-called "defences" were actually desperate attempts to *overcome* and *recover from* states of despair and terror. They carried, that is, elements of basic developmental needs: for protection, for preservation, a sense of urgency and potency, and even revenge and justice" (ibid., p. 78). In addition, she found that it was not enough to "give them" good experiences in the analytic relationship, but it was also necessary to point out that they like, need, and wish for those experiences.

To some extent, feeling understood requires an expectation that understanding exists and a sufficient number of experiences of having felt understood by another to make paying attention to the other to find out what they are thinking, feeling, and noticing worthwhile. These are matters of experience and attention. However, "Some children who have been rarely or never understood do not know what understanding is. The more advanced ones, when they first notice the therapist 'understanding' them, often ask, 'How did you know that? Are you a mind-reader?'" (ibid., p. 151).

Alvarez further notes that "Attention, ... before it can be held, sometimes has to be caught and elicited ... For alpha function to operate, the object has to be seen to be worth attending to in the first place" (ibid., p. 142). Consequently, she writes, "We have to find ways of helping these children to attend to us, and have to sustain their attention; ... emotionally heightened interest is central to this process" (ibid., p. 173). The analyst may have to provide something vitalising and intensified to attract the patient's attention to the analyst as a live object, to up-regulate affect in the situation and to insist on meaning "calling the child into contact with an object, and also recalling ... [the child] to himself when there is a severe deficit in both the [child's] self and internal object" (ibid., p. 147).

V

Returning to Power's (2017) essay we note that:

> Non-neurotic states of mind and the mental processes that characterise them are of great interest for contemporary psychoanalysis. Weakened capacities to represent one's mental life, difficulties with symbolisation, reliance on evacuation, erasure and foreclosure as well as other direct forms of discharge to manage psychic distress, and activation of annihilatory levels of anxiety, all present the practicing analyst with significant challenges in creating an analytic process, managing and maintaining an analytic frame, and dealing with the countertransference. Patients who present with these difficulties place great demands on the analyst to be a lively, engaging presence, to be flexible and spontaneous, to trust in and rely on reverie despite profound challenges to the analyst's own representational capacities, and to be willing to employ these capacities in the service of assisting patients' efforts to "weave psychic patches" in response to holes or tears in the psyche. The task nowadays is often one of helping to fill in psychic voids where representation of experience is absent or weak, and less often one of simply

uncovering repressed, conflictually laden but symbolically represented content (Levine, Reed and Scarfone, 2012; Mitrani, 1995; Roussillon, 2011).

These difficulties, both conceptual and technical, are especially highlighted in psychoanalytic work with patients who demonstrate a variety of autistic disturbances, whether they are formally diagnosed as autistic or on the Asperger's Spectrum or described as manifesting autistic states or barriers (Klein, S., 1980; Tustin, 1986). Though the differences between these various types of clinical presentations may be vast, important similiarities arise from the fact that for each, *endogenous autosensuousness* (Tustin, 1992, p.18) dominates mental life to an extent that mental development is endangered by the limit that sensory life places on the growth of subjectivity. Said slightly differently, in all these disorders sensory life becomes an obstacle to, rather than a springboard for, emotional growth and psychological development.

(pp. xv–xvi)

It is striking that auto-sensuousness and other forms of turning away from contact with external reality in favour of varieties of self-stimulation have been implicated in the aetiology and development of psychosomatic disorders (Aulagnier, 2001; Miller, 2015) and psychoses (De Masi, 2020) and are prominent in drug and alcohol addictions and many sexual perversions. While not "autistic" in the literal or formal sense of the term, these conditions all have in common the potential of being ego distortions and organisations that attempt to protect the self by screening one's self off from contact with emotions and awareness of one's internal states and intensely withdrawing from contact with and awareness of the subjectivity and selfhood of objects in the external world. This forces psychoanalysts who attempt to treat these patients to confront the limits of language in addressing and describing these conditions and internal states.

In *Learning from Experience*, Bion (1962b) asserted: "The problem presented by the psycho-analytic experience is the lack of any adequate terminology to describe it" (pp. 67–68). There is an uncertainty inherent in the infinite complexity of human development and personal relations that renders emotional truth fleeting: transient and always in transit (Bergstein, 2019, p. 4). Consequently, efforts to report or describe the *experience* of the psychoanalytic process, such as we have attempted to convey in this book, and the claims of psychoanalytic theories in general, inevitably challenge and may appear to fall short of our everyday views of causality and evidence. The latter are limited by and appear in a context of the three-dimensional perspective to which human consciousness is restricted, while the realm of psychic reality and the unconscious, especially the unrepresented, unrepressed, and inaccessible unconscious, is multi-dimensional, perhaps infinitely dimensional (Bion, 1970; Bergstein, 2019).

Added to this fundamental limitation in the extent to which any of us may be able to come to know the domain of the psyche is an all too human foible that each of us shares. We tend to hate any limitations in what we can know and so create "explanations" that attempt to negate and deny the painful fact of our ignorance.

In his Tavistock Seminars, Bion (2005) put it this way:

> when we are at a loss we invent something to fill the gap of our ignorance—this vast area of ignorance, of non-knowledge, in which we have to move. The more frightening the gap, the more terrifying it is to realise how utterly ignorant we are of even the most elementary and simplest requirements for survival, the more we are pressed from outside and inside to fill the gap.
>
> … in a situation where you feel completely lost; you are thankful to clutch hold of any system, anything whatever that is available on which to build a kind of structure. So from this point of view it seems to me that we could argue that the whole of psychoanalysis fills a long-felt want by being a vast Dionysiac system; since we don't know what is there, we invent these theories and build this glorious structure that has not foundation in fact—or the only fact in which it has any foundation is our complete ignorance, our lack of capacity.
>
> However, we hope that … psychoanalytic theories would remind you of real life at some point in the same way as a good novel or a good play would remind you how human beings behave.
>
> (p. 2)

I have tried to show—and readers will discern in the many clinical descriptions in the chapters that follow—how over and above any *content*-related interpretations, the inter-affective, intersubjective responsiveness and vitality of the analyst seemed to play a key role in the reclamation (Alvarez, 2010) and reanimation of deeply withdrawn, perhaps regressively undrawn, desertified patients. The question of whether the kind of interventions described are analogous or identical to what has been proposed as essential environmental provision in the mother–infant relationship are moot and probably unanswerable.

So too, the relationship between inter-affective reclamation and activation of the patient's psychic capacities for representation, symbolisation, affective and associative linkage, objectalisation, etc. The achievement and consolidation of each of these capacities has been described in various analytic theories as following from interactive, inter-affective, and/or intersubjective relational experiences with primary objects. Each has been indicated as playing some role in the life-long process of binding internal (e.g., drives and their derivatives) or external (e.g., perception and sensation) excitation and making sense of and creating meaning from one's own knowable experience. Bion's (1962b, 1970) description of alpha function and container/contained is but one of the many available theoretical formulations that attempts to put these processes into words.

In the case of Thomas, whose treatment I have described at length elsewhere (Levine, 2020), I proposed that the inter-affective and intersubjective stimulation afforded by *my* affect-laden memories that underlay my intervention—I suggested something he might actively do to forestall and prevent a looming depressive isolation and withdrawal—helped enliven Thomas by sparking his own capacities for thinking, imagining, and dreaming into action. In retrospect, that intervention functioned as a "Hey" interpretation, priming the "pump" of Thomas' psychic apparatus. At the same time, the emergence of my memories in the session at that time was also unconsciously defensive and self-restorative for me in the face of Thomas' barrenness and despair, as well as a hopeful conveyor of my positive parental countertransference towards him. Once his attention was attracted ("Hey!"), his own previously limited representational capacities could be said to have emerged or come back on line in the service of thinking through a solution to the problem at hand. My intervention helped catalyse and restore his capacity for "thought as trial action", a capacity that is heavily dependent upon processes of representation and figurability, enabling him to do some research, think through the possibilities, and put into action an actual decision to follow up on my suggestion.

My description of my work with Thomas also illustrates the role of construction and myth in the analytic dialogue. Readers who go back to the more extensive case report may or may not agree with the pragmatic value of my formulations as they compare my comments with their own personal experience. My hope, as in Bion's remark, is that my description may remind some of you of "real [analytic] life" and how humans behave, the way a good play or novel might, and in doing so, may help you negotiate a useful path in a future encounter with your patients.

References

Alvarez, A. (2010). Levels of analytic work and levels of pathology: The work of calibration. *IJPA, 91*: 859–878.

Alvarez, A. (2012). *The Thinking Heart*. London: Routledge.

Alvarez, A. (2019). Extending the boundaries of psychopathology and of its psychoanalytic treatment: A review of *Engaging Primitive Anxieties of the Emerging Self: The Legacy of Frances Tustin* edited by H. B. Levine and D. G. Power. *Psychoanalytic Quarterly, 88*: 867–882.

Aulagnier, P. (2001). *The Violence of Interpretation*. London: Brunner Routledge.

Bergstein, A. (2019). *Bion and Meltzer's Expedition into Unmapped Mental Life*. London: Routledge.

Bion, W. R. (1962a). A theory of thinking. In: W. R. Bion (1967), *Second Thoughts*. London: Heinemann.

Bion, W. R. (1962b). *Learning from Experience*. London: Heinemann.

Bion, W. R. (1965). *Transformations*. London: Heinemann.

Bion, W. R. (1970). *Attention and Interpretation*. New York: Basic Books.

Bion, W. R. (2005). *The Tavistock Seminars*. London: Karnac.

De Masi, F. (2020). *A Psychoanalytic Approach to Treating Psychosis*. Abingdon, Oxon: Routledge.

Eaton, J. (2011). *A Fruitful Harvest: Essays After Bion*. Seattle: The Alliance Press.

Ferro, A. (2002). *In The Analyst's Consulting Room*. London: Routledge.
Freud, S. (1920g). *Beyond The Pleasure Principle*. S.E., 18: 7–66.
Freud, S. (1923b). *The Ego and the Id*. S.E. 19: 3–68.
Green, A. (2005). *Key Ideas for a Contemporary Psychoanalysis: Misrecognition and Recognition of the Unconscious* (trans. A. Weller). London: Routledge.
Klein, S. (1980). Autistic phenomena in neurotic patients. *International Journal of Psychoanalysis*, 61(3): 395–401.
Laplanche, J. (1987). *New Foundations for Psychoanalysis* (trans. D. Macey). Oxford: Basil Blackwell, 1989.
Levine, H. B. (2020). Reflections on therapeutic action and the origins of psychic life. *JAPA*, 68: 9–26.
Levine, H. B. (2022a). *Affect, Representation and Language: Between the Silence and the Cry*. Abingdon, Oxon: Routledge.
Levine, H. B. (Ed.) (2022b). *The Post-Bionian Field Theory of Antonino Ferro*. Abingdon, Oxon: Routledge.
Levine, H. B., Reed, G., & Scarfone, D. (2013). *Unrepresented States and the Construction of Meaning*. London: Karnac/IPA.
Marty, P. (1980). *L'ordre psychosomatique*. Paris: Payot.
Miller, P. (2015). Piera Aulagnier, an introduction: Some elements of her intellectual biography. *IJPA*, 96: 1355–1369.
Mitrani, J. L. (1995). Toward an understanding of unmentalized experience. *Psychoanalytic Quarterly*, 64: 68–112.
de M'Uzan, M. (1984). Slaves of quantity. *Psychoanalytic Quarterly*, 72: 711–725 (2003 trans. R. Simpson).
Power, D. G. (2017). Introduction. In: H. B. Levine & D. G. Power (Eds.), *Engaging Primitive Anxieties of the Emerging Self: The Legacy of Frances Tustin* (pp. xv–xxx). London: Karnac.
Reed, G. S., & Levine, H. B. (Eds.) (2018). *Representation and the Work of the Negative: Andre Green Revisited*. New York: IPA/Routledge.
Roussillon, R. (2011). *Primitive Agony and Symbolisation*. London: Karnac.
Tustin, F. (1986). *Autistic Barriers in Neurotic Patients*. New Haven, CT: Yale University Press.
Tustin, F. (1992). *Autistic States in Children* (revised edition). London: Routledge.
Tustin, F. (1993). On psychogenic autism. *Psychoanalytic Inquiry*, 13: 34–41.

Winnicott, D. W. (1960). The theory of the parent–infant relationship. In: *The Maturational Processes and the Facilitating Environment* (pp. 37–55). New York: IUP, 1965.

Winnicott, D. W. (1974). Fear of breakdown. In: C. Winnicott, R. Shepherd & M. Davis (Eds.), *Psycho-Analytic Explorations* (pp. 87–95). Cambridge, MA: Harvard University Press, 1989.

CHAPTER TWO

Finding the wavelength: tools in communication with children with autism*

Anne Alvarez

Listening is a complex art. A few years ago, there was a series of letters in *The Times* on the subject of blackbirds and their song. Here is one from 14 June 2000:

> Sir—Blackbirds are joyful in May and sing in A major. In July, they are content and sing in F major.
>
> I've waited 68 years to say this, Beethoven's Seventh and Sixth Symphonies supporting my theory.
>
> Sincerely, D. F. Clarke

---

*An earlier version of this chapter was published as Anne Alvarez (2004). Finding the wavelength: Tools in communication with children with autism. *Infant Observation*, 7(2–3): 91–106. DOI: 10.1080/13698030408405045

Copyright © Tavistock Clinic Foundation, reprinted by permission of Taylor & Francis Ltd, http://www.tandfonline.com on behalf of Tavistock Clinic Foundation. The editors thank Routledge and *Infant Observation* for permission to reprint.

The writer is clearly a good listener and seems to like listening. Here is a rather different attitude to listening, this one by Fernando Pessoa (1981):

> Cease your song!
> Cease, for along with
> It I have heard
> Another voice
> Coming (it seemed) in
> Interstices
> Of the charm, softly strong
> Brought by your song as
> Far as us

The last stanza reads:

> No more song! Must
> Now have silence,
> To sleep clear
> Some remembrance
> Of the voice heard,
> Not understood,
> Which was lost
> For me to hear.

Note the insistence that what he needs in order to listen is *silence*, not song. Children with autism are notoriously poor listeners: indeed, they are often thought to be deaf. The established triad of symptoms includes, as well as impairments in social relatedness and the use of the imagination, impairments in communication and language development. It is important to identify symptoms, yet a nosology which relies too exclusively on a one-person psychology—that is, which sticks to describing attributes of the child's self—may tell only a part of the story. I think a fuller descriptive psychology of autism is provided by a two-person (and eventually three-person) psychology. Such an approach involves a study of intrapersonal relations: in a model of the mind which involves a two-person psychology, the mind contains not just a self with particular qualities and orientations and possible deficits; it also contains a relation to, and relationship with, what are called "internal objects" (Klein, 1959) or "representational models" (Bowlby, 1988), and these too may contain deficits. A more personal, intrapersonal view of autism carries the implication that the self is in an emotional, dynamic relationship with its internal representations, figures, objects—no matter how skewed, deficient, or odd this relationship may be. (There is no aetiological implication here: it is the child's inner world of figures and representations that is at issue. Many psychoanalysts use the term "internal object", rather than "representation", as the latter may sometimes be taken to imply an exact copy of external figures, whereas the former carries no such implication. Internal objects are thought to be amalgams of both inner and outer factors.) If the child treats us as a piece of furniture, he may be *seeing* us as something like a piece of furniture, and he may also *feel as though we are like* a piece of furniture. If he does not listen to us, it may be in part because he does not have the habit of listening, but it may also be because he finds our talk uninteresting, or intrusive, with too few of Pessoa's silences. How, then, are we to cease our song and still be heard? Also, if he does not talk to us, it may be in part because he does not think we are worth the effort of speaking to, or because he feels our listening capacities are limited. Or else he may feel we want to pull his words out of him so that, in some sort of terrible way, they will become ours and no longer his. His "theory of mind" (Leslie, 1987) may assert that minds are basically unmindful: this can do major damage to processes of introjection, learning, and internalisation.

Yet symptomatology and pathology are not everything: each person with autism can usually be found to have an intact, non-autistic part of the personality interwoven with their autism. Bion described the importance, in psychoanalytic work with psychotic patients, of making contact with the "non-psychotic part of the personality" (Bion, 1967). There is also now a growing body of research on "spared function" in autism (Hobson & Lee, 1999). For all its apparent stasis, the autistic condition is less static and more mutable than it sometimes appears. While a micro-second's interested glance by a child at a person, say, or a new toy, may be followed by an instantaneous return to old rituals, the quality of the child's glance may nevertheless offer a clue, a faint signal that can be amplified and built upon tactfully. It is important to assess what the developmental level is at which this apparently more normal part of the self may be operating. The child's chronological age may be five or ten years, but, because of habitual life-long interference from the autism, the healthy, related, object-seeking part may be functioning at ten months or even three weeks of age. Traces of early preconceptions (Bion, 1962)—or of not so much a "theory of mind" (Leslie, 1987) or of person (Hobson, 1993) but a proto-theory of mind or a proto-sense of person—may still be detectable. It is on this foundation that a treatment—precisely calibrated to the level of emotional communication of which the child is capable—may build.

Normal infant development, vision and proto-language

William, thirteen months old, heard his father getting up at 5 a.m. outside his door. William called "Ey!" The father said it sounded like, "Hey! What are you doing! Where the heck are you going?!!!" Dad opened the baby's bedroom door, and was greeted with another demanding "Ey!!!" Dad whispered, in order not to wake the mother, "I'm going to work, William, you go back to sleep now." William said, "Awhhhh", and went back to sleep.

From the moment of birth, as the psychoanalyst Klein maintained, and developmental psychology research has subsequently demonstrated, normal babies are now known to be extremely precocious socially (Klein, 1959, p. 249; Newson, 1977, p. 49). They have all the basic equipment they require to begin to engage in face-to-face interpersonal communication—initially of a nonverbal kind. They prefer to look at face-like patterns, to listen to the sound of the human voice, and they have a remarkable capacity for finely tuned interpersonal exchanges (Stern, 1985, p. 40; Trevarthen & Aitken, 2001). Clearly, emotional communication involves a whole orchestra of "instruments" in which eye gaze (Fogel, 1977; Koulomzin et al., 2002), emotional engagement (Demos, 1986), level of attention and interest, expressive bodily gestures (Hobson, 1993), and vocalisations (Trevarthen & Aitken, 2001) all play their part. Most of these instruments are used both expressively and then communicatively, or, to put it in psychoanalytic terms, via different types of projective identification. They are also used, however, for purposes of introjection and internalisation. Vision, for example: at birth, the infant has a set of visual structures highly sensitive to those aspects of stimulation that emanate from other people's faces (Papousek & Papousek, 1975). Schore (1997, p 10) points out that the caregiver's emotionally expressive face is by far the most potent visual stimulus in the infant's environment, and the child's intense interest in her face, especially in her eyes, her brightening and dulling gaze (Robson, 1967), leads him to track it in space and to engage in periods of intense mutual gaze. Eyes, after all, have what Robson calls, immense "stimulus richness" to the newborn: their shininess, mobility, and the micro-second by micro-second changes in the size of the pupil attract attention, at first only fleeting but nevertheless frequent (Fogel, 1977). After the second month, fixation on the mother's eyes increases (Maurer & Salapatak, 1976). At seventeen weeks the eyes are a more attracting feature of the mother's face than her mouth (Uzgiris & Hunt, 1975).

Language and triadic skills involving visual regard

Towards the end of the first year of life, infants begin to extend the use of an earlier skill: the capacity for gaze monitoring. Scaife and Bruner (1975) have shown that even very young infants will turn their heads to follow the mother's line of regard. In the last quarter of the first year, following the trajectory of another's gaze and gazing at the object of the gaze is intensified, as the baby is motivated to keep track of his mother and her comings and goings. This is followed by the emergence of the more proactive activity of proto-declarative pointing between the ninth and fourteenth month (Scaife & Bruner, 1975). Bruner (1983) was one of the first to point out that language arose in the context of interactions between infant and caregiver. It was here that the infant learned to understand that there was more than one perspective, but that differing perspectives could be linked (and see Urwin, 2002 for a discussion of language development as an emotional process). Burhouse (2001) has offered suggestions as to the emotional pre-conditions which might explain why gaze monitoring seems to precede proto-declarative pointing. She points out that the baby has learned to value mother's return of gaze during the early months of face-to-face dyadic mutual gazing, and this interest in and valuing of her attention leads the baby to follow her gaze when it goes to someone such as an older sister. Eventually, the baby finds active ways of getting this attention back, through communicative pointing and expressive sounds. These are emotionally laden events, and the grammar of emotional events structures language There are huge differences in communicative intention between a "Hey there!!!", a "C'mon give us a smile …", an "Oh look at the lovely bright sun!", a teasing, "I'm coming to catch youuuuuu!", a "You've been a very naughty boy!", a "Oh you really like that banana puree, don't you, oh yes yum yum", and an imperative "Don't touch that socket—it is VERY dangerous!" Language, as Bruner (1983) taught, emerges always *in contexts* and, as developmentalists have shown, is accompanied by emotion (Demos, 1986). Burhouse describes a moment when the baby seems to be thinking, *she (mine) is talking to and looking at her, not to me.* Psychoanalytic theorists and developmentalists alike have suggested that early two-person relationships lay the foundation for the later three-person social capacities (Klein, 1945; Winnicott, 1958; Trevarthen & Hubley, 1978). Recently Striano and Rochat (1999) have demonstrated empirically that the link between triadic social competence and earlier dyadic competence in infancy is indeed a developmental one. You don't follow the trajectory of someone's gaze unless you find his or her gaze *worth having in the first place.*

Therapeutic implications of impairments in communication: getting on the right developmental wavelength

The question of the psychoanalytic treatment of children with autism has been surrounded by controversy. Some psychoanalysts and psychotherapists have themselves described the need for changes in technique with these children (Meltzer, 1975; Tustin, 1981; Alvarez 1992; Alvarez & Reid, 1999). The impairments in symbolic capacity, play, and language make an understanding of more ordinary explanatory interpretations very difficult for them. Where the autistic symptomatology is especially severe, and where not only the child's sense of the existence of other people, but also his sense of self is weak, the concepts of transference and countertransference may *seem* too advanced: transference may seem to be non-existent, and a countertransference of frustration or despair in the therapist can lead to indifference. Yet close observation may begin to reveal faint or disordered signs of relatedness which can then be amplified.

The view of the Autism Workshop at the Tavistock Clinic is that, regardless of aetiology, a disorder of the capacity for social interaction may benefit from a treatment which functions via the process of social interaction itself, provided this takes account both of the nature and severity of the psychopathology and the particular developmental level at which the child is functioning. The therapeutic approach is three-pronged: it addresses the child's personality, the autistic symptomatology (disorder and sometimes deviance), and the intact or spared "non-autistic" part of the child, however developmentally delayed this may be (Alvarez & Reid, 1999). The psychotherapy is thus psychoanalytically, psychopathologically, and developmentally informed.

1. The psychoanalytic perspective offers the close observation of the transference and countertransference. This can alert the therapist to personality features in the child that accompany, and may act to exacerbate or reduce, his autism. (Some children with autism develop quite deviant personalities that are in no way an essential feature of the autism itself.) The psychoanalytic theory of the need and capacity of every ordinary child first to relate intensely to, and gradually to identify with, both of his parents contributes greatly to the understanding of normal child development. So also does the theory of the Oedipus complex, the understanding of the ordinary child's disturbance at, but also enormous interest in and stimulation by, those aspects of the parental couple's relationship that exist independently of him (Houzel, 2001; Rhode, 2001).
2. The psychopathological perspective helps the therapist to understand the power and pull of autistic repetitive behaviours, and the ways in which (as psychoanalysts, too, have suggested), addictive and concrete non-symbolic behaviours differ profoundly from simple neurotic mechanisms and defences (Kanner, 1944; Joseph, 1982; Tustin, 1981).
3. Clinical intuition can be both confirmed and supplemented by the study of very young infants both by the methods of naturalistic observation (Miller, Rustin, Rustin, & Shuttleworth, 1989) and of developmental research. Therapists try to identify and facilitate the precursors of social relatedness: the technique draws on findings into the ways in which mothers communicate with their babies,

and into how this facilitates the infant's capacity for communication and relatedness. The developmental research emphasises a number of factors: the normal baby's need for his level of stimulation and arousal to be carefully modulated (Dawson & Lewy, 1989; Brazelton, Koslowski, & Main, 1974) and his attention channelled; the power of "motherese" (softer, higher inflections with particular adagio rhythms during pre-speech/pre-music dialogues) (Trevarthen, 2001), and particular grammars (coaxing rather than imperatives) (Murray, 1991); differing proximity of faces at different ages for eliciting eye contact (Papousek & Papousek, 1975); and, depending on developmental level, the child's readiness for primary intersubjectivity (face-to-face communication and play in a dyadic situation) *vs.* secondary intersubjectivity (shared play with objects, where the baby glances at the caregiver seeking moments of "joint attention" to a toy, for example—a triadic situation) (Trevarthen & Hubley, 1978).

Yet many severely autistic children have never played, nor developed a capacity for joint attention (Baron-Cohen, Allen, & Gillberg, 1992). They may have no language at all; worse, they may never have babbled playfully. It may be a real achievement in the therapy when the non-speaking child begins to play with sounds, to make sounds that are more contoured than before. The technical issues for the psychotherapist are difficult: how can we reach a child with little or no language? How should we talk to such a child? I now want to describe work with a child where the use of both "motherese" and something which might be called "fatherese" combined to facilitate communication between us and to help his communicative capacities to grow. In both situations I often found that I had to contain and dramatise feelings that were either unfamiliar or unmanageable for Joseph. Yet he showed growing interest in my reactions.

Joseph

Joseph was referred to me at the age of eight by his music therapist. He had been born two weeks overdue and had been induced. His older brothers were normal. Joseph was a placid baby, happy to be held by anybody, and he made eye contact until about the age of three.

The parents only suspected something might be wrong when they tried to toilet train him at the age of two and he seemed not to understand. When they started to try to put pressure on him to communicate, he "closed down", and eye contact reduced. He was always content, but he cut himself off and would not play with other children. He had always been tactile, cuddly, and loved being sung to. He could sing numerous songs, but his spoken language was very limited. Joseph's mother wrote that his early pretend play was good: from the age of two years, he held two dolls facing each other and made them have "conversations" with each other, and dance together. Joseph did this in his sessions with me, but for much of the time the quality was very closed and shut-off, and I think by now it was no longer real pretend play. It was too *real* for him: he seemed to believe he really was those people talking and playing together. Most of the language I heard in the early sessions was of this private type—conversations between various video characters, lively, interested, yet very repetitive and, for much of the time, impossible to understand. Occasionally a question could be heard, or an exclamation. But to his parents and me, the only real word I heard directed to them or me, was when we asked him if he would like to use the toilet, and he responded with an excessively light, quite disembodied "No". It was so light and impersonal, un-aimed and unlocatable, that you could easily imagine you hadn't heard it.

I saw Joseph together with his parents for three consultations. He occasionally responded to his mother's songs, in the sense of joining in on the last word, but much of his positive connection with her was through cuddling. He was a big eight-year-old, but I did begin to note how easy it was to see him as younger than his age, and to want to be protective of him: he was an attractive boy, with a sweet, rather unformed face, and a very loose-limbed body, which in the room was much of the time horizontally laid out on the couch, half in his mother's lap. He did examine the toys a bit, but avoided most suggestions or directives from her or me regarding any play activity. When walking, he tended to drag his arms and legs, especially his feet, after him as though they did not belong to him. I was cheered by more signs of alertness and life in a teasing game he began to play, in which he said, suddenly, "Night-night" and then liked it when I did an exaggerated startle and expressed my disappointment that he was disappearing under the blanket *again*.

He made a little fleeting eye contact after these moments. It was clear that Joseph was a very loved child, but there was also a sense in which he had never really woken up to the world. He seemed to need to discover his bones and muscles, his verticality (his pleasure in standing and stretching up into the world, to jump, and his capacity to move forward and explore it). There was far too much passivity in his life, and yet, as he so easily collapsed into a sort of panicky temper-tantrum when challenged or stretched, it was easy for everyone to suppose that his autism had made him far too delicate for ordinary life and ordinary demands. On the other hand, it was clear that both his parents and the school were able to be firm about certain things, as Joseph was in many respects a reasonable and easy-going child.

After two months or so of psychotherapy I got the impression that the talk between the video characters, or between the toy animals, was not always as totally absorbing to Joseph as it seemed, that in fact he was often quite aware of my attention on him as he carried out these repetitive activities. I also began to think he was enjoying my feelings of exclusion, so I began to dramatise my countertransference: "Oh, Joseph won't talk to me, it's not fair, nobody will talk to me, and they are having such a good time over there talking to each other". I also added sometimes, "Oh, please talk to *me* Joseph, not to them!!" This was all quite emotional—coaxing/pleading/protesting. I was beginning to suspect that he thought of talking as something other people did together, with a third always excluded, but had no idea of the real pleasures of face-to-face talking in a twosome. I felt I needed to give the third a voice, and yet attract him back to real relationships. One day, after my coaxing, he looked straight at me, put his head up and back, starting to shake it just like a toddler, saying "No! Nononononono!", really relishing his power to tease and thwart me. But this had at least a bit of give and take: he was, after all, looking at me, and it was a genuine "no", with some real oomph in it. Like his "Night-night", it was full of mischief, and really made me laugh.

Not all of my countertransferences were so obliging, however. I sometimes found myself feeling very annoyed by his complacent assumption that only he and his shadow were interesting, or that he was not really bored silly by his unending conversations, or that he knew what was behind a particular wall in the room. Eventually I felt our relationship was strong enough for me to begin to challenge these assumptions. I began saying things like "Oh no, you *do not* know what is in there behind that wall. You'd love to know, but you don't!" I said it strongly, but I kept it lively and fun and rhythmic, so it accompanied or responded to his sing-song style. Except that his was high and expressive, whereas I was bringing him down with my voice to a more earthbound but, I hoped, more interesting place. It was flatter and lower than his, but still quite humorous. I also persisted with the idea that his talk was *not* real, and that I knew he was dying to talk in a real way!!! The people in his pretend conversations seemed always to be having fun—or at least a dramatic and interesting time. But in order to become *like* someone, you also have to become aware that you cannot *be* that person.

However, you also have to feel that other people give you permission to be like them. Therefore, on occasions when he came in very wild and excited, I echoed the excited/aggressive element in his utterances. If there were sudden growls and stamping of his feet, I copied and amplified both, which delighted him. I felt he needed to discover his musculature as well as his own boy's voice. I also encouraged the toy animals to take longer journeys. They were often sitting around kissing each other most tenderly, but they never went for even a simple walk! I'm certain that even Anthony and Cleopatra went out for a breath of fresh air sometimes! I had frequently accompanied the animals' large rather assertive steps (they always remained in the same place, or moved in the tiniest of circles) with even more assertive stamps of my own feet, but eventually, I began to get a bit tougher over their unadventurousness. I began to insist that they were not scared, they *did want to go further*, that *he* was holding them back. He began to climb them up the back of the sofa and, unlike the days when all I could see was their backs, he placed them to face me from the top.

As the first year progressed, Joseph took more and more pleasure in discovering his deeper voice, and a more powerful and muscular self. His parents reported that he was making more eye contact and had begun occasionally to use spontaneous speech at home. Not long after the end of the second year, he began to engage in what I think was real pretend play. He lay on the couch, shouted "Yee-ikes, 'elp, save me!!!" as he "fell" onto the rug. Although this scene may have come from one of his videos, it was not carried out in isolation as in the doll conversations where he usually kept his back to me: here he fell off the couch right in front of me, looking at me often, and if I was too slow to call out, "Help, this poor boy is falling off the cliff, we've got to rescue him, hurry, hurry!!!", he pulled my arm to get it to reach out to his. The sequence was repeated, but somehow was never boring, perhaps because of Joseph's delight in the high drama. Certainly, my involvement in the game was quite intense too: lack of a capacity for pretend play and for joint attention is one of the early markers for autism, and it is moving and cheering when they begin, however immature they may be in relation to the chronological age of the child. The game seemed heavy with meaning: sometimes I told him that I agreed—he did indeed need rescuing from his self-imposed autistic isolation, and to be brought up and out onto firmer ground where there were other real people.

Discussion

The technical issues in talking to a child like Joseph are difficult. Needless to say, I have only cited parts of sessions where I think I managed to find a way of being heard, encouraging proto-speech between us. Working with these children is never easy, and the power of their autism is awesome. However, it is interesting to think about how to talk to these children, and why particular methods may be more useful than others. I think there were many different motives for Joseph's repetitive talk. Sometimes he did seem totally absorbed in it but, as I said, I began to think that at times he was definitely monitoring my response to it. And he did become less autistic when I gave urgent voice to this excluded third. This suggests that there was a communicative element in the projection at such moments. Or should we call it a proto-communication? He may not have expected a response, but he recognised it and seemed delighted by it when he got it. At other moments, when I felt his "talking" was more arrogantly self-indulgent, I challenged it. I think he needed both the more receptive coaxing "motherese" from me, and also the more challenging "fatherese". There seem to have been two aspects to the father's voice in the room: first, a father who declines to indulge omnipotence, who makes demands on his child to learn and grow, and who makes it clear that the child is not the same as the grownups; second, the father who invites and permits identification (with the strong voice and the potency of the stamping). Both only worked when I got the tone right. I suspect that when I challenged him too strictly, it may not have permitted the kind of identification he needed with a strong father. What seemed to work better was a firm, slightly bored tone, or a more humorous teasing. Some identification processes seemed to be beginning with his deeper growls, strong stamping, and standing tall. Some identification with father certainly aids the tolerance of oedipal rivalries, and enables omnipotent methods to be replaced by a more realistic sense of agency and potency.

I have described elsewhere the need to approach the child with autism on the right band of intensity (Alvarez & Reid, 1999), but it is interesting that Barrows (2002) has been even more specific in introducing aggressive play to a child with autism.

To return to the more receptive or maternal function: Bion talked about "alpha function", a function of the mind that makes thoughts thinkable and lends meaning to experience. He suggested that the mother's reverie provided the necessary emotional containment of experience that enables babies to think. He described this in terms of the mother's containment of the baby's distress which had been projected into her and then transformed there by her capacity to think about and process feelings (Bion, 1962). But as developmentalists like Stern (1985) and Trevarthen and Aitken (2001) remind us, these processes do not concern only moments of distress. Babies need to impress, to delight, to bring a light to the parents' eyes, to surprise and astonish them, to make them laugh. And they also need to be given room and space and time in which to do all this. We all may need to learn to keep our distance, know our place, wait our turn, and bide our time—and, especially important, respect the child's space and the child's timing. I think it was important for this child that I could hold the experience of being left out, unwanted, helpless, and especially, powerless, and give him space and time to feel that he had the power to keep me waiting. Of course, the risk in such a technique is of being experienced as masochistically colluding with his omnipotence: it needed vigilant monitoring on my part, so that when it felt more self-indulgent on his part, I could be firmer.

I also want to mention another point concerning the strength of my voice when I coaxed Joseph to talk to me, rather than to his imaginary (or delusional?) friends. I feel there was a kind of process of "reclamation" at such moments, possibly because Joseph didn't really believe his objects minded when he disappeared (Alvarez, 1992). Even the most loving and devoted parents, teachers, and therapists can get very demoralised and give up a little under such conditions. Joseph did seem to appreciate my staying power, but only when I kept it mock-desperate, playful/needy: as soon as there was a hint of unprocessed frustration or directive pulling on my part, he retreated. (His teachers have independently developed similar non-controlling methods with him.) I also think the drama in my voice got through to the developmentally delayed proto-speaker in him. (These active elements in the technique were informed by developmental thinking and also by awareness of the powerful hold of the repetitive preoccupations. The technique was by no means strictly psychoanalytic.) We have to find ways of helping these children not only to attend to us, but also to sustain their attention; and emotionally heightened interest is central to this process.

In conclusion, it is important to say that Joseph had dedicated parents, teachers, and speech and music therapists, with whom I have liaised regularly, so this has been a co-operative effort. I have simply tried to outline some techniques and concepts that seem to have been helpful in my particular part of the work. Our task continues to be enormously difficult.

References

Alvarez, A. (1992). *Live Company: Psychoanalytic Psychotherapy with Autistic, Borderline, Deprived and Abused Children*. London: Tavistock/Routledge.

Alvarez, A., & Reid, S. (Eds.) (1999). *Autism and Personality: Findings from the Tavistock Autism Workshop*. London: Routledge.

Baron-Cohen, S., Allen, J., & Gillberg, C. (1992). Can autism be detected at 18 months? The needle, the haystack, and the CHAT. *British Journal of Psychiatry, 161*: 839–843.

Barrows, P. (2002). Becoming verbal: autism, trauma and playfulness. *Journal of Child Psychotherapy, 28*(1): 53–72.

Bion, W. R. (1962). *Learning from Experience*. London: Heinemann.

Bion, W. R. (1967). Differentiation of the psychotic from the non-psychotic personalities. In: *Second Thoughts*. London: Karnac.

Bowlby, J. (1988). *A Secure Base: Clinical Applications of Attachment Theory*. London: Routledge.

Brazelton, T. B., Koslowski B., & Main, M. (1974). The origins of reciprocity: the early mother–infant interaction. In: M. Lewis & L. A. Rosenblum (Eds.), *The Effect of the Infant on its Caregiver*. London: Wiley Interscience.

Bruner, J. (1983). From communicating to talking. In: J. Bruner, *Child's Talk: Learning to Use Language* (pp. 23–42). Oxford: OUP.

Burhouse, A. (2001). Now we are two, going on three: Triadic thinking and its link with development in the context of young child observations. *Infant Observation: The International Journal of Infant Observation and its Applications*, 4(2): 51–67.

Dawson, G., & Lewy, A. (1989). Reciprocal subcortical-cortical influences in autism: The role of attentional mechanisms. In: G. Dawson (Ed.), *Autism, Nature, Diagnosis, and Treatment*. New York: Guilford Press.

Demos, V. (1986). Crying in early infancy: An illustration of the motivational function of affect. In: T. B. Brazelton & M. W. Yogman (Eds.), *Affective Development in Infancy*. New Jersey: Ablex.

Fogel, A. (1977). Temporal organization in mother-infant face-to face interaction. In: H. R. Schaffer (Ed.), *Studies in Mother–Infant Interaction*. London: Academic Press.

Hobson, P. (1993). *Autism and the Development of Mind*. Hove, Sussex: Lawrence Erlbaum.

Hobson, R. P., & Lee, A. (1999). Imitation and identification in autism. *Journal of Child Psychology and Psychiatry*, 40: 649–659.

Houzel, D. (2001). Bisexual qualities of the psychic envelope. In: J. Edwards (Ed.), *Being Alive: Building on the Work of Anne Alvarez*. Hove, Sussex: Brunner-Routledge.

Joseph, B. (1982). Addiction to near death. In: M. Feldman & E. Spillius (Eds.), *Psychic Equilibrium and Psychic Change*. London: Tavistock/Routledge, 1989.

Kanner, L. (1944). Early infantile autism. *Journal of Paediatrics*, 25: 211–217.

Klein, M. (1945). The Oedipus complex in the light of early anxieties. In: *The Writings of Melanie Klein Volume 1: Love, Guilt and Reparation and Other Works*. London: Hogarth, 1975.

Klein, M. (1959). Our adult world and its roots in infancy. In: *The Writings of Melanie Klein, III: Envy and Gratitude and Other Works*. London: Hogarth, 1975.

Koulomzin, M., Beebe, B., Anderson, S., Jaffe, J., Feldstein, S., & Crown, C. (2002). Infant gaze, head, face and self-touch differentiate secure vs. avoidant attachment at 1 year: A microanalytic approach. *Attachment and Human Development*, 4(1): 3–24.

Leslie, A. M. (1987). Pretense and representation: The origins of "theory of mind". *Psychological Review*, 94: 412–416.

Maurer, D., & Salapatak, P. (1976). Developmental changes in the scanning of faces by young infants. *Child Development*, 47: 523–527.

Meltzer, D. (1975). *Explorations in Autism: A Psycho-analytic Study*. Perthshire: Clunie Press.

Miller, L., Rustin, M., Rustin, M., & Shuttleworth, J. (1989). *Closely Observed Infants*. London: Duckworth.

Murray, L. (1991). Intersubjectivity, object relations theory and empirical evidence from mother–infant interactions. *Infant Mental Health Journal*, 12: 219–232.

Newson, J. (1977). An intersubjective approach to the systematic description of mother–infant interaction. In: H. R. Schaffer (Ed.), *Studies in Mother–Infant Interaction*. London: Academic Press.

Papousek, H., & Papousek M. (1975). Cognitive aspects of preverbal social interaction between human infants and adults. In: *CIBA Foundation Symposium*. New York: Association of Scientific Publishers.

Pessoa, F. (1981). Cease your song. In: *Selected Poems* (2nd edition). Penguin: London.

Rhode, M. (2001). The sense of abundance in relation to technique. In: J. Edwards (Ed.), *Being Alive: Building on the Work of Anne Alvarez*. Hove, Sussex: Brunner-Routledge.

Robson, K. (1967). The role of eye-to eye contact in maternal–infant attachment. *Journal of Child Psychology and Psychiatry*, 8: 13–25.

Scaife, M., & Bruner, J. (1975). The capacity for joint visual attention in the infant. *Nature*, 253: 265–266.

Schore, A. (1997). Interdisciplinary developmental research as a source of clinical models. In: M. M. Moskowitz, C. Monk, C. Kaye, & S. Ellman (Eds.), *The Neurobiological and Developmental Basis for Psychotherapeutic Intervention*. London: Aaronson.

Stern, D. N. (1985). *The Interpersonal World of the Infant: A View from Psychoanalysis and Developmental Psychology*. New York: Basic Books.

Striano, T., & Rochat, P. (1999). Developmental links between dyadic and triadic social competence in infancy. *British Journal of Developmental Psychology, 17*: 551–562.

Trevarthen, C. (2001). Intrinsic motives for companionship in understanding: Their origin, development, and significance for infant mental health. *Infant Mental Health Journal, 22*(1–2): 95–131.

Trevarthen, C., & Aitkin, K. J. (2001). Intersubjectivity: Research, theory and clinical applications. *Journal of Child Psychology and Psychiatry, 42*: 3–48.

Trevarthen, C., & Hubley, P. (1978). Secondary intersubjectivity: Confidence, confiding and acts of meaning in the first year. In: A. Lock (Ed.), *Action, Gesture and Symbol: The Emergence of Language*. London: Academic Press.

Tustin, F. (1981). *Autistic States in Children*. London: Routledge and Kegan Paul (revised edition, 1992).

Urwin, C. (2002). A psychoanalytic approach to language delay: When autistic isn't necessarily autism. *Journal of Child Psychotherapy, 28*(1): 73–93.

Uzgiris, I. C., & Hunt, J. M. V. (1975). Infancy: *Ordinal Scales of Psychological Development in Infancy*. Illinois: University of Illinois Press.

Winnicott, D. W. (1958). Transitional objects and transitional phenomena (pp. 249–242). In: *Through Paediatrics to Psychoanalysis: Collected Papers*. London: Tavistock.

CHAPTER THREE

"Making a person": clinical considerations regarding the interpretation of anxieties in the analyses of children on the autisto-psychotic spectrum*

Joshua Durban

Over the past 88 years, psychoanalysts, beginning with Melanie Klein (1930), were fortunate to glean a significant amount of understanding from their pioneering work with psychotic and autistic child patients. A recurring theme in these findings is the central role of unconscious anxiety in the formation and symptomatology of autistic states. Analysts discovered that alongside more organised anxieties and their concomitant defence mechanisms, which could be classified as borderline or psychotic, there are more primitive sets of anxieties and defences belonging to autistic states (Winnicott, 1962; Tustin, 1968, 1972, 1981, 1990; Meltzer, 1974, 1975; Levine & Power, 2017). Thus, to paraphrase Bion's differentiation between psychotic and non-psychotic parts of the personality (1957), we may expand our work to include the

---

*An earlier version was published as Joshua Durban (2019). "Making a person": Clinical considerations regarding the interpretation of anxieties in the analyses of children on the autisto-psychotic spectrum. *The International Journal of Psychoanalysis*, 100(5): 921–939, DOI: 10.1080/00207578.2019.1636254. Copyright © Institute of Psychoanalysis, reprinted by permission of Taylor & Francis Ltd, http://www.tandfonline.com on behalf of Institute of Psychoanalysis. The editors thank Routledge and the *IJP* for permission to reprint.

interplay between the often-overlapping autistic, psychotic, and non-psychotic aspects of these patients. If we are to apply the vast knowledge gained by Kleinian psychoanalysis regarding the centrality of object relations, anxiety, and unconscious phantasy in autism (Rhode, 2018) and the pioneering work done simultaneously by the French psychoanalysts concerning the role of psychotic structures, pre-psychotic structures, and structures of deficit, the role of corporality, of language, and of the desire of the other in the creation and destruction of the infant's development (Lacan 1966; Haag, 1993, 1997; Bursztejn et al., 2003; Lechevalier, 2003; Houzel, 2004, 2018; Laznik, 2007, 2013), then we must consider that these findings carry major and far-reaching clinical implications.

Any expansion of our psychoanalytic approach, however, confronts us with numerous diagnostic, theoretical, and technical challenges. This is especially the case when we work with children and adults who exhibit a mixture of autistic and psychotic anxieties on what might be called the autisto-psychotic spectrum. Analysts thus face the complicated task of trying to integrate the insights gained from both the Kleinian and the French schools into their daily clinical work. My aim in this chapter is to demonstrate how such integration might be achieved by trying to follow the various, often confusing and intertwined levels of anxieties within the session and trying to speak their language.

The autisto-psychotic spectrum and the autistic psychic retreat

A considerable number of the children who are nowadays diagnosed as suffering from autistic spectrum disorder (ASD) often reveal themselves during psychoanalytic treatment to be suffering from a combination of autistic and psychotic anxieties, defended against and masked by an autistic pathological organisation. The pathological organisation described by Steiner (2011, 1993) as a rigid, nearly impenetrable set of narcissistic defences serves as a double protection from persecutory paranoid–schizoid anxieties regarding the object as well as from the inevitable anxieties and psychic pain involved in the depressive recognition of reality and loss. The autistic psychic retreat, however, is non-symbolic, bodily very concrete and observable, due to the disturbance in symbol formation and the regression to symbolic equation (Segal, 1957). It is characterised by hyper-cathected senses, inadequate or failed splitting, and fragmentation of both self and object. The autistic pathological organisation serves as a concrete container of a fragile constitution, which is plagued by various deficits and is, therefore, often symbiotically oriented (Bleger, 2013). Furthermore, these children's multiple developmental deficits create parent–child vicious circles of projections and counter-projections of despair, depression, and un-mentalized psychic content (Alvarez, 1992; Durban, 2014). This vicious circle is often enacted in the analysis and projected into the analyst's internal objects (Brenman Pick, 1985) and into his body. This creates a bewildering and often overwhelming emotional seesaw between despair and hope in both patient and analyst (Durban, 2014).

The autistic psychic retreat is created through an unconscious phantasy of active "mantling" by the object (Durban, 2014, 2017a) and of annexing forcefully its external layers (Rhode, 2012a) as a defence against "dismantling"—that is, a passive crumbling of the psyche's connective tissues (Meltzer, 1974, 1992). Mantling, which is the frantic search for concrete bodily and sensorial covers, protects the child from the dread of falling into bits, dissolving, losing shape, freezing, burning, suffocating, falling, losing his membrane, his sense of cohesiveness and of orientation. The child then concretely acts out this unconscious phantasy by covering himself up with autistic objects and sensation-shapes and thus, in phantasy, avoids relationship, communication, and an unbearable reality (Tustin, 1981, 1990). The autistic psychic retreat has two phases: it appears initially as autistic encapsulation into the body parts or onto inanimate objects. As the analysis progresses, it appears as a more developed mantling when the child, snail-like, begins to emerge from his primary encapsulation only to retreat again into his shelter. Nevertheless, in this secondary mantling, the shelter is constructed with the help of vital, annexed parts belonging to a living object.

In the course of the psychoanalyses of ASD children, it is important to try and distinguish between the different forms of autistic psychic retreats and interpret accordingly. The primary autistic retreat of encapsulation is bodily sensorial, concrete, using autistic objects and sensation-shapes. It is characterised by a massive confusion between self and object as a defence against separateness from the object and its proper internalisation. The secondary psychic retreat of mantling implies the beginning of object perception and relatedness. Primary encapsulation protects the child from nameless dread and catastrophic annihilation following a lack of sufficient sense of "the body-as-a-safe-mother" (Durban, 2017b). Secondary mantling protects against catastrophic change and psychic pain in a dawning reality of dependence, transience, and otherness. The object, rather than the body in the case of primary encapsulation, then becomes the traumatising agent. The primary encapsulated retreat wards off "anxieties-of-being" and paralyses the movement towards paranoid anxieties. The retreat of secondary mantling prevents the movement towards depressive anxieties and mourning. Thus, these two lines of autistic defensive organisations tragically bring to a halt not only the fluctuations between paranoid and depressive anxieties (PS–D) and the possibility of psychic equilibrium (Joseph, 1978, 1989) but mainly between "anxieties-of-being" and paranoid anxieties (B–PS).

Klein (1952) described the constant interaction and fluctuations between different constellations of anxieties vis-à-vis the internal and external objects, accompanied by typical defence mechanisms and unconscious phantasies. To highlight the non-linear nature of these interactions, she conceptualised them as positions rather than phases or stages. Klein's understanding of the constant to-and-fro movement between different anxiety situations has been further investigated, described, and developed by her followers. They came to understand the process of mental development as consisting of a capacity to contain, tolerate, and modify these various interacting anxiety situations so that thinking, creativity, and integration (Bion, 1963), feeling, emotional equilibrium, and reality testing (Joseph, 1978, 1989) may evolve. Furthermore, necessary movements towards temporary states of disintegration were seen not only as a defence against integration but as an inevitable part of development (Bion, 1963). Simultaneously, apparent states of more organised depressive states of being were discovered to be defensive organisations against change with all the psychic pain and further arousal of anxieties it brings about (Steiner, 1987; Britton, 1998). From a clinical perspective, Brenman Pick (2018) describes the many difficulties the analyst encounters in trying to "bring things together" when facing these oscillations between the different positions.

She points out the importance of the timing of interpretation and the painful nature of the process for both the analyst and the patient as they struggle with murderousness, envy, jealousy, and guilt. In the case of the autisto-psychotic child, this oscillating movement is constantly attacked due to an influx of archaic bodily anxieties-of-being and failed attempts at binary splitting. This tragically interferes with the emergence of thinking, feeling, and transformation.

As Brenman Pick describes, the way to approach these unconscious anxieties and "bring them together" is through interpreting them for the patient, thereby supplying him with a network of meaning, thinking, object-relatedness, and facilitating holding and containing functions. In the case of the autisto-psychotic child, the very act of interpretation also rescues him from his extreme, debilitating isolation or devastating loneliness. However, the main difficulty with these children is not only in deciding the right timing for interpretation but in selecting the appropriate level of interpretation, suitable for such states characterised by massive confusion or lack of self–object differentiation (Alvarez, 2012) and impaired processes of identification (Rhode, 2005). Interpretation is often made difficult, if not impossible at times, due to intense adhesive identification and the freezing of the analyst's free associations. These are equated with the child's own experience of being frozen, with the threats of parental intercourse producing a baby, and with the autistic horror of bodily disintegration. Thus, the analyst's mental movements resonate with the child's fear that movement, whether physical or mental, means losing parts of the body and is to be avoided at all costs (Rhode, 2015).

The manifest pathology in the autisto-psychotic spectrum child is primarily an autistic one. It consists of withdrawal and of "shutting off" the mind against separateness, fragmentation, and chaos, initiated by the death drive. In the course of the psychoanalyses of these children we often witness an opening up of the impenetrable, obsessive autistic defensive organisation and an emergence of vivid psychotic material. This indicates an underlying, previously buried, better-developed self–object differentiation, a better capacity for splitting mechanisms, and even symbolic thinking. The child then erects a second line of defence in the form of secondary mantling. He fluctuates in-between the two forms of mantling, and development is seriously jeopardised.

In the analyses of children who are primarily autistic, however, such a movement is rare and appears, if at all, much later in the analysis.

Haag (1993) supplies us with further insight into these conditions. She writes:

> In my experience, those encapsulated autistic children who emerge from their armor seem to do so in rather long transitory stages and following one of two principal tracks … either into post-autistic obsessionality or into a more boisterous manner, so-called psychotic or schizophrenic, and in any case of hyperpenetrating symbiosis, which is quite destructive.
>
> (pp. 71–72)

She tries to differentiate between the schizophrenogenic elements characterised by an explosion into minute splitting and those elements derivative of manic-depressive problems, characterised by non-explosive projective identification which uses the different bodily compartments for the purpose of re-penetration and sexualised co-excitation.

This attempt at differentiation between childhood schizophrenia, autism, and psychosis has historical roots. Melanie Klein was struggling with this problem while analysing her patient Dick (Klein, 1930), whom she half-heartedly diagnosed as suffering from childhood schizophrenia. Although today Dick would have been diagnosed as an ASD child, it might very well be that Klein was in a way right. Although at the time of Dick's analysis the diagnosis of autism did not exist, clinically speaking, Dick was exhibiting a confusing array of autistic and psychotic anxieties and defences, related to a tragic developmental history of deficit and loss.

Throughout the years that followed, many attempts were made at clarifying the differences between schizophrenia, psychosis, and autism in the psychiatric, developmental, and psychoanalytic fields (Houzel, 2018; Rhode, 2018). Clinically, however, when analysing a child with manifest autistic symptoms, we are still confronted daily with the need to understand the nature of their anxieties, defences, unconscious phantasies, and object relations.

One might argue that the problem today is mainly one of an inaccurate or a too-all-inclusive initial diagnosis of the child, inspired by the psychiatric ASD criteria. Furthermore, such diagnosis is influenced by many political, financial, social, and pharmaco-medical considerations. In Israel, for example, the numbers of diagnosed ASD infants are constantly on the rise, and these children are entitled to considerable financial support from the government and have excellent analytically informed treatment facilities from a young age. This is not the case with childhood psychosis. Curiously, there is also less stigmatisation of autism than of psychosis since the latter somehow arouses more conscious and unconscious anxieties.

Our experience in Israel shows that many times the underlying structure of the child, who is initially diagnosed as autistic, is only revealed in the course of analysis. This is a unique and distinguishing feature of child analysis: the child not only develops but in a way is being "created" as the analysis proceeds. Thus, as the analysis progresses there are often oscillations between mantling—that is, acquiring some sort of a container, albeit often concrete, false, annexed, or precarious (Rhode, 2012a; Durban, 2014, 2017a)—and psychosis. These constant oscillations differentiate the children on the autisto-psychotic spectrum from the more stable situations described by Haag (1993, 1997), where children emerging from autistic states may move in the direction of schizophrenia, manic depression, or obsessionality; or by Tustin (1990) in her last book where a subgroup of children are said to use "an autistic straitjacket" to hold psychotic anxieties in check (but not the other way around). There is a constant, rapid, and often confusing back-and-forth movement between emerging and withdrawal, followed by the formation of primary and secondary autistic pathological organisations. These children are not post-autistic but rather, to follow the French method of classification, borderline autistic: a "mixed bag" of paranoid–schizoid and autistic "anxieties-of-being". They hover between autistic fragmentation and withdrawal characterised by adhesive identification and sensorial hyper-cathexis, and between better-formed psychotic mechanisms such as splitting and projective identification. These borderline autistic organisations defy linear etiological explanations. Houzel (2018) writes:

> It is not easy to accept that one does not know what the next stage will be or when it will occur. And yet it is the condition for making room for the processual aspect of psychic development. It is not a matter of a linear development, but rather of an evolution in the form of a spiral going through progressions and regressions. The team of caregivers must engage in intense elaborative

work to evaluate this evolution correctly and to avoid taking a necessary regression as a sign of deterioration, or the emergence of inevitable psychic suffering for an outbreak of symptoms that must be suppressed.

(pp. 737–738)

An article published recently by Larson et al. (2017) from Cambridge University in the *British Journal of Psychiatry* provides important research-based support for the existence of such a subgroup. The authors claim that there may be a specific subtype of ASD linked to comorbid psychosis. Their results indicate that the spectrum of psychotic illness experienced by adults with ASD may be different from that experienced by those without a diagnosis of ASD. They further propose that their observations support the existence of an underlying neurodevelopmental vulnerability to developing psychosis in some people with ASD, driven perhaps by a not-yet-understood genetic mechanism, compounded by elevated rates of depression and anxiety.

Larson et al.'s article has confirmed my impressions gained from many years of analysing ASD infants, children, and adolescents and supervising many other such cases. I believe that there are, in fact, two spectrums: one is purely autistic and the other one is autisto-psychotic. The main difference between these two spectrums lies in the nature of the anxieties and defences involved. The child on the autisto-psychotic spectrum manifests a mixture of paranoid–schizoid and less well-differentiated anxieties-of-being, such as liquefying, dissolving, having no skin or a skin full of holes, freezing, burning, losing a sense of time and space, and existing in a bi-dimensional world. The autistic child shows mainly the latter. The seeming overlap of these two spectrums, or the overshadowing of the psychotic structure by autistic defences and vice versa, often leads to a theoretical and clinical confusion and an overuse of phenomenological-psychiatric diagnostic language instead of a psychoanalytic one.

Some technical considerations

When analysing a child on the autisto-psychotic spectrum, we experience constant fluctuations between different levels of anxieties, defences, and of self–object differentiation and integration. Thus we may encounter in the same child, and often in the same session, anxiety states ranging from archaic anxieties-of-being, to more clearly defined anxieties concerning object relationships of the paranoid–schizoid and depressive kind, and even some rudimentary forms of autistic oedipal anxieties (Rhode, 2012b). Psychotic anxieties might cover up and bind primitive anxieties-of-being, while the latter might serve as a retreat from psychotic anxieties. These dynamics are embodied in unconscious phantasies characteristic of early malformed mental states.

Anne Alvarez (2012) in her influential work proposes to think about these primitive states along the lines of different levels of meaning, corresponding to different levels of self and object integration. Such understanding, she claims, necessitates different levels of interpretations which move from the higher explanatory mode, through the descriptive mode, and down to what she calls the vitalising mode. Furthermore, she points out the important need to differentiate between two kinds of anxieties: one that is based on projective mechanisms (such as projective and counter-projective identification), and another more primitive one, in which no projective identification is possible. This second kind of anxiety triggers the analyst's response to a devastated state of mind in the infant without the infant even being aware of its devastated-ness. Following her work, I have realised, over many years of working with such states, that the key to understanding the child and to the creation of shared meaning lies for me primarily in adhering to the Kleinian principle (1932, 1948, 2017) of detecting the most urgent, deeper anxieties and in their interpretation in what might be described as their own "language" or syntax (Amir, 2014). Nevertheless, this calls not only for a widening of our understanding regarding the nature of these deepest anxieties, ranging from autistic signal anxieties-of-being to better differentiated paranoid–schizoid and depressive ones, but also of what we define as interpretations.

I wish to share some observations gained from my experience in the analysis of one such child when, often intuitively and unawares, I have found the need to shift between these different forms of anxiety and modes of interpretations. This involved brief resorts to very primitive, concrete, and fragmented interpretations in order to establish some immediate contact with these deep unconscious anxieties of the withdrawn, fragmented, pre-corporal, nonverbal, and pre-symbolic child

(Durban, 2014). These interpretations in action (Ogden, 1994; Durban, 2014, 2018; Pollak, 2017) or pre-symbolic realisations (Sechehaye, 1951) reflect a special countertransference in the analyst and assume different forms: verbal, nonverbal, and sometimes a concrete act. They do not qualify as symbolic play but might be regarded as acting in and out of the sessions and as a deviation from traditional technique. Nevertheless, I believe they form an inevitable part of the psychoanalytic technique required when treating such unreachable mental states. These moments are familiar to child psychoanalysts and are more traditionally incorporated into their play technique. There are other moments, however, which cannot be regarded as symbolic play since the child's level of self–object differentiation and capacity for representation is still undeveloped, attacked, or destroyed. In this way, certain aspects of the child's shattered mind might be reassembled, repaired, and sometimes even virtually created by an "analytic object implant"—that is, by introducing the analyst as a new, concrete object that can substitute for developmental deficits. I think one of our main challenges as psychoanalysts today is to modify and apply these shifts between various kinds of interpretations into our work with adult patients who exhibit, momentarily or for extended periods, the same or similar states of being.

Rafael

Rafael is a fourteen-year-old boy who has been in a five-sessions-per-week analysis with me since the age of nine. Referred to me by a colleague from another country, Rafael was born to an Israeli mother and a European father. At the age of three, he was diagnosed with low functioning ASD. He exhibited all the major symptoms of such a diagnosis: minimal and bizarre use of speech; no eye contact; avoidance of people, including his parents; lack of bodily co-ordination and integration; alternation between states of limpness and rigidity; psychomotor agitation; self-stimulation by the use of autistic objects, autistic sensation-shapes, and masturbation; rigidity and obsessive-compulsive repetitive behaviours; lack of play; lack of empathy; and no imagination.

Rafael began his first psychotherapy in parallel with behavioural therapy and was prescribed anti-psychotic medication for his violent outbursts. By the time he turned five, there had been little improvement; in fact, his condition seemed to be getting worse. Rafael had frequent violent tantrums, resulting in occasional self-harm. His aggression also took the form of physical attacks against his mother and his baby brother (born when Rafael was four). His speech developed slowly and bizarrely. He would mainly scream for food, the toilet, and television. Following the appearance of speech, the parents realised that he was hallucinating. He would report seeing various shapes and colours, he would see the air twisting around him, and he saw holes in the floor and in the walls, which seemed to be cracking and crumbling whenever he touched them. He also complained about loud noises and voices in his head telling him to kill himself and his brother. Although at that stage he had been closely watched at all times by his parents and various caretakers, he attempted several times to throw himself out of the window and tried to harm his brother, once by suffocating him with a pillow and once by trying to drown him in the bath.

Neurological tests indicated nothing. At that point, the devastated parents agreed to admit him to a psychiatric hospital ward for children, where he was diagnosed as suffering from childhood schizophrenia. This diagnosis resulted in Rafael receiving a maximal dosage of antipsychotic medication, after which he withdrew into a catatonic, autistic state. Both parents sought help as they became severely depressed and anxious. They perceived Rafael's diagnosis as a kind of "death sentence" for the child. In the initial interview with them, I was struck by their use of this expression, instead of saying "a life sentence", for example. This choice of words, as it turned out, was not accidental.

The grandparents on both sides exerted great pressure upon the parents to have Rafael admitted to a special institution for mentally ill children, claiming that he would ruin the life of the whole family since he was unmanageable at home. There were several cases of mental illnesses on both sides of Rafael's family. The mother's twin brother committed suicide, following his release from the Israeli army, where he served as a high-ranking officer in the fighting units. The brother was described as "being poisoned by the army", which is an Israeli expression used to describe extreme devotion to and admiration of the militant actions. The mother's father died from cancer while she was still pregnant with Rafael. The child was therefore born into and out of a death-saturated family womb, with all its hereditary psycho-genetic, internal and external, manifestations (Durban, 2011). Complicated grief and stunted mourning were constant shadowy companions for Rafael and his family.

The parents, who in the meantime started psychoanalytic psychotherapy, insisted on keeping Rafael at home. They took turns staying with him and initiated home-schooling. They both described Rafael as lovable in spite of his enormous difficulties. From various things they said during our initial interviews, it became clear that Rafael had a triple unconscious function for the parents: he was a cork-child who was supposed to fill up the void created by loss; a pipe-child into which the mother projected her un-mentalized toxic materials (beta elements) thus turning him into an open-ended leaking pipe. Rafael often suffered from bouts of vomiting and diarrhoea. In addition, both parents were trying to repair something through him and thus deal with their numerous losses and grief.

The mother decided she wanted to go back to Israel to be closer to her mother and the rest of her family. She also wanted to provide Rafael with psychoanalysis. It was not that she believed especially in psychoanalysis or knew much about it, but a childhood friend of hers had an autistic girl who had been in analysis with me and had benefited from it. She also found out about the possibility of getting considerable financial support from the Israeli government for Rafael's treatment (through the National Health Service and the Ministry of Defence). It was then that the family contacted me and, following my advice that Rafael begin analysis, the whole family moved to Israel. So, in addition to the obvious pressure exerted on me by Rafael's pathology and the slim chances of its cure, there were also the family's intense idealisations of and expectations from the treatment.

At the beginning of the analysis, I was pleasantly surprised by Rafael's co-operation. I was also encouraged by the presence of early oedipal anxieties concerning rivalry and competition with his brother and envious possessiveness towards the mother. Although incomprehensible and quite unmanageable and withdrawn most of the time, Rafael would occasionally tell me things.[1] He didn't seem to know how

---

[1] Rafael's analysis was conducted at first in English, then in a mixture of English and Hebrew, and finally in Hebrew.

to play. During sessions he would just move about the room in an agitated manner, making unintelligible noises, waving his arms, scratching violently, banging his head against the wall, and sometimes running towards me and trying to bite or scratch me. His hands were often bandaged to prevent him from scratching and biting himself, tearing out pieces of skin. At other times he would slump into a heap on the floor and rub his saliva and mucus all over his body.

He carried with him a hard, plastic Superman toy, which he mainly waved about. At that time, I took it to be his autistic object, providing protection but blocking out communication. However, during one session Rafael bit and eventually pulled out Superman's arms. He then got into a panic and mumbled, "Repair, repair", proceeding to push different materials and other torn parts from other toys into the holes created by the mutilated arms. When this failed, he pointed at the Superman symbol on the toy's chest and said, "button", insisting that I push the button and make Superman whole again. Rafael's anxiety resonated in me mainly in the form of a deep confusion. Eventually, I managed to interpret this confusion and said, "All confused. Rafael, Superman, arms, chest, mommy, daddy, dead, alive." Rafael kept pushing the button and grabbed my arm so that I would push, too. I then said, "Rafael wants Joshua to repair Superman, repair, Rafael, repair daddy and mummy. Rafael bit the button off mommy's breast and daddy's wee-wee. Daddy and mommy are angry and tear Rafael apart. Now Rafael wants to stick it back into place and wants Joshua to help him. Rafael wants to be whole again." At that point, there were two main anxiety states intermingled. At a deep autistic level, there was the anxiety of falling apart and leaking out through what Rafael experienced as his body full of holes. At the same time, there was the more clearly defined and object-related anxiety of Rafael causing harm to the breast and to the penis through his aggression and greed, resulting in retaliation and mutilation of his own body. To complicate things further, I perceived Rafael also as an open-ended, leaking "pipe-child" (Durban, 2018), through whom the projections and traumatisation of the former generations lived on. From this perspective, the destroyed Superman toy also stood for his maternal uncle, the soldier-hero who committed suicide. Due to the intermingled nature of his anxieties, and of the primary and secondary autistic defences employed against them (his withdrawal into his bodily fluids, the bandages, the hard Superman toy), it was difficult for me and often quite impossible to reach for the appropriate anxiety and interpret it.

Rafael's sadism and aggression, exacerbated by his internal, attacked persecutory objects, were deflected outwards, albeit in a passive way. He would limp in and out of the consulting room, treading as if unaware of the flower beds, tearing out leaves without as much as looking at his hands, appearing to be totally oblivious and distracted. Toys were frequently broken and whenever he approached me his hands would swing and hit me.

Rafael was terrorised by and terrified of his destructiveness and felt equated with an omnipotent, deadly superego who reigned supreme. He soon introduced me to secret "things" which were very bad, persecutory, and dangerous. These "things" were composed of even and odd numbers. Even numbers, especially two, four, and twenty-two, were considered to be good and protective, albeit equated with a primitive sadistic superego. He claimed they often took away his speech and forbade him to look at other people. He would then become mute and roll his eyes upwards so as not to see, or be seen by anyone. The odd numbers three, five, and seven were particularly vicious and harmful. Number one and zero were considered to be very good since one was similar to two ("Almost twins," he said), and zero was a sign for him to relax and be quiet. When he was under the influence of the zero number, Rafael appeared catatonic and impenetrable.

At that time, I mainly interpreted Rafael's symbiotic wish to be one with his mother and me, without any differentiation or competition. This was represented by the even "twin" numbers, which were replicating one another. Any threat of separation or differences was perceived as an attack. Rafael would then strike back, trying to annihilate either the threatening agents of separation or his perception and mind. The zero number stood for his wish to reach the symbiotic unity and thus get rid of reality, where things were separate from him and from each other, incontrollable. It also expressed his death wish: to cease to exist so as not to feel so much fear and hatred. Rafael responded well to these interpretations and started calling me "Mr no-number" and at other times "Mr Zero". I became a figure who was outside the reach of the evil numbers, but at the same time stood for a death-like, frozen state.

He said that I was stupid, a zero, thereby equating me not just with help and relief but with annihilation and mindlessness. At other times he said I was three people at once. I thus became also the threatening number three, standing for the dreaded oedipal triangulation.

As the analysis progressed, Rafael's behaviour at home improved, his violent outbursts subsided and eventually he was even able to attend a special school. It turned out that he was an intelligent child and thus excelled in his studies. Inside the consulting room, however, he seemed to be getting even more fragmented. He would stay silent for long stretches of time, hardly recognising my existence, mumbling to himself, playing with his fingers raised in the air, spitting and licking himself and hiding under the armchairs. I thought that Rafael's improvement outside of the consulting room was precarious. It was made possible only by his splitting himself further and by encapsulating his madness, which he then deposited within the analysis. He retreated into his primary autistic shelter and occasionally used me and the analysis as a second mantling. Thus, when he momentarily emerged from his withdrawal and his use of self-generated sensation-shapes, he started imitating me, repeating my interpretations, and insisting on covering himself up with a blanket which lay on my couch. After staying covered for a few minutes, he would start crumbling the blanket, throwing it on the floor and trying to shove it underneath the couch. He said that the blanket was bad and stinking. He said this in Hebrew and the way he pronounced the word "blanket" (*Smicha*) sounded like the word "conversation" (*Sicha*). It was very difficult for me to bear it. Like Rafael, I felt split between what was going on in the analysis and the external favourable feedback from his parents, who were very appreciative and thankful. I sometimes doubted what was real and what was not and became suspicious of this external "blanket" in a paranoid way. Upon further reflection, I understood that I was saturated with and invaded by Rafael's experiences of paranoia and de-realisation, the result of massive splitting and projective and adhesive identification. Like him, I found myself drifting into numbness and mental paralysis alongside psychomotor agitation and hypersensitivity.

Up to this point in Rafael's analysis, the majority of his anxieties belonged to the paranoid–schizoid position, with quite a lot of material relating to the early oedipal situation, and I therefore attempted to establish contact with his unconscious through interpreting the anxieties directly within the transference. When working in these areas, where there is a certain degree of differentiation between self and object and an ability to use splitting and projective mechanisms, it is effective to interpret within the total transference situation. These "explanatory interpretations", as Alvarez (2012) calls them, are usually thought of as: what is the content of the patient's unconscious anxieties and phantasies; who does what to whom and why; and what is the role and positioning of the analyst within this drama of object relationships? Rafael indeed responded well to such interpretations. However, the persistence of Rafael's symptoms in the analysis, alongside the existence of a considerable amount of anxieties-of-being, indicated that there was a lot of unconscious material against which he defended himself by fragmentation and with which, at that time, I could not yet establish better contact.

"What is a person?" The further emergence of primitive anxieties-of-being

During the second year of the analysis, Rafael would often ask me, "Are you a person? What is a person? Am I a person?" He would start screaming, biting himself, and say, "There's blood everywhere, where is the blood? Is it in or out? Are you bleeding? This is AIDS." The parents told me he often bit himself in order to see that "there was blood inside" and upon seeing it would tell them, "I have AIDS." I interpreted his fear that he was paper-thin, with nothing between inside and outside. Only when he saw the blood could he believe that he has an inside and is therefore human. However, upon inflicting so much harm and pain upon himself he also realised how ill he was and was afraid that his illness might be incurable, like AIDS. This was a sentiment that I, at that time, secretly shared with him. I also bore in mind the story about his uncle's "poisoning" by death and the army, which led to his suicide. I wondered whether Rafael was unconsciously attacked by too much psycho-genetic death in his psychic system.

As Rafael's anxieties regarding having no inside and leaking out subsided, he would arrive for the sessions and say that now he is Joshua and I am Rafael. This did not sound like a game but rather a conviction. It was then that I realised that he was trying to merge us and reverse our roles to ward off feelings of separateness and dependence that were beginning to appear inside of him. This violent merging through the annihilation of our separate existence assumed the form of perverse homosexual phantasies, in which we were penetrating one another, thus creating a combined, dangerous bizarre object, resulting in our death. He would try and aim imaginary missiles at me, mainly at my eyes, mouth, and anus. He would then run to the toilet and defecate, crying that his insides were exploding. I interpreted his fear that I penetrated him to punish him and explode his insides. I also thought that he was describing a problem with his and his mother's psychic immune systems whereby there was a failure in transforming (digesting) the death-infused external and internal maternal environment during pregnancy. I think he probably experienced the mother's placenta and her immune system as attacking cell-missiles. The mother had reported "some odd sensations" during the first term of her pregnancy. Rafael often claimed that he did not know her and that she was not his mother. Thus, the familiar and the unfamiliar were all confused, as in some auto-immune failure (AIDS). Furthermore, once Rafael was born, the mother, who was usually a quite verbal and fluent person, found it extremely difficult to talk to her non-responsive baby, therefore exacerbating another failure in mutual transformations.

I understood that Rafael was deteriorating to ensure that we would not be separated by the end of the treatment. By confusing him and me, inside and outside, creating one bloody mess, he was also saying that the analysis and I became a part of him, like blood, and that losing it would kill him. Nevertheless, this could only be experienced in a concrete psychotic fashion, not as affects accompanied by thoughts. I interpreted this to him over many sessions and this brought about a certain relief. The visual hallucinations calmed down. During one session when he was biting his hands, I noticed that he was looking intently at the bites, as if he were searching for something inside of his body. He also took out the bits of bitten skin and held them very carefully in both hands. Since he did not speak at that time, and having already interpreted his archaic anxiety of leaking out and liquefying, I now said that he was looking for what went on inside of him. I was encouraged by this new budding distinction between inside and outside and decided to interpret in terms of internal object relations. I suggested that, as a result of his unrelenting attacks on his mother and her body, which he equated with his own, he was leaking out, having no container or skin to hold him together. He also felt that his mother and father were bleeding to death inside of him and that he was trying to get them out and perhaps even save them. I said, "Having no mother with a body and no father to protect her is the same for you as having no body, being nobody."

Following this phase of the treatment, he came up with what seemed like a rudimentary game. Rafael would touch my nose and then his, my mouth and then his, my ears, hands, and legs and then touch his own. I was initially taken aback by this physical contact and tried to stop it, as I would have done with any patient's attempt to touch me. Rafael kept on insistently trying to initiate this ritual, which he called "making a person". He did this, as was not his custom, in a very gentle and non-eroticised way, while maintaining unusually long eye contact. I was greatly helped at that time by the contributions of two prominent French clinicians working with ASD infants and children. The first was Marie Christine Laznik's work on the role of the invocatory drive (2013) and the crucial role of the maternal prosody within it. Laznik, following Lacan (1966), claims that the child is being called into the realm of relationships and identifications by the desire of the other. It is the absence of this call in autistic children that she sees as the basis of autism. The autistic child fails in seeking to attract the attention and approval of his caretakers. The second inspiration was Genevieve Haag's extensive works on intracorporal identifications (1985), and the autistic child's failure in establishing a background object of identification (1985). Following Grotstein (1986), she describes the importance of the possibility of communicating with the other through one's gaze while having the feeling that what is projected is reflected back after touching a solid background. In the analysis of withdrawn children, this is often experienced when the psychoanalyst succeeds in communicating with the infant and their eyes meet. As a consequence, a psychic skin can gradually be constituted, allowing the infant to gain access to tri-dimensionality and symbolisation, and the infant feels contained.

I gradually came to understand this as yet another attempt to create himself as a separate, differentiated entity, through me. This time he used comparison with my own body. It is important to add that Rafael's differentiation between bodily parts and functions was impaired from the outset. He would very often close his eyes when there was a loud noise or put his hands to his ears when he saw something frightening. Right and left were always confused and he often got disorientated, bumping into things. Nevertheless, this emergence of a very basic confusion between his body parts took place after more developed anxieties about his internal objects were interpreted. There was a clearer movement between paranoid–schizoid and more archaic anxieties-of-being dealing with his very sense of existence as a bounded, separate being in time and space.

As we were approaching the summer break, Rafael's growing recognition of his and my existence as separate, albeit connected, entities developed. It was then that he became terrified again of people, perhaps out of conscious awareness of the dangers of losing them. Although he made some friends at school, he severed all contact with them, refused to go to school, and withdrew again from human contact. One day he told me that he killed his mother because she was not his mother and very bad. He threatened to kill me, too. He resumed his self-mutilation, this time as a result of unbearable psychotic guilt about his aggression and murderousness towards his objects. I interpreted that he prefers killing to being killed by loss and guilt. It was tempting to interpret these anxieties-of-being at the paranoid–schizoid level, but I soon discovered that this was unhelpful at best, and served only to deepen the gap between myself and Rafael, at worst.

Some improvement was gradually achieved through a special kind of analyst-based interpretation utilising my immersed state of mind: his memories, experiences, bodily sensations, and my capacity to think, feel, relate, and integrate. In other words, it is the analyst's task to provide mantling and linking functions for the child that will lead to a safe in-dwelling in his mind. Linking means actively and concretely reconnecting the disintegrated proto-elements of unconscious phantasy. This is one of the most complicated tasks in the sense that the analyst needs to constantly and actively link together fragmented senses, feelings, actions, intentions, and thoughts into a single sequence or string.

To attain the analyst's function as a mantling and linking object to be internalised by the child, he/she might need to consider an active construction of a bodily container (Pollak 2009) for patients with a disintegrated or confusional bodily representation. Interpretations should aim at helping the patient differentiate between body parts, inside and outside, self and object, before more well-integrated interpretations make sense. Rafael's creation of the "making a person" game, and my active participation in it for many sessions before an interpretation could be fully formed in terms of "you" and "I", would be one example.

In addition, the analyst needs to use moments of reparation or interpretation in action. That is, to initiate an action, a gesture, which signifies in a near-concrete way the possibility of understanding the preverbal and pre-symbolic experience and promotes integration and reparation. As Rafael's analysis commenced, further anxieties came to the surface as a result of my previous interpretive work. These brought about another change in technique.

Rafael's crossing

During the third year of the analysis, I was back after having been away for a week. While waiting for him, I could hear Rafael screaming and crying outside. I opened the door and saw him standing as if paralysed, unable to get in. "What's wrong?" I asked him. He trembled and pointed to the ground. "Are you scared of something here?" I continued to ask, not being able to think or to comprehend his crying. Rafael nodded and kept on pointing to the ground. When I followed his finger, I saw a crack between my entrance door and the paved path leading to it. I had never noticed it before. "A crack?" I asked. Rafael shouted, "The Grand Canyon, the Grand Canyon!" It was only later that his father told me about a film he had been watching over the weekend. The protagonist gets caught in a big canyon because a rock blocked his way and trapped his arm under it. To save himself, the hero needed to amputate his arm with the help of a pocket knife. The father realised too late that Rafael was standing trembling at the door and was watching that horrifying scene. I said to Rafael, "You're telling me that the crack under my door appears to you like the Grand Canyon, un-crossable, dangerous." Rafael was crying, and I thought he was hallucinating again. He kept shouting that it was the Grand Canyon. I felt very anxious, not least because Rafael's shouting was loud enough for the entire neighbourhood to hear. I said, "We haven't met for such a long time, and it feels like there's an unbridgeable canyon between us. But now we're both here. I'm waiting for you; please come in." Rafael did not move and kept crying and screaming. "How shall we cross?" I asked, quite devastated by then. Rafael reached out his arms towards me. I turned and offered him to climb on my back. He quickly jumped on, and we entered the room.

It was intuitively clear to me at that moment that Rafael needed my physical support to enter the room. He needed to feel that I was unharmed by our separation and that I was there for him. Furthermore, I wanted to do what a father would intuitively have done—take him in my arms. This, however, was quite impossible as he was a big boy and heavy, and also because I did not wish to create an over-excitation by being face to face with him. It was only later on, once I learnt what happened from the father, that I was able to link this act of "crossing over", of bridging the gap and reaffirming my presence, with Rafael's violent unconscious phantasies of our separation as a mutually vengeful mutilation: an amputation of limbs. In addition, there was enough material presented in the following sessions to support the understanding that while I was away Rafael felt he was swallowed by a void inside his mother, which turned out to be the deadening number zero. In the next session, he initiated a game in which both of us had to walk very carefully so as not to fall into a bottomless, dangerous pit in the room. He claimed the pit was inside a huge spaceship from which tiny aliens came out to destroy the world. He then drew it, and it looked like a big zero. Only then could I go back to a full verbal interpretation, linking up the whole process we underwent from the moment I went on my holiday.

This criss-cross movement within the sessions between the different anxieties and their interpretation led to a major improvement in Rafael's condition. He is currently attending a regular school, treated with a minimal dose of anti-psychotic medication, has no violent bouts and is gradually becoming more connected to the turbulent reality of an adolescent his age, or in his own words, "becoming a person". However, this improvement is ever-precarious as the rapid oscillations between anxieties-of-being, psychotic and depressive anxieties, and between autistic and psychotic defensive retreats continue, albeit in better contained and better-communicated ways.

Some concluding thoughts

In this chapter I have tried to demonstrate that:

1. In the course of analysis, some children who are initially diagnosed as suffering from ASD turn out to move along an autisto-psychotic spectrum. This spectrum is characterised by a mixture of paranoid–schizoid anxieties and less differentiated autistic anxieties-of-being. Thus, these children could be described as borderline autistic.
2. The interpretation of unconscious anxiety and its accompanying defences is central for the psychoanalytic curative process with children on the autisto-psychotic spectrum.
3. One needs to consider the constant interplay between depressive, paranoid–schizoid anxieties and "anxieties-of-being". The child on the autisto-psychotic spectrum is characterised by an overwhelming influx of intermingled anxieties. Thus, it is the analyst's difficult task to try and trace the dominant, most urgent anxiety and interpret it in its own "language". Furthermore, it is helpful to interpret and show the child how autistic withdrawal defends against further fragmentation, and how fragmentation prevents an influx of paralysing anxieties-of-being.
4. Different anxiety states demand different technical considerations and means. This is especially so when the type of anxiety is related to disintegrated or unintegrated states of the body.

The main difficulty has to do with the absence or the repeated destruction of space and time in autism and in severe psychosis. Inside and outside, self and object are all blurred, confused, or attacked. As a consequence, the localisation of experience (Freud, 1900a), what happens to whom, why, and where, is diffuse, elusive, and often untraceable.

When working in the domain of such autistic or psychotic transferences, one has the feeling of living in a nightmarish virtual reality where anything human is not really human and a sense of the uncanny prevails (Freud, 1919h). Furthermore, since speech and symbolism are hardly existent or based on autistic equations, and unconscious phantasies slowly disintegrate into their components, the analyst is sometimes lost completely in the sphere of the ineffable (Bion, 1979).

Complexity, links, and multiplicity, characteristic of mental space, collapse into concrete "things" and actions. This exerts huge pressure upon the analyst who is equated and sometimes identified with this "thing-ness", with excitations and actions. What occurs in the session is very often in the realm of sensations, perceptions, and actions. In the analysis, verbal interpretations, instead of establishing contact, might be experienced by both analyst and child as unreal, incomprehensible, intrusive, or psychotic acting in and out of the session.

Accumulated experience acquired through the analyses of psychotic and ASD adults and children, such as Rafael, indicates that we must create and use different levels of representation-promoting and object-building interpretations in action. This entails the movement between different levels of non-symbolic and symbolic interpretations, according to what kind of anxiety and developmental level are present. These interpretations start at the most basic, primitive levels of bodily experience and integration. They require a very concrete movement between what Klein, in her clinical seminars (2017), called "absorption" in the patient's unconscious material, and disentangling from it so as to be able to form an interpretation. At the same time, it is the gradual construction of a good internal object, through the use of the total body–mind presence of the analyst, that eventually promotes representation and internal good-object consolidation.

When oedipal content seems to be dominant, it is transference interpretations, alongside historical reconstructions, that prove to be especially helpful. When depressive or paranoid–schizoid anxieties are at their most intense, then it is the interpretation of the total transference situation that establishes direct contact with the patient. But when the session is saturated with anxieties-of-being, there is a need to rely mainly on the stability, continuity, and boundaries of the setting. Patients who suffer from a preponderance of anxieties-of-being should be encouraged to come for analysis for as many sessions during the week as possible. It is my experience that five to six sessions per week analyses bring about a significantly quicker and deeper change for the better than those with fewer sessions per week. It is with such patients that we should aim to utilise some additional modes of anxiety interpretations.

References

Alvarez, A. (1992). *Live Company: Psychoanalytic Psychotherapy with Autistic, Borderline, Deprived and Abused Children.* London: Routledge.

Alvarez, A. (2012). *The Thinking Heart.* London: Routledge.

Amir, D. (2014). *Cleft Tongue: The Language of Psychic Structures.* London: Routledge.

Bion, W. R. (1957). Differentiation of the psychotic from the non-psychotic personalities. *The International Journal of Psychoanalysis, 38*: 266–257.

Bion, W. R. (1963). *Elements of Psycho-Analysis.* London: Heinemann.

Bion, W. R. (1979). *A Memoir of the Future, Book Three: The Dawn of Oblivion.* London: Karnac, 1990.

Bleger, J. (2013). *Symbiosis and Ambiguity: A Psychoanalytic Study.* London: Routledge.

Brenman Pick, I. (1985). Working through in the countertransference. *The International Journal of Psychoanalysis, 66*: 157–166.

Brenman Pick, I. (2018). Bringing things together. In: F. M. Davids & N. Shavit (Eds.), *Authenticity in the Psychoanalytic Encounter: The Work of Irma Brenman Pick* (pp. 192–209). London: Routledge.

Britton, R. (1998). Before and after the depressive position: PS(n) →D(n) →Ps(n+1). In: *Belief and Imagination: Explorations in Psychoanalysis* (pp. 69–81). London: Routledge.

Bursztejn, C., Golse, B., & Misès, R. (2003). Classifications en psychiatrie de l'enfant. In: Encycl Méd Chir, Psychiatrie/Pédopsychiatrie, 37-200-B-10, 2003, 1–9. Paris: Éditions Scientifiques et Médicales Elsevier SAS.

Durban, J. (2011). Shadows, ghosts and chimaeras: On some early modes of handling psycho-genetic heritage. *The International Journal of Psychoanalysis, 92*: 903–924.

Durban, J. (2014). Despair and hope: On some varieties of countertransference and enactment in the psychoanalysis of ASD (autistic spectrum disorder) children. *Journal of Child Psychotherapy, 40*: 187–200.

Durban, J. (2017a). "The very same is lost": In pursuit of mental coverage when emerging from autistic states. In: H. B. Levine & D. G. Power (Eds.), *Engaging Primitive Anxieties of the Emerging Self: The Legacy of Frances Tustin* (pp 129–150). London: Karnac.

Durban, J. (2017b). Home, homelessness and "nowhere-ness" in early infancy. *Journal of Child Psychotherapy, 43*: 175–191.

Durban, J. (2018). The pipe child. Paper read at the Psychoanalytic Institute Berlin, 28 September, 2018.

Freud, S. (1900a). *The Interpretation of Dreams. S. E.*, 4: 1–310. London: Hogarth.

Freud, S. (1919h). The uncanny. *S. E., XVII*: 217–25. London: Hogarth.

Grotstein, J. (1986). *Splitting and Projective Identification*. Northvale, NJ: Jason Aronson.

Haag, G. (1985). La mère et le bébé dans les deux moitiés du corps. *Neuropsychiatrie de l'enfance et de l'adolescence*, 33(2–3): 107–114.

Haag, G. (1993). Fear of fusion and projective identification in autistic children. *Psychoanalytic Inquiry*, 13: 63–84.

Haag, G. (1997). *Psychosis and Autism: Schizophrenic, Perverse and Manic-Depressive States During Psychotherapy*. In: A. Dubinsky & H. Dubinsky (Eds.), *Psychotic States in Children* (pp. 189–211). London: Karnac.

Houzel, D. (2004). *The Psychoanalysis of Infantile Autism. Journal of Child Psychotherapy*, 30: 225–237.

Houzel, D. (2018). Autism and psychoanalysis in the French context. *The International Journal of Psychoanalysis*, 99(3): 725–745.

Joseph, B. (1978). Different types of anxiety and their handling in the analytic situation. *The International Journal of Psychoanalysis*, 59: 223–228.

Joseph, B. (1989). *Psychic Equilibrium and Psychic Change*. London: Routledge.

Klein, M. (1930). The importance of symbol formation in the development of the ego. In: *Love, Guilt and Reparation and Other Works* (pp. 219–233). London: Hogarth.

Klein, M. (1932). *The Psychoanalysis of Children: The Writings of Melanie Klein, Vol 2*. London: Hogarth.

Klein, M. (1948). On the theory of anxiety and guilt. In: *Envy and Gratitude and Other Works 1946–1963* (pp. 25–42). London: Hogarth, 1975.

Klein, M. (1952). Some theoretical conclusions regarding the emotional life of the infant. In: *Envy and Gratitude and Other Works 1946–1963* (pp. 61–93). London: Hogarth, 1975.

Klein, M. (2017). *Lectures on Technique* (edited by J. Steiner). London: Routledge.

Lacan, J. (1966). *Écrits* (translated by B. Fink). New York: Norton, 2006.

Larson, F. V., Wagner, A. P., Jones, P. B. Tantam, D., Lai, M.-C., Baron-Cohen, S., & Holland, A. J. (2017). Psychosis in autism: Comparison of the features of both conditions in a dually affected cohort. *The British Journal of Psychiatry*, 210(4): 269–275.

Laznik, M. C. (2007). Joint mother–baby treatment with a baby of 3 months who shows early warning signs of autism. In: S. Acquarone (Ed.), *Signs of Autism in Infants: Recognition and Early Intervention* (pp. 139–170). London: Karnac.

Laznik, M. C. (2013). Lacan et l'autisme. *La revue lacanienne, 14*: 81–90.

Lechevalier, B. (2003). Autistic enclaves in the dynamics of adult psychoanalysis. Unpublished paper.

Levine, H. B., & D. G. Power (Eds.) (2017). *Engaging Primitive Anxieties of the Emerging Self: The Legacy of Frances Tustin*. London: Karnac.

Meltzer, D. (1974). Adhesive identification. In: A. Hahn (Ed.), *Sincerity and Other Works: Collected Papers of Donald Meltzer* (pp. 335–350). London: Karnac, 1994.

Meltzer, D. (1975). The psychology of autistic states and of post-autistic mentality. In: D. Meltzer, J. Bremner, S. Hoxter, D. Weddell & I. Wittenberg (Eds.), *Explorations in Autism* (pp. 6–32). Strath Tay, Perthshire: Clunie Press.

Melzer, D. (1992). *The Claustrum: An Investigation of Claustrophobic Phenomena*. Strath Tay, Perthshire: Clunie Press.

Ogden, T. H. (1994). The concept of interpretive action. *The Psychoanalytic Quarterly, 63*: 219–245.

Pollak, T. (2009). The "body-container": A new perspective on the "body-ego". *The International Journal of Psychoanalysis, 90*: 487–506.

Pollak, T. (2017). Interpretation-in-action. Unpublished paper.

Rhode, M. (2005). Mirroring, imitation, identification: The sense of self in relation to the mother's internal world. *Journal of Child Psychotherapy, 31*(1): 52–71.

Rhode, M. (2012a). Whose memories are they and where do they go? Problems surrounding internalization in children on the autistic spectrum. *The International Journal of Psychoanalysis, 93*: 355–376.

Rhode, M. (2012b). The "autistic" level of the Oedipus complex: Some implications for problems surrounding sense perception. *Bulletin of the British Psychoanalytical Society*, March 2012.

Rhode, M. (2015). "Paralysed associations": Countertransference difficulties in recognising meaning in the treatment of children on the autistic spectrum. *Journal of Child Psychotherapy, 41*(3): 218–230.

Rhode, M. (2018). Object relations approaches to autism. *The International Journal of Psychoanalysis, 99*(3): 702–724.

Sechehaye, M. A. (1951). *Symbolic Realization: A New Method of Psychotherapy Applied to a Case of Schizophrenia* (translated by B. Würsten & H. Würsten). New York: International Universities Press.

Segal, H. (1957). Notes on symbol formation. *The International Journal of Psychoanalysis*, 38: 391–397.

Steiner, J. (1987). The interplay between pathological organisations and the paranoid–schizoid and depressive positions. *The International Journal of Psychoanalysis*, 68: 69–80.

Steiner, J. (1993). *Psychic Retreats: Pathological Organizations in Psychotic, Neurotic and Borderline Patients*. London: Routledge.

Steiner, J. (2011). *Seeing and Being Seen: Emerging from a Psychic Retreat*. Hove, East Sussex: Routledge.

Tustin, F. (1968). *Autistic Barriers in Neurotic Patients*. London: Karnac.

Tustin, F. (1972). *Autism and Childhood Psychosis*. London: Hogarth.

Tustin, F. (1981). *Autistic States in Children*. London: Routledge & Kegan Paul.

Tustin, F. (1990). *The Protective Shell in Children and Adults*. London: Karnac.

Winnicott, D. W. (1962). Ego integration in child development. In: *The Maturational Processes and the Facilitating Environment* (pp. 56–64). London: Hogarth, 1965.

CHAPTER FOUR

The birth of emotional experience under the sea: a clinical case*

Jani Santamaría

> Somewhere in the analytic situation, buried under masses of neurosis, psychosis, and so on, there is a person struggling to be born.[1]
>
> —W. R. Bion (1992)

In this chapter I wish to write about the psychoanalysis of a child who is fighting to get out of an autistic state. When Eric[2] first came to my consulting room, he was three years old. He had developed a fascination with mermaids, feminine dolls, and female clothing. This triggered fears in the family, especially his parents and maternal grandparents, who demanded and begged me to "help Eric not be homosexual".

---

*An abbreviated version of this case appeared in the *Colombian Psychoanalytic Association Review* (Santamaria, 2013). https://dialnet.unirioja.es/servlet/articulo?codigo=4726622. I am grateful for their permission to reprint and expand upon it.

[1] Translated from Spanish.

[2] As readers will see, in this presentation, I chose the name "Eric" for this patient, because it is the name of the prince in the Disney film (Clements & Musker, 1989) who rescues the mermaid, Ariel.

I started his psychoanalysis with four sessions per week and also met occasionally with Eric's parents for some time. What I came to recognise and hope to describe was that what his family feared was a matter of sexual orientation or looked initially like it might be a gender identity disorder, came to be understood as an autistic state or defence.

The advances in psychoanalytic theory that took place from the time of the rich observations of Melanie Klein's (1930) case of Dick opened doors in working with children as they shed light on primitive states of mind and the constitution of the psyche. Extraordinary work by authors such as Tustin (1972, 1981, and 1986), Meltzer (1975), Alvarez (2012), and Durban (2020), among others, have given rise to a number of theories relevant to the treatment of patients whose problems do not conform to the expectations of classical analysis. Houzel (2020) described how some autistic children tend to make a very early split between the male and female components of psychic bisexuality. They present with a mixture of different anxieties, ranging from the neurotic to less differentiated autistic anxieties of being (Durban, 2020). In such cases, one needs to consider the constant interplay between the three conceptual levels of intervention suggested by Alvarez (2010)[3] in order to explore the reasons why one type of therapeutic understanding can work rather than another. In addition, it is necessary to interpret and show the child how autistic withdrawal defends against further fragmentation, and how fragmentation prevents an influx of paralysing anxieties of being. In the words of Levine (2020), these patients are "beyond neurosis" (p. 11).

As Anne Alvarez (2012) pointed out, "psychoanalytic theory is today much better equipped than before to explain change, development, novelty, and growth of the mind" (p. 31). An important collection edited by Levine and Power (2017) covers a variety of theoretical and technical efforts needed to address extremely severe levels of developmental arrests with the psychoanalytic method. These and similar contributions are part of contemporary psychoanalysis' further refining very powerful theories to guide us in our psychoanalytic work with non-neurotic states of mind and the mental processes that characterise them. In 2020, Levine noted:

---

[3] See also Chapters One and Three, this volume.

One of the changes in theory is that analysts have increasingly come to recognise the importance of understanding, formulating and learning to clinically catalyse the processes through which the self is vitalised, representations are formed, and psychic regulatory processes are strengthened and created.

(Levine, 2020, p. 17)

In this sense, the analyst's task nowadays is often one of helping to fill in psychic voids where representation of experience is absent or weak (Levine, Reed, & Scarfone, 2012; Mitrani, 1995; Roussillon, 2011)

At our first meeting, Eric's parents told me that he only played with mermaids, had a preference for princesses and did not play with anything else. His parents blamed the housekeepers for this behaviour, and said that his two older sisters (seven and nine years old) did not play with dolls. They also mentioned that his external world was "impoverished", that he was hypersensitive, had no friends and did not socialise with anyone at school; he only drew mermaids. If the mermaids were hidden from him, he would become irritated and exasperated, "as though we would have hidden part of him, like an arm or a leg".

A few months prior to these interviews, a member of their extended family had publicly "declared" their choice of a homosexual partner. This event triggered a series of projections, which "led to" Eric's parents' divorce (legally) and "caused" Eric's maternal grandparents' divorce. And all of this led the family to bring Eric to treatment with a feeling of great urgency to address their wish for Eric "not to become a homosexual".

My response to Eric's parents' insistent questions as to whether or not Eric, too, would become a homosexual, was to tell them that psychoanalysis would reveal important configurations and anxieties, and that Eric's psychic pain would be the starting point. I offered to see him four times a week, which they accepted. And that is how Eric began treatment.

At our first meeting I was surprised to see a slim, white boy with curly hair, and big, sad eyes that avoided eye contact. He walked in on tiptoe, as though he was being forced by someone and I felt that in some way, he did not exist. He did not look back at his mother and walked down the stairs into my consulting room. Without asking questions, he sat down, looked at the toys for boys on the table with disgust and with an annoyed look asked me, "Do you have mermaids or toys for girls? I don't like these." He remained quiet and did not look at me; he did not initiate any interaction. I felt an unsurmountable wall, and decided to remain silent and observe. The session ended and he left without saying goodbye.

At the next session, he cried until he found a small notebook with princesses on the cover. He took it in his hands, but did not write anything in it. He stroked the pages as though he were "touching" the princesses.

Before his third session, I heard screaming from far away. I opened the door and found Eric clinging to his mother. He shouted, "I don't want to, I don't want to!" He was crying and didn't want to go in to the consulting room. His screams were like the expression of the last glimpses of hope. When he finally came in, he threw himself on the floor and started kicking around. He was still crying, and he told me over and over again, "I want to go with my mum. It's cold here, it's freezing! I don't like it! My mom's car is warm. It's cold here. I don't want you, go away! Go away!"

While on the floor, he hugged his legs and then started kicking again. Eric was in a severe state of disorganisation, a traumatic state. I had the impression that he was still part of his mother's body and wasn't fully born. I told him, "I understand, Eric. Mommy's belly is warm, but you are out of her belly and feel cold."

He shouted at me, "It's cold here. I hate you. I hate you. I want to go with my mum!" To which I replied, "I understand, Eric. That's how you feel when you're not with Mommy, you feel cold and alone. But you're not in her, you have come out. Do you want a blanket?" Eric didn't listen and was shouting the same thing over and over until he slowly calmed down. I offered the blanket again. He nodded, I covered him with the blanket, and so he remained throughout the session. Eric cried in the darkness, looking for light. His only communication was crying.

Eric's terror seemed only partially contained by the blanket. Although he was severely withdrawn into himself, I felt that at the same time he was also yearning to make contact with me. Caught in the intensity of that transference position, Eric came into these early sessions in silence. He walked next to me as though I didn't exist and avoided eye contact.

He walked down to the consulting room, looked at my hair, hugged his legs, and curled up into a ball on the couch (as though he were in the womb?). He didn't talk, he only gently touched the cover of the princess notebook and showed no other sign of interaction. I felt his silence as an armour he had created to protect himself from any sort of stimulus in the session. Any attempt to get close could trigger in him a threat of annihilation and terror. Thus, I remained a silent witness for months. As Bick (1962) wrote:

> One may have to sit with children for a long time completely in the dark ... until suddenly something comes up from the depth ... It imposes on the child analyst a greater dependence on his unconscious to provide him with clues to the meaning.
>
> (Bick, 1962, p. 329)

Almost four months into the sessions, Eric finally entered the area with more toys. He was showing small signs of curiosity about that place and that's how he found mermaids in a box. He quickly grabbed them and asked for a brush. He said, "Should we brush their hair?" I accepted and saw how he was drawn mainly to their long hair, which he constantly stroked.

His play at this time was very mechanical: he brushed the mermaids' hair, put them to sleep, covered them with a tissue (which was their blanket), put them in water, took them out of the water, put them in their pyjamas, and put them back to sleep. There were no words or dialogue. The objects seemed rich in surface qualities but lacked meaning. Eric expressed himself through actions and conveyed the sense of a very sad environment. His mother had told me that when Eric was born, he was constantly ill and she was depressed, because she didn't know how to take care of him. I wondered if he was trying to turn me into a part of himself, an object with no life of its own, so as "to avoid becoming aware of separateness and to deny life with all its uncertainties" (Bergstein, 2019, p. 80).

Amidst these first movements, slowly a mermaid became present, both as a sign of primitive agony and also linked to a mythical entity with a strange power of seduction with its hair and singing; a shy mermaid from *The Odyssey*, which now appeared in the interaction of the analytical pair.

Another activity Eric began to do over and over again was colouring, tracing, and drawing stories. Eric had a special talent for drawing and he really enjoyed it. He traced princesses on sheets of paper for sessions on end. He really concentrated on making them as exact as possible. He coloured images of princesses, and if he added a prince to the picture, he would tell me, "You do him and I do her." He did not allow me to touch or come close to the princess with my crayon.[4] When I tried to intervene or make a comment, he would tell me, "No talking, just drawing."

Even though he invited me to participate—it is questionable whether our activities at this point could be referred to as "play"—I had the impression that he plunged into a world I could not be part of, a world where sensations predominated—touching hair, touching water, touching tissue—as though he was "an embryo of the psyche". The mermaids seemed to be an armour he created to protect himself from human contact. He didn't respond to them as personified *objects*, but rather to the sensations they triggered on his skin. For Eric, the sensation was the object.

In Eric's life, mermaids seemed essential, but they were not used to identify or "play" with. They had a stereotypical quality whose role was static and did not lead to new playful scenes or actions. It was as if he and they had no internal space. Only the surface of the object and the self were experienced.

A few months went by; I respected the time, rhythms, and space where Eric would only sit down in silence and I saw that he enjoyed the sensations he got from touching the texture of the mermaid dolls' hair. I increasingly felt that the problem was not as centred on gender identity or sexuality as the school and his family had insisted.[5] Everything seemed to indicate that Eric's "obsession" with mermaids had more to do with his need to use the mermaids as autistic objects (Tustin, 1986) than a "desire to be a woman."

---

[4] Tustin (1978) noted that "autistic children have developed rigid cuts between 'clean' and 'dirty,' full/empty, wet/dry. If they experience the contrary together with the opposite state, they are afraid one of the opposites will destroy the other" (p. 293).

[5] Houzel (2020) calls autism a pathology of otherness "and traces a link between this pathology and primary defects in the integration of psychic bisexuality: on the one hand, the combined object is split into its masculine and feminine components and on the other, there is absolute separation between self, experienced as soft and vulnerable, and not-self, felt to be hard and threatening".

In the transference at this time, Eric was fascinated by the texture and red colour of my hair, but not interested in me as an alive human object. As Meltzer (1975) pointed out, in bi-dimensional object relations, the object is perceived as no more than the sensual characteristics of its surface (similar to the way at the beginning of development that the objects are experienced as a sense of softness and warmth emanating from the tactile sensation of the infant's cheek on its mother's breast). In the countertransference, there seemed to be no sense of twoness; my analytic function felt sterile.

Eventually, Eric found a story in a book that helped us a great deal. It was about yummy (tasty) food and unpleasant food. He used the word "gross" for the latter and laughed a lot when he said it. He would ask me to read this story to him in every session and when I did, I saw how much he seemed to like not so much the story, but the *sensory quality* of the words "yummy" and "gross". Despite this, I told him that with the "tasty and gross" food he was telling me he felt he was nourishing the experience of getting to know each other, but that we had to get to know what food (experiences) nourished him and what food didn't; just like the body needs food, he needed to be understood. He just nodded and kept on pointing at "yummy and gross" food.

What I wish to emphasise is that, in these initial movements, there was a gradual creation and acceptance of nonverbal interaction spaces. I thought that Eric still needed to be in the sensory realm, to use his omnipotence and create objects, as a prelude to relating to objects and demonstrating a more developed capacity for play.

Gradually, Eric stopped limiting his touch to the mermaids and began touching fabric. He would put them on his face and say, "Nice". His favourite fabric was velvet. He rejected hard things like sandpaper.

Tustin (1978) had written of the importance and use of hard and soft objects in autistic states:

> Gradually, soft sensations become associated with "taking in", "with receptivity, "hard" sensations become associated with the infant's bisexuality. "Hard" trusting becomes "male" and "soft" receptivity becomes "female". When, on the basis of a co-operative suckling experience, the "hard" entering nipple and tongue are experienced as working together with the "soft"

receptive mouth and breast, then a "marriage" between "male" and "female" elements takes place.

(Tustin 1978, p. 8)

In a new development, Eric began to notice and touch my hair, which was red like the mermaid in the Disney film. He said, "Your hair is like Ariel's, my favorite mermaid." He would put the doll next to my hair and say, "You're both the same." Thanks to these moments of more object related contact[6]—*you* are like *her*—I started to see a glimmer of hope.

In later sessions, he invited me to *play* Disney's *Little Mermaid*; he was Ariel (the mermaid) and I was Sebastian (the crab), and we talked with Flounder, a fish that was always with Ariel. He would closely listen to me talk about Ariel's fear of losing her voice. I would say, "Ariel's voice is precious. We will protect it from Ursula trying to steal it." Eric listened and put his hands on his throat just like Ariel does in the movie. In the meantime, we (Sebastian and Flounder) would sing *Under the Sea*. Eric looked at me bewildered and slowly started singing and dancing with me. He was surprised I knew the whole movie and would ask me questions, like an exam, to confirm that I had, in fact, seen the movie. He got very excited every time I answered correctly. These elements drew his attention to me as an alive object and drew us closer together.

At home, his parents had waged war on gender. They would no longer let him play with mermaids and he was not allowed to use anything that could be related to "being a girl". They filled his room with cars, swords, action figures, etc. When he came to sessions, he told me, "My mum said I could only play with mermaids with you. I'm a boy but I like girly things." He seemed to be being "bombarded" with external messages on gender to which he responded by trying to show "he no longer liked pink".

Eric kept a small mermaid inside a *Cars* (Disney film, 2006) box, which he pushed down a slide-shaped chair. As he did so, he looked up at me and said, "I'm not playing girl, ok? It's a car." I could sense the falsity and compliance behind his statement and I told him that he didn't need to pretend, and that the most important thing was to "be".

---

[6] In addition to the more obvious meaning of "contact with me as an object", did not this identity in Eric's mind also indicate that *he* was making contact with Ariel and with me *as objects, in his own mind*?

I wasn't sure he understood what "be" meant and I regretted being so "technical" with him. However, he responded to my spontaneous comment by taking the mermaid out of the *Cars* box, throwing the *Cars* box away, and starting to play with the mermaid on the couch. Using a chair as a makeshift slide, he pushed the mermaid from the top and ran to catch her at the bottom. As Eric ran around the consulting room with all the mermaids, I felt he was genuinely happy. It was nice to see him smile. I told him that he might feel that if he didn't do what his family said—play with cars—he would lose their love, and that at the same time he tried to show me what he really wanted to do—play with mermaids. He was quiet after I talked, but seconds later he threw the *Cars* box to the other side of the couch and broke out laughing.

A year later, the mermaid games, drawing, and cutting out princesses began transforming into games where we separated "pink" and "blue" things, sorted and ordered things, talked about sexual differences and he sometimes played with a Spiderman house. After still more time in our work together, more than two years into the analysis, the following game evolved.

He would switch off the light and we would play "going down the mountain" (my couch). He then opened a vault in the Spiderman house and said, "This is where I keep my fears." He kept opening little boxes and doors of the houses. He made ropes by interlinking little monkeys and he used them to go up or down the mountain. The exciting part was the darkness, having the lights off; he would switch off the light and we used a flashlight. This game of "exploring underneath" led me to formulate interpretations that pointed to the core of the transference, to "being inside me". At the end of the sessions, I asked him, "What does it feel like being inside?" Eric replied, "Inside you? It feels nice."

The intimacy that rolled out in every session maintained the interweaving of various relationship levels. The excitement and play in the dark as we became closer *as objects* can be inferred to also have meaning on an object related, sexual level. More immediately, however, the rope he created on which the characters could go up or down was understood at a more primal level as a lifeline (Alvarez, 2002, p. 107), an umbilical cord, or a tie that provided support and continuity.[7]

---

[7] See Winnicott's article on string (1960).

By the third year, Eric enjoyed ringing the doorbell and when I opened the door, he would hide behind his mother or driver. I had to notice his absence, ask where he was, and after a few minutes he would jump out and say, "I'm here!" In sessions, there was a palpable change in the level of his mental functioning. While he still experienced what Durban (2020) called *anxieties-of-being*—that is, fears of fragmentation, annihilation, and nameless dread (Bion, 1957)—there also appeared separation anxiety and fears of object-loss.

Prior to our third summer vacation break, Eric's mother told him "by mistake" that he wouldn't be seeing me and he responded with night terrors. In the first session after the break, he acted as though we had not stopped seeing each other, mentioned watching the film, *La Llorona*[8] and then told me about two dreams he had had.

"I dreamt there were two dimensions. Coraline's[9] mum was in one of them and she wanted to sew a button on my eye but she didn't. I managed to run away and escape through the tunnel."

He continued: "I cried and woke up crying. I ran to my mum. This dream didn't have a happy ending. The other dimension was La Llorona. She didn't get me because San Juanito showed up and killed La Llorona. Juanito is in the movie. Have you seen it?"

I jotted down these dreams on a piece of paper and we put them in a plastic container. We put it on the highest shelf and he said, "I'll take them with me when I finish therapy. But right now, let's keep them there because they scare me."

---

[8] La Llorona is a Mexican legend about an indigenous woman who falls in love with a Spanish gentleman. They have three children and then he leaves her for a woman of high social standing. When she finds out about this, she goes mad and takes her children to the river and drowns them. She can't stand the guilt and takes her own life. From that day on, legend has it that she always appears dressed in white on the shore of Lake Texcoco crying and saying, "Oh my children", and then disappears.

[9] *Coraline* (2009) is a movie about an eleven-year-old girl. She moves house with her parents who are always busy working and don't pay attention to her. She feels very lonely so she explores the house and finds a closed door in their living room. Her mother said she couldn't go into it, but the following day she takes the keys to the door, opens it, and finds "another mother" and "another father". They are almost the same as her real parents, except they have buttons instead of eyes, which make them look like dolls and not people. She later goes back to try to save them and has to go through a tunnel that takes her to another other dimension.

These dreams led me to think about the different dimensions Eric functioned in. The break between sessions clearly had shattered the precarious feeling of continuity and his fear of disappearing was a clear sign that this experience of separation had gone beyond what Eric could tolerate and had awakened his most primitive fears. But the fact of the dreams also showed that Eric had an "apparatus to symbolise" dreams. They not only reflected his agony and terror of becoming a thing—buttons instead of eyes—but expressed other important elements in his family's life: the depressed mother (La Llorona), who cried day and night when she and Eric's father separated.

The dreams seemed to be complex amalgams. On the one hand, they were clear indicators of the repetition of a trauma. It was highly likely that Eric had felt the only way to survive was through a symbiotic stage (the tunnel), and the dreams expressed his wish for his father—the paternal San Juanito—to save him from La Llorona (his depressed mother). But in regard to his previously autistic presentation, the dreams showed that Eric had started to live "in his own mind". He now had inside of himself different levels of reality (different "doors", like in Coraline's dream), and was able to transform sensory experiences into visual images that had meaning.

At first, I chose to not interpret these dreams so as not to risk forcing my meanings upon him. Eric had gone through a moment of terror when he was telling me about the dreams and I thought it was more important to respect and just accept his level of anxiety. I saw a great sign of relief on his face when I put the container with his dreams away on the highest shelf. In these moments of vulnerability, as Durban (2020, p. 23) has pointed out, the silent recognition and acceptance of the affects in itself constitutes an intimate interpretation. I felt that this active exchange with Eric reflected a moment of deep intimacy as he moved closer to the capacity to experience psychic pain (Joseph 1983).

Towards the end of the third year, Eric came into session crying. He seemed very sad.

E: Jani, I'm not happy.
J: I understand. [Silence.]
E: I'm a boy but I like girly things. [Silence.] I can't be both. I have to choose; I can't be a boy and a girl.

J: I think you're right.
[Eric was still crying. I gave him a box of tissues and put his chair in front of me.]
E: I don't know what to choose.
J: Take your time. It hurts a lot.
E: Yes … What if I die? That way I wouldn't be anything … Or I could be a unicorn, neither one or the other. [Silence.]

These sessions deeply touched me. I wanted to stop the pain through an action—by holding, soothing him—but I knew that that moment was a critical one for Eric, one that he would have to resolve for himself.

The legend of Ulysses and the Sirens came to my mind. My sense of hopelessness seemed like the mermaids' songs, seducing me to symbiosis, to my wish to hold and soothe him. That singing was pushing me to act, but I knew I had to stand firm at the mast of my analytical role and trust that Eric would tolerate and cross the sea of psychic pain. I sensed that if I didn't take the risk of waiting and containing the pain, we would not get to safe harbour. We had to stay on the ship (the emotional experience) and navigate (tolerate) towards the sea of transformations (Bion, 1965), otherwise Eric would not be free, he could not *be*.

The sessions during this period were very painful and he left them feeling sad. He would come to the session, sit in front of me, cry and tell me, "I'd rather die …" How can one tolerate the turbulence, the luminous darkness of silence? It wasn't about resignations and discarding, but about painful, slow changes.

I noticed Eric kept his "used" tissues in his trouser pockets and would leave with them. I told him one day, "Eric, the tissues are like those blankets you used to cover the Barbies with. The tissues wrap up your tears and you can leave them here, just like you leave your fears in that container [I pointed to the top shelf]. Your pain can also stay here."

He replied embarrassed, "But there's a lot of them and they're dirty." I said, "Dirty, clean, few, many, everything you are is well received and is part of you. This is you." Eric opened his eyes, impressed and at the end of the session he put all the tissues in the trash can. I felt it had been important to make space for the experience of "dirtiness" that resided in Eric, because I wanted him to know that it, too, was part of him and could be accepted. We were trying to help him create and/or find an inner space in which he could integrate these painful experiences into his psyche.

In the midst of this, Eric's mother called me on a weekend and told me that he was either crying or sleeping and didn't want to leave his room. I told her it was important to be close to him, and she added, "This is what you told us when he started therapy, right? It's the sadness you told us he held inside?" I said it was and she was relieved to hear that Eric's emotional state corresponded to the process.

A few weeks went by and on a Monday, I opened the door to find Eric jumping towards me and telling me in a very excited way, "Hi, Jani. I have chosen! I'm a boy, I'm a boy! Smell me …" The consulting room smelled of that "manly smell" and he added, "I'm using an aftershave my grandfather gave me! We men use aftershave!" I smiled and said, "You chose to be alive. Congratulations."

Different moments had intertwined. Eric had experienced the rhythmic continuity of his existence. Being alive was the arrival point of a series of psychic operations. It seemed to be the first step to multiple transformations. This approach of celebrating the importance of being alive was crucial to me, since Eric had worked a lot and his universe had broadened. The powerful explosive energy liberated was transformed and now being used in the service of representation and symbolisation. In subsequent sessions, he asked for paper to draw on and showed how much he now liked drawing animals and his family. He also asked me to read him stories.

Then came more vacations. In the second to last session before a break, Eric and I made figures out of play dough. He made a doll called Jani and I made a figure named Eric. He was happy at the end of the session and took Jani with him.

In the next session, he entered the consulting room, said "hi" to me, walked across the play area, looked for some drawings he had "traced" a few years back, and started to throw them around. He shouted at me, "Some drawings are missing, Jani. I made a lot of them and they're not here. Where did you put them? Did you throw them out or what? I worked very hard on them and you don't value it. Where are they? Did you give them to another kid? Where is everything I made?" With his feet firmly planted on the ground, Eric threw books and looked in drawers for the drawings we kept in a folder.

Anger, expressed in the transference, provided an opportunity to analyse the feeling of not being valued, of being a ghost (of walking on tiptoe). I pointed out the importance of expressing his anger. Eric, the "child ghost", felt he had the right to exist, to demand, and he looked for bridges made of co-operation with foundations of pain and tears; he demanded a relationship with someone. I tried to show him that he managed to demand because he had felt free and confident that we had a relationship based on trust. I added that he seemed to be showing me that we had built something more important than drawings, that we had built a relationship and that perhaps he had been afraid of losing it. It was clear that this "active" search out of sadistic and intrusive curiosity (opening all the drawers violently) in search of the truth gave access to a more integrated position (depressive). As Ogden (1989) pointed out, the beginnings of true "contact might entail as well the anxieties associated with dangerous human errors and misunderstandings".

I was impressed by the liveliness of Eric's voice and the fact that instead of withdrawing as he did at the beginning of treatment, he was able to demand. Clearly, his response to the absence (vacations) also showed the horror of differentiation, separation, and loss. His anger seemed to also serve to reclaim his aliveness and pull himself out of his frozen state. I felt that his anger revealed a moment of deep vitality and authenticity and I considered that any attempt to link the angry experience with other thoughts—for example, to its symbolic connections—would have been at best redundant, at worst, an interference with a new development.

Eric stopped crying. He came close to me and said, "I also lost Jani" (the play dough doll). He asked, "Do you still have me?" I replied, "Yes, I have you." He turned to the wall, saw his figure in the same spot as the previous week, smiled, and told me, "Yes, you didn't lose me." He calmed down and we played with skateboards and play dough. "We can rebuild what is lost," I told him. So, we "made another Jani" and at the end of the session I pointed to my head and said, "I may be already inside you. And if you lose this one [the play dough doll], I will still be inside you." He looked at his body as though he was trying to understand what I was saying. He touched his head on his way out like he was attempting to "keep me in there". He took his play dough doll and left.

As we have seen, the process of emerging from autistic isolation and gaining some awareness of the separation can be quite traumatic.

The changes achieved, on their own, also became a source of new pain. As a "dream-work-alpha" (Bion, 1991) settled into the analytical process, Eric was able to make sense of these experiences. Oedipal expressions began to occupy an important place in the transference. He asked if I had children, who slept on the bed (on the couch), who lived above the consulting room; all questions that showed curiosity and concern about the other.

The psychic birth of Eric's emotional experience was seen in the following session. His sixth birthday was coming up, he brought a small cake to the session and I sang "Happy Birthday" to him. He then asked, "Were you born here?"

J: Yes. What about you?
E: So was I. I was also born here, Jani.
J: Yes. How do you feel?
E: Well, very well. Should we play that I lay down and was born?

He lay down on the couch and we recreated everything he knew about birth. He asked me to tell him a story about birth. We switched roles: first, he was "the mum" who had a daughter (me); then, I gave birth to him; and then, he was "the third one", my husband, and enjoyed seeing the birth of his child (of a baby in the consulting room). At the end, he asked me to read him *The Three Little Pigs*. He hugged me and said, "You're warm."

I think the "live company" (Alvarez, 2012) was important in this session on the different levels of identification of the experience and I believed it announced a weaning process. A few months later, the sessions were different: Eric took out all the princess and mermaid drawings, the stories, and everything related to "pink". He said, "I don't need this anymore, put it up there."

I understood that through this request, Eric was showing his interest for "everything human" (the interaction), and that the devitalised, repetitive, and controlled autistoid relationships to which he had adhered could be "uploaded" to another portal of his mind.

He "resolved" his separation anxiety due to the next upcoming vacation with his Nintendo. He would draw me first, put the drawing in his trouser pocket, then take a photo of me, and say, "I have you now." I responded, "Oh, it seems you want to keep me in your little box [little head] now that vacation is close." He would laugh and say, "Yes, that way you won't get lost." It seemed evident that Eric wanted to "take a piece of me" with him via those photos. He seemed to have developed or reconnected internally with an internal space that contains memories of objects and relationships and that helped make separations tolerable for him (Meltzer, 1979).

This interplay and communication also seemed to serve as a transitional phenomenon, an intermediate path of experience between the purely narcissistic illusion that everything belongs to oneself and the mature awareness of separation, where a symbolic thought may be constructed. We could "play" with that "camera" at a symbolic level. Games were no longer two-dimensional and static and led to new associative chains. A few months later, he took some images of princesses and said, "I know, let's give them [images of princesses] to the cat outside [my neighbour's cat was always at my door]." I asked astonished, "To the cat?" There was a spark of joy in his eyes and he said in a mischievous tone, "Yes. Let's put them in his milk. The cat will smell it and drink it. He'll get confused and become a female cat." (He laughed a lot).

J: Could we think that you felt that this happened to you? That once you drank Mom's milk and thought that you had to be a girl?
E: [He laughed.] Yes, but it's not like that anymore. I drink Dad's milk now.
J: Do dads have milk?
E: No, of course they don't! [He laughed a lot.] My dad gives me Gatorade when I go with him to the gym.
J: What if I drink it? What would happen to me?
E: There's no point, you're already a girl. What if [with a mischievous look] you drink it and become a cat?! Ha, ha.

Eric was discovering the magic of milk as food for the mind, and recognition of identity. Experiences with his father[10] who promised identity

---

[10] Eric's mother had started a legal battle against his father. She said she wanted to "expel" him from the country so that he would never see him again. But after several sessions with her, she withdrew the legal claim, began a therapeutic process, and allowed Eric to meet with his father frequently.

and contact games beyond the sensual—popped up; an interesting present was coming to life. He transformed his thoughts in search of himself; he could be spontaneous and enjoy play.

Grotstein (1990) described how "infants must develop a feeling of safety from their background object of primary identification". Eric's playful discourse about cats and milk and Gatorade reflected maternal and paternal identifications and indicated how they could be united in a harmonious relationship. Renouncing bisexuality allowed Eric to be "fed" by the parental couple and he was now capable of incorporating both male and female elements (grandfather's aftershave and the taste of milk). It was a lovely example of the importance of integrating psychic bisexuality (Houzel, 2020) in the therapeutic relationship in which the masculine elements reinforced the feminine ones.

Some reflections on my work with Eric

Patients like Eric "threaten to break therapists' hearts, because they themselves are heartbroken … and the feeling of brokenness goes into the fabric of their being" (Tustin, 1978, 1986). Their withdrawal, despair and encapsulation "places great demands on the analyst to be a lively, engaging presence, … [who must] trust in and rely on *reverie*". In the discussion that follows, I would like to consider my work with Erik in the light of Alvarez' (2010) three conceptual levels of intervention: the explanatory, descriptive, and vitalizing levels.

During the initial phases of Eric's treatment, I was forced to endure periods of almost overwhelming deadness, feelings of hopelessness and the sense that it was impossible to have any impact on Eric. I felt we were enmeshed in a chronic apathy about relating which went beyond despair; nothing was expected. Assuming he was more undrawn than withdrawn (Alvarez, 1992, 2010), I found it very useful to work at the reclamation level where "Attention, … before it can be held, sometimes has to be caught and elicited. … For alpha function to operate, the object has to be seen to be worth attending to in the first place" (Alvarez, 2010, p. 142). Once the child's attention is "caught", then "We have to find ways of helping these children to attend to us, and have to sustain their attention; ... emotionally heightened interest is central to this process" (p. 173).

This level of work engages the very foundations of mental and relational life. As Alvarez (2010) insists:

> This is not a question of one or two tracks, this is a question, first, of helping the patient to get on track, or back on track, in situations where he has been profoundly lost (not hiding).
> (Alvarez, 2010, p. 8)

Thus, the act of reclamation or claiming by a therapist in response to a powerful countertransference sense of urgency may be an extreme form of the mother's normal activity of awakening and alerting the normal, mildly depressed, or slightly distracted, infant.

In a similar vein, Durban (2020) suggests that the analyst can serve as a *developmental reparational object* through whom an "object-implant is achieved into a black hole where bad objects masked a neuromental experience of no object."

In regard to Eric's autistic defences, I tried to show the importance of respecting those defences (or "protections", to quote Tustin (1981), not challenging them or trying to break through them but to wait and wait for a tiny relaxation or opening and then make some tiny moves. So, for example, at the beginning, I offered a blanket, and later, fabrics, to help begin processes of comforting, containment, and discrimination. I was working predominantly at the descriptive level: ascribing or amplifying meaning through sensations.

Bion (1962) indicated that some projective identifications took place not simply for defensive or destructive reasons, but for purposes of needed communication. Consequently, I tried to explore the nature of the missing parts of the patient as they resided in me, until the patient was able to own or re-own them. I kept trying to meeting Eric where he was, at his level, rather than attempting to coax him out of encapsulation or enthrallment with mermaids (as the school and family had tried to do). I waited and waited without intruding and didn't interpret his dreams, but responded to the terrible anxiety in them.

It was only in the later sessions that we were able to work in the first, explanatory level: offering alternative meanings. These interpretations tended to replace one meaning with another, the conscious with the unconscious, or the disowned with the re-owned. For example: "What if you felt that drinking mother's milk will transform you into a girl? Do you think that this was the reason you felt that you needed to be a girl?"

In retrospect, I would say that Eric's interest in mermaids was *pre-gender*, and maybe their legless bodies and capacity to slide smoothly down or forward rather than to have to walk or crawl, signified that they weren't just "girly" or defensive, but represented a foetal, intrauterine existence or some ideal state he'd never had.

Summarising my stance, perhaps we can say it was "an under the sea technique" (Alvarez, 2021) in the sense that with children like Eric, you need to work at primordial levels in order to build a mind. Our process did seem to involve a kind of awakening from autism or life-long dissociation—or both. As a cautionary note, Molinari (2007) has pointed out that one would not want to advocate such a technique with the shell-type autistic child, with whom we must not be intrusive.

As a final illustration and a testament to Eric's growth, I would like to conclude with material from the fourth year of his analysis.

Eric pulled out two Troll dolls that were stuck together; one had pink hair and the other blue.

E: Jani, can I borrow a pair of scissors? I'm going to cut them apart; they can't be stuck together anymore.
J: They can be together, but not stuck together anymore.
E: Yes, Jani, I'll be starting the first grade.
J: It seems you're saying we can be together but we shouldn't be stuck to each other anymore.
E: Yes, I don't throw tantrums anymore. Do you remember when I liked girly things? … I've grown up, Jani.
J: I agree, you have grown up … Do you remember why you started coming here?
E: Yes, I came because I was lonely, because I needed you … And well, because of the other things I just said. I deleted everybody from my

Nintendo; I only left the important ones: you, my mum, my dad, my sisters, and my grandparents.

Eric had started seeing his father on a regular basis. He would show me the presents he got from him and he liked telling me about the new friends he played Avengers with. Eric was seven at that time. Soon after, Eric noticed photos of Sigmund Freud on the bookshelves and asked, "Is that your dad?" I smiled and before I could say anything, he interjected, "No, it can't be your dad, he's too old to be your dad, It must be your grandpa."

His comment upon discovering Freud's photo allowed me to infer Eric's attempt to place himself in an order of generations and in the distribution of conflicts. He was thus beginning to write his own version of his story; a story that did not have to be the same as the one given to him where he felt he had to disappear (like in the La Llorona dream) or to function as a "thing" with black buttons (black holes?) instead of eyes (like in the Coraline dream). I think that this session may also inadvertently remind us how important it is for the container/analyst to have the internal support of a paternal identification (exemplified in symbolic form in the photograph of Freud that I have in my office).

Still later, Eric sorted through all the material we had produced and I told him, "It looks as though you're going through (revisiting) the path we have built." He said, "Yes, we've done a lot but a few things still need to be finished … I'm pulling toys out from this drawer to make room for new things." Eric seemed to be in tune with what Alvarez (2012) emphasised: "We need symbols not only to tolerate losses and dusks, but also to configure the beginnings of new tomorrows"[11] (p. 168).

Eric's emotional experience comprises many topics that we could elaborate on. He has shown me that the path in the process to "be" (Durban, 2020) is infinite. I enjoy his smile and his spontaneity, but I think that what I enjoy the most is seeing that Eric is now the owner of his own mental truth.

---

[11] Translated from Spanish.

References

Alvarez, A. (1992). *Live Company: Psychoanalytic Psychotherapy with Autistic, Borderline, Deprived and Abused Children*. London: Routledge.

Alvarez, A. (2002). *Una presencia que da vida*. APM Biblioteca Nueva Vision: Madrid.

Alvarez, A. (2010). Levels of analytical work and levels of pathology: The work of calibration. *IJPA*, *91*: 859–878.

Alvarez, A. (2012). *The Thinking Heart: Three Levels of Psychoanalytic Therapy with Disturbed Children*. London: Routledge.

Alvarez, A. (February 2020). Mexico Autism Conference. Autismo y Estados No Representados. CDMX, México. Personal communication.

Bergstein A. (2019). *Bion and Meltzer's Expedition into Unmapped Mental Life*. London: Routledge.

Clements, R., & Musker, J. (1989). *The Little Mermaid*. Buena Vista Pictures.

Bick, E. (1962). Symposium on child analysis. *International Journal of Psycho-analysis*, *43*: 328–332.

Bion, W. R. (1957). Differentiation of the psychotic from the non-psychotic personalities. *International Journal of Psycho Analysis*, *38*: 266–275.

Bion, W. R. (1962). *Learning From Experience*. London: Heinemann.

Bion, W. R. (1965). *Transformations: Change from Learning to Growth*. London: William Heinemann.

Bion, W. R. (1991). *Cogitations*. London: Routledge.

Bion, W. R. (1992). *Seminarios clinicos y cuatro textos*. Lugar Editorial. Buenos Aires Argentina.

Disney Pictures (2006). *Cars* (Lasseter, J. Ranft, J. & Klubien, J.).

Durban, J. (21, 22 February 2020). From chaos to Caravaggio: Technical considerations in the psychoanalysis of autisto-psychotic states in relation to sensory-perceptual fragmentation (Conference). Autismo y Estados No Representados. CDMX, México.

Grotstein, J. (1990). Nothingless, meaningless, chaos and the "black hole". II. *Contemporary Psychoanalysis*, *26*: 377–407.

Grotstein, J. (2007). *A Beam of Intense Darkness*. London: Karnac.

Houzel, D. (February 2020). Splitting of psychic bisexuality in autistic children. Lecture given for the Frances Tustin Memorial Trust series of lectures.

Joseph, B. (1983). Towards the experience of psychic pain. In: J. S. Grotstein (Ed.), *Do I Dare Disturb the Universe? A Memorial to W.R. Bion* (pp. 93–102). London: Routledge.

Klein, M. (1930). *Caso Dick*. Obras completas. Buenos Aires: Paidós.

Levine, H. B. (February 2020). Making the unthinkable thinkable: Vitalisation, reclamation, containment and representation. Paper presented at the II International A. Santamaría Foundation Conference. CDMX, México.

Levine, H. B., & Power, D. G. (Eds.) (2017). *Engaging Primitive Anxieties of the Emerging Self: The Legacy of Frances Tustin*. London: Karnac.

Levine, H. B., Reed, G. S, & Scarfone, D. (Eds.) (2013). *Unrepresented States and the Construction of Meaning*. London: Karnac/IPA.

Meltzer, D. (1975). La dimensionalidad como un parametro del funcionamiento mental: su relacion con la organización narcisita. In: *Exploración del Autismo* (pp. 197–209). Buenos Aires: Paidós.

Meltzer, D. (1979). *La psicología de los estados autistas y dela mentalidad pos autista*. In: *Exploraciones del autismo*. Buenos Aires: Paidós.

Mitrani, J. L. (1995). Toward an understanding of unmentalized experience. *Psychoanalytic Quarterly, 64*: 68–112.

Molinari, E. (2007) Aprender a danzar en el desierto del "no-pensamiento". In: *Soñar el análisis. Desarrollos clínicos del pensamiento de W. R. Bion*. Buenos Aires: Ed Lumen.

Roussillon, R. (2011). *Primitive Agony and Symbolization*. London: Karnac.

Santamaría, J. (2013). Transformaciones y dolor psíquico. *Colombian Psychoanalytic Association Review, XXIV*(1–2): 1–148. https://dialnet.unirioja.es/servlet/articulo?codigo=4726622

Selick, H. (2009). *Coraline*. Focus Features.

Tustin, F. (1972). *Autismo y psicosis infantiles*. Barcelona: Paidós Ibérica.

Tustin, F. (1978). Psychotic elements in the neurotic disorders of childhood. *Journal of Child Psychotherapy, 4*: 5–18.

Tustin, F. (1981). *Autistic States in Children*. London: Routledge.

Tustin, F. (1986). *Autistic Barriers in Neurotic Patients*. New Haven, CT: Yale University Press.

Winnicott, D. W. (1960). String: A technique of communication. *Journal of Child Psychology and Psychiatry, 1*: 49–52.

CHAPTER FIVE

The third topography: a topography of the bond, a perinatal topography

Sylvain Missonnier and Bernard Golse

Can a biography that starts with the day of being born be a serious enterprise? No, it cannot, no more than can an anamnesis that excludes the subject's history before birth.

After several decades devoted to the elucidation of the parent–infant relationship, it is at last time for a psychoanalytical psycho(patho)logy that is genuinely *perinatal*.

The cries and whispers of the living and the dead meet and intermingle here, in a subtle choreography of bodies, affects, and fantasies. But what can we say about the undead?

Auguste: the ghost of the intimate Atlantis

I saw Auguste at the age of six in consultation for night terrors.[1] Accompanied by his parents, he told me in a spontaneous, lively, but anxious manner, that a weasel would bite his feet during the night, waking him up terrified. The parents had brought him to consult on the advice of

---

[1] Consultation conducted by S. M.

their community paediatrician. They reported "complete failure to understand" these frequent night terrors in which Auguste, with his uncontrollable crying, had been waking the whole household for nearly two years. I soon learnt that Auguste was one of triplets resulting from in vitro fertilisation. The parents also remarked on the recurrence of frequent episodes of fever, which had led them to often frequent paediatric emergency departments or to call emergency medical services.

Auguste, very attentive, listened to what his parents had to say, but by the quality of his presence appeared from the outset as the main protagonist. Because I immediately perceived his implication, I felt I should offer to see him on his own for a while.

Once alone with me he immediately returned to the attack by the weasel. Chitta, a woolly monkey that Auguste chose among the toys on offer, played the part of the attacker. During this play sequence, I remembered something: as a child I witnessed a rather unusual hunting episode, where an old man, a friend of my grandfather's, had come with a trained weasel in a wooden box and had put it down rabbit burrows to drive them out and catch them in a net at the entrance to the burrow. This memory was accompanied, in a transferential manner, by a dulled anxiety and a degree of depressive feeling. This led me to ask Auguste what he knew about weasels. His answer was "Weasels kill chickens." He then explained that in his grandmother's house in the country he had seen a stuffed weasel, and that she had explained to him that before it was killed, it used to raid the hen-run, which Auguste knew well having been there to collect eggs. At the end of the session, Auguste asked me if he could take Chitta home with him. I asked him why, and he replied that Chitta would help defend him from the weasel.

As an exception I agreed, on condition that he return the toy at the next appointment set for ten days later. It was the intensity of the distress—mine and his, intermingled—that justified this loan that went against the usual rules in my office.

At the second appointment Auguste started the session alone with me. Spontaneously he explained to me that he wanted to keep Chitta to help him in the night with the weasel, which was still coming to bite him. That was why he had not brought the toy back.

"Were you afraid I would take Chitta back?" I asked. "Yes," he replied sheepishly. He then played with a small vehicle that launched missiles, and enthusiastically killed numerous weasels, represented by the waste bin.

When a missile hit the bin, Auguste made it utter cries of acute pain.

The parents then joined us. To break the initial silence, the mother talked about her guilt at having contracted a sexually transmitted disease before their marriage. This disease was the reason for her infertility, and especially for the "ordeal" of fertility treatment, culminating in the announcement of quadruplets which she said at once dismayed and delighted her, so great was the jump from "nothing" to "four".

Seeing my astonishment at the figure of four, the mother sobbed for a long time. The father then explained to me the "procedure" required: an "embryo reduction", because there was not enough room for four, only for three.

His wife then resumed the conversation, and recounted in great detail, and "for the first time in front of Auguste", the loss "of one of their children".

"You can't be unhappy and at the same time produce three babies," commented the father, underlining the fact that he himself had contributed to the professionals' attempts to minimise things to prevent the appearance of parental mourning, mourning that had clearly remained congealed in a destructive terror, and I was beginning to realise that the weasel was the possible messenger of this terror in Auguste's nightmares.

Auguste had ceased playing with the garage and the missile-launcher, and had come close to his mother, his head in her lap. I suggested: "Maybe the weasel that bites Auguste's feet at night is the dead baby alongside the three that were alive—he wants to come back to the family."

Like an echo, calm silence set in. The mother stroked her son's hair with one hand and with the other wiped away a few tears. The father looked at them both protectively.

I suggested an encounter with all the family next time to commemorate the memory of the dead child.

In my notes I wrote: "Let's hope the weasel child is relinquishing its role of a ghost drifting through the family fantasies."

It was only later that I discovered that (in French) *fantasme* (fantasy) and *fantôme* (ghost) have the same Greek root, *phantasma*—apparition, phantom, ghost. Indeed, in fourteenth-century French, *fantasme* could mean either an illusion or a ghost.

At the third appointment, Auguste laid legitimate claim to his role of initiator, and spent the first quarter of an hour with me. He proudly told me he was now sleeping very well. He returned Chitta, putting it carefully back on my desk. Rather solemnly, he then surveyed the walls of my office and said: "The weasel is nice to me now, he doesn't bother me anymore."

The artistic talents of the father of the triplets (an interior designer) proved very valuable. After explaining that he was actually present for the procedure, on my suggestion he made a drawing of the embryo reduction procedure, representing "Mummy" and her "belly where the babies are". As we watched, drawn together by emotion, he drew four little people "cramped in like sardines", and wrote the three names at their feet. When he hesitated a moment before the fourth, Auguste decisively announced "Chitta", which the father, moved and smiling, wrote down. He then mimed the gesture of the puncture procedure.[2] The mother began to weep again for a short while, and then exclaimed: "I'm sure it was a girl", drying her years. (It can be noted in passing that in thirteenth-century French *belette* (weasel) was the diminutive of *belle* and meant a "pretty creature".) She then became more lively, ruffling the heads of her "little scoundrels".

First hypothesis: the engram of proto-representative sensory traces imprinted during Auguste's intrauterine life exists and is active. The traces concern the foetal epigenesis in general, and the embryo reduction and its spatial consequences in particular. They cannot be symbolised directly, but they are active in a psychosomatic homeostasis and in the numerous affective, intrapsychic, and interpersonal conflicts that for him regularly commemorate the primordial content/container dialectic.

Second hypothesis: explicit narratives and implicit references, here concerning the embryo reduction, are at the centre of family narratives

---

[2] There are two techniques: either aspiration of the embryo through the cervix or a potassium chloride puncture that "disconnects" the embryo which remains in place and is absorbed or converts into a *fetus papyraceus*. It is important to know the technique used so as to capture the symbolic. Here the foetus that was killed was indeed *papyraceus*, that is to say changed into a "papyrus, the secret guardian of thought" (Maupassant, *La vie errante*, 1890).

and generational transmission (Golse & Missonnier, 2005). The first bonds between parents, foetuses, and children are inseparable from prenatal loss and the inertia of its imprint.

Do Auguste's night terrors relate to the first or the second hypothesis?

To bring them together and avoid polarisation, a third hypothesis can be suggested, that of *an intrauterine virtual object-relation*, which we consider is present throughout life (Missonnier, 2009).

This hypothesis could be based on a preconception of the damaged bond with the surviving foetus as a result of the removal of the other foetus.

We now need to define matters more clearly, in order to envisage the specific features of the *ghosts of the intimate Atlantis*[3] through this prism.

Mourning the "hidden child"

Initially, this theorisation of the intrauterine virtual object-relation is clearly linked to my practice in maternity departments, which has two aspects: attending to parents on the occasion of a miscarriage, a stillborn baby, or a baby who died immediately after delivery; and following up "expectant" parents who are confronting abortion for medical reasons as a result of the detection of a foetal anomaly.

This clinical practice confronts professionals with fertility issues, and with the limitations to the validity of the well-known Freudian theme developed in "Mourning and melancholia" (Freud, 1917e), where loss concerns a *total* object constituted *outside* the body itself, while the specificity of perinatal mourning for what I have called the "hidden" child is well upstream in psychoanalytic object theory. To say here that the dead being is encrypted in the person in mourning is not metaphor for a psychic reality, but a fully fledged raw fact of material reality. In this context, when there is a medical abortion, it is a genuine *variable amputation* for the mother-to-be and the couple.

---

[3] Atlantis is a mythical island mentioned by Plato in two of his texts (The Timothy and the Critias). In Greek mythology, the island was swallowed up by the waves in a cataclysm caused at the instigation of Zeus.

Dominique Blin and Marie-Josée Sobieux (1997), in Freudian terms of nostalgic yearning, conceptualised this as the loss of a "non-object object", "half self, half other", situated in-between narcissistic investment and object investment.

In the WAIMH Fr group "Le premier chapiter",[4] we have extensively discussed a polemic study (Hugues et al., 2002) published in *The Lancet*. This research, highly disputable both in its form and in its content, questions the legitimacy and the psychological efficacy of the accompaniment scenarios offered for decades to parents who have lost a child during pregnancy.

Without entering into detail on this interesting debate, it seems to me that there is considerable danger in systematising procedures for presenting the foetus, naming it, and for the civil and religious rituals, etc. by deciding whether or not to undertake them merely in reference to the chronological term of a pregnancy. Quite clearly, all things being equal, the parents—individually and as a couple—are at a psychic moment in the pregnancy that differs in every case. The embryo, and then the foetus, is positioned, from the point of view of the parents at the time of the event, somewhere between nothing and everything, between a thing and a person in the on-going perinatal process of humanisation. The ritualisation offered thus has meaning if it is tailored to this process of maturation. Adopting a "ready-made" protocol is dangerous if it is linked solely to the term of the pregnancy, or systematised without any pathological or psychological evaluation.

It is precisely at this point in our reflection that the notion of the *intrauterine virtual object-relation* arises. Rather than taking a *photographic*, static view of the embryo or foetus, non-historical, fixed in its status of a non-object object, half-self, half-other, I prefer the *cinematographic*, dynamic view of a parental investment that is evolving, located for each individual at a precise point somewhere between the narcissistic zero and a genuine pre-objectal state, rather than the emergence of the classic oral, anal, or genital object-relation. This variable factor between an extension of one's own body and inclusion in the self of an otherness-in-the-making corresponds only to the maternal side of the intrauterine virtual object-relation.

---

[4] www.rap5.org

An intrauterine virtual object-relation?

This prenatal virtual object-relation is indeed, strictly from the viewpoint of the object-relation, a new concept that concerns the "expectant" parents, the unborn child, the embryo, and later the foetus.

Since in psychoanalysis we refer to a "typical" object in reference to the oral, anal, or genital relation, as original characteristics, the virtual object-relation is, for its part, *uterine*. The fantasies of men and women becoming parents form the fabric of these object relationship.

I see this relationship as the matrix of all later development, from the partial object-relation to the total object-relation. Its prime function is to *contain* this development, and to potentiate the evolving dynamics at work. It is useful to consider that this intrauterine virtual object-relation corresponds to a prenatal version of the "containing function" (Bion, 1962; Anzieu, 1993) as it was initially conceived by the English psychoanalytic school, which is distinct from the Freudian conception of a conflict that is solely intrapsychic, favouring, rather, conflict that is at once intrapsychic *and* intersubjective.

If we consider the framework of "primary intersubjectivity" rooted in the prenatal period (according to Trevarthen & Aitkin, 2001), the uterine virtual object-relation can be described from the aspect of the embryo/foetus/baby (nidation) and then from the aspect of the parents-to-be (nidification), on condition that we do not forget that these are just two sides of the same process.

For the foetus and the expectant parents, we can therefore say that the uterine virtual object-relation relates—with considerable individual variability—to a process that runs from extreme narcissistic investment (tending towards the object zero) to the progressive emergence of a (pre) object-relation.

Basically, this uterine virtual object-relation is an interface between "becoming a parent" and "being born a human", which precedes—and potentiates—the parent–baby relationship. Its persistence and coexistence *throughout life* with other modes of object relations should of course be envisaged.

On this point, it is probable that the hypothetical proto-representative sensory traces embedded in the uterine virtual object-relation may not later be directly open to symbolisation, but may nevertheless be active in the subject's psychosomatic homeostasis, and the numerous intrapsychic and interpersonal affective conflicts that recall the primary dialectic of content and container.[5]

The universality of the original fantasy of intrauterine life in Freud (1915b) is an excellent argument in favour of the persistence of the uterine virtual object-relation. We still lack data on the genetic equation in order to decipher the phylogenetic transmission theorised by Freud. However, in this nostalgic recurrence (both pregnant with meaning and the systematic object of massive repression), we can reasonably detect a cultural constant of this uterine signifier and the dynamics structuring its generational, nonverbal transmission.[6]

Mourning, melancholy, and embryo reduction

For Auguste, we can hypothesise that his sleep disorder reflects an intersubjective foetus/baby/child/parent plural assemblage.

For the parents, there is unresolved parental mourning in which the ambivalent conflict takes precedence, and which is compounded by a saturation of the guilt of infanticide.

The fantasised and ghostly presence of the child that has been "put to death" is omnipresent in day-to-day relations between the parents and their triplets.

For Auguste, the uterine virtual object-relation could carry proto-representative memory traces that are not open to direct symbolisation. They probably crystallise in the aftermath when coming into contact with the generational representations inherent in the many nonverbal inter-relationships, and the parent/foetus/baby narratives.

There is also the ever-present threat of a non-represented scenario of parental infanticide (which is therefore not contained in perceptible time-space), which is probably very damaging in this instance.

---

[5] See Jean Bergeret and Marcel Houser (2004)—"souvenirs/non-souvenirs".
[6] The four strata of original fantasies described by Bergeret and Houser (2004) cast light on this debate: Level 1, the closest to the manifest register of a sexual and oedipal order at work in reconstructions after the fact; Level 2, latent, of the narcissistic type; Level 3, more archaic, rooted in intrauterine life; Level 4, a phylogenetic register (Bergeret & Houser, 2004, pp. 284 and following).

This threat can probably be described as a morbid, traumatic, and enigmatic signifier reflecting the inability of the adults themselves to put it into words (see Laplanche, 1987). The symptom experienced by Auguste is the "ambassador" of this effect.

In this context, consultation with Auguste, the vehicle of family repressions, provides scope for an attempt to trap the family "papyrus" ghost concealed under the appearance of a stuffed weasel.

Only individual and family work on the bereavement can place this ghost in an accessible mental space, free from guilt, so as to enable it to disappear. This is as if Freud's killing of death in "Mourning and melancholia" could correspond to killing the ghost, and breaking the pact with melancholia. Nicolas Abraham and Maria Torok would express it as relinquishing the melancholic *incorporation* of death (refusal to mourn) in favour of the process of *introjection* making mourning possible.

Yet in the area of embryo reduction, things are generally regulated by consensus and protocol, for the caregivers and for the family, precisely to ensure that a work of mourning is banned (Garel et al., 2004, 2010). The amplification of the fundamental paradox of humanness—the simultaneity of the metabolisation of death and the enhancement of life—is here so extreme that it cannot entertain thought. For this reason at least, embryo reduction all too often relies on an experimental protocol intended to cater for pathological mourning, with the conversion of the dead embryo into a wandering ghost. The prenatal mourning for the virtual child-to-be always favours melancholic encrypting (Abraham & Torok, 1987). Clearly, the scenario of embryo reduction is radically singular for each of the parents.

Paradise lost

To complete our commentary, we would like to converge on a famous text by José Bleger (1966) in which he defines the framework of psychoanalysis.

This author puts emphasis on the fact that in the cure, the framework relates to the most "undifferentiated" part of the archaic history of the analysand. He states that the patient's framework is the expression of his most primitive merging with his mother's body, and the framework of the psychoanalyst needs to re-establish this original symbiosis in order to be able to alter it. The framework is the "receptor" of the symbiosis with the mother (non–self-immutability) enabling the child to develop his ego.

According to Bleger, in reality, there are two frameworks: one that is proposed and maintained by the analyst and consciously accepted by the patient; and one onto which the patient projects his psychic reality.

However, what is crucial for our theme is what Bleger calls "the ghost world", the part of the framework onto which the patient projects his conflicts.

This ghost world framework offered by the therapist and onto which Auguste and his family project the most archaic part of their personalities to my mind corresponds precisely to the shared resonance of the cries and whispers of the primitive symbiotic relationship in the uterine virtual object-relation.

In other words, the psychoanalytic setting (typical cure, face-to-face, family therapy, etc.) is in itself an elective invitation to take in the resonances of the uterine virtual object-relation and its ghosts … so long as the analyst remains hospitable in countertransferential mode towards them.

This being so, the caricatured resonances of the uterine virtual object-relation in perinatal and childcare therapeutic consultations appear merely as an amplification of an element that is identical in all psychoanalytic settings, frequently present and frequently unobtrusive and masked.

This is why these consultations clearly form a heuristic laboratory for psychoanalysis, because they offer a real-time window on certain environmental elements underpinning the aquatic archaic of the foetus, and thereafter their reiterations in the open air in the transference of the parents and the countertransference of the psychoanalyst.

Ultimately, this opening onto the first prenatal chapter of human biography and its ghosts is an opportunity for the psychoanalyst. If this charming elderly lady allows her sons and daughters to explore her own uterine content and leaves room for the uterine virtual object-relation alongside oral, anal, or genital object-relations, she will finally be able to accommodate the many ghosts of the intimate Atlantis, and be better able to foster the recognition and symbolisation of the cries and whispers of their repeated tragic wanderings.

Theoretical considerations—a perinatal metapsychology

The two topographies proposed by Freud, that is, the first (the unconscious, the preconscious, and the conscious) and the second (the id, the ego, and the superego), formalised from 1920, both relate to a conception of the psyche as being organised in psychic locations or systems resulting from a process of intrapsychic differentiation.

These two topographies are clearly still relevant, and their heuristic dimension is well-recognised in the clinical, technical, and theoretical domains when working with "fully fledged" subjects (children, adolescents, and adults). When working with babies, however, or with subjects that are not fully differentiated (such as patients presenting so-called "archaic" pathologies), the use of these two topographies should be subject to caution, as they belong to an essentially intrapsychic metapsychology.

Indeed, while a baby does not require us to renounce our usual psychoanalytic markers (the drive theory, the anaclisis theory, or even the "afterwardness" theory, provided that the changes proposed by Diatkine[7] for the latter are made), the baby's fundamental incompletion, his basic immaturity, his psychic and physical neoteny require us to rethink the topographical viewpoint, which here needs to be from a strictly intrapsychic perspective.

This is why we propose what could be termed a third topography, a topography of the mental representation of the bond with the idea—paradoxical in appearance only—that primitive bonds could be invested even before the subject and the object are clearly delineated.

In all events, this is our proposal, also knowing that this hypothesis of a third topography has already been envisaged by certain authors (Brusset, Dejours, Kaës) but in other fields than that of early development, and this is a subject to which we will return.

We in fact set out to plead for a perinatal metapsychology, which is to some extent the main aim of this work.

---

[7] It is indeed important to underline that the "afterwardness" theory is fully useable in work with babies, whether it is contracted by envisaging it within the same early interactive system, as did Diatkine (1979), or diffracted over several generations, since what can be valid as the first moment of trauma for the child can always be the nth moment in the history of the child's maternal or paternal filiations (Golse, 2007).

A third topography and its confrontation with the dyad and triad

"There is no such thing as a baby." Winnicott's statement is well known and often overused. It means that a baby cannot be apprehended outside the bonds he forms with his first environment.

Infant psychology, psychopathology, and psychiatry have been developing fast in recent decades, as has our knowledge of dyadic and triadic functioning.

This being said, if we talk in terms of dyad and triad we are necessarily in the interpersonal register, not in the intrapsychic register. We are aware that the historical setting of the emergence of these two major theoretical corpuses, psychoanalysis and attachment theory, has meant that the former is mainly centred on the intrapsychic and the latter on the interpersonal.

Indeed, these two corpuses arose in very different historical settings: the end of the nineteenth century for psychoanalysis and the latter part of the twentieth century for attachment theory (Bowlby, 1978).

The latter part of the nineteenth century was preoccupied with the inside of things (with the discovery of X-rays by Rötgen in 1895 in the area of the curiosity towards the inside of bodies, and the drafting the same year by Freud and Breuer of their *Studies on Hysteria*, marking the start of psychoanalytic reflection in a form of curiosity towards the inside of the mind). In contrast, in the latter part of the twentieth century, after the Second World War, which upset a whole range of social relationships, there was more preoccupation with questions of interpersonal security.

Thus, psychoanalysis quite naturally came to be characterised by intrapsychic issues, while attachment theory for its part was centred on the interpersonal question and the theme of security.

There was then fierce debate between proponents of psychoanalysis and proponents of attachment theory, and it is well known that Widlöcher (2000) suggested the idea that these conflicts resulted from a failed encounter between English and Hungarian psychoanalysis, an encounter which, via Balint's concept (1971) of primary love, could have enabled the opposition between the primary characteristic of attachment and the secondary characteristic of love according to psychoanalysis to be overcome.

Whatever the history of this debate, it is clear that there is a dead end: that of an intersubjective topography (dyadic or triadic) including a baby whose internal world is not yet sufficiently differentiated for the metapsychology relating to him to be genuinely intrapsychic.

Nevertheless, the very term "intersubjective topography" is to some extent a hybrid, a heresy, since the concept of intersubjectivity calls on the interpersonal register, while it is the concept of subjectivation that calls on the intrapsychic register and that is legitimately the concern of metapsychology in the classic meaning of the term.

It is to overcome these contradictions that we propose to focus on what are probably very early developments: the interpersonal bond and the modes of intrapsychic representation among babies.

Representing the bond before representing the object

This proposal is less paradoxical than it might seem, in particular if we take account of the investment of the early interactions of babies.

The long-standing debate between R. D. Stolorow and L. Friedman in the USA

At a time when there was as yet no debate on the precedence of the representation of the bond over the representation of the object, it was the question of the very nature of internal objects that led to a debate—the internal objects theorised by Stolorow above all as mental representations of the self-interacting with the other, and which he thought possessed their own energy, enabling them to be updated in thought or action.

This author considered that there was no representation of the self that was not a representation of the self in interaction with another, and no representation of the other that was not a representation of the other in interaction with the self.

It is well known that here the position of Widlöcher was closer to that of Stolorow than to that of L. Friedman, who for his part was in favour of a relatively holistic conception of the psyche as having no elementary psychic objects, but as being subjected to a global energy drive. (This concerns the debate of 1978–1980, which in a way preceded and prepared the way for the now famous 1984 debate in the Association psychanalytique de France on the theme "What is the role of the drive?")

From this perspective, subjectivation appears as an interiorisation of intersubjective representations, and in babies as a progressive interiorisation of representations of interactions (in the area of attachment or affective tuning), but with a gradual perfusion into the system of the unconscious parental dynamic, the parent's whole infantile history, their oedipal conflicts, their psycho-sexual history, their inter- and trans-generational issues and all the accompanying "afterwardness" effects.

The object is invested in before being perceived

Even before this somewhat forgotten debate, Lebovici as early as 1960 made the following remark, leading to much comment: "The object is invested before being perceived".

Almost as if in the *fort–da* game, it was the string that mattered for the child more than the spool itself.

A first reading of Lebovici's statement can relate to the narcissistic/objectal balance, in the sense that the object can be invested although it is still perceived as being part of the self (a narcissistic object) before being fully perceived as being outside the self (objectal object). This in a way recalls Winnicott's distinction between subjective and objective objects, even if his distinction is above all based on the survival of the external object in the face of attacks directed towards the mental representation of that object.

A second reading of the statement can also link to attachment theory, here again with the idea that one can become attached to an object that is still perceived as not distinct from the self, so that the first attachments could have the subjective value of self-attachments.

In all events, this investment in the object before it is perceived as such in a way appears as the reverse of the "*désobjectalisation*" drive studied by Green as a death drive.

Disobjectification of the object, according to this author, is a consequence of a devitalising investment, while for Lebovici it is the vitalising investment of the pre-object that prepares its objectification in the perspective of a life-drive.

This being so, the idea that the object can be invested in before it is perceived leads us to reflect on the possibility of an investment of bonds before access is gained to intersubjectivity, and this in our view is precisely what opens the way to the hypothesis of a perinatal metapsychology, provided we accept a degree of deconcentration of the concept of object representation.

The three levels of object representation

When considering object representation, a frequent and classic notion, the concept often appears too global, and it is probably useful to break it down into several distinct levels.

The representation of the place of the object is one thing, the representation of bonds with the object is another and the representation of the object itself is a third.

The place of the object

The place of the object probably possesses its own level of representation, and there are several arguments in support of this.

Those of us who work in nurseries, for instance, know how children who are placed from birth in view of adoption appear early on to possess the notion of what a "parent" is. It is true that after a while they can have had occasion to see the visits of parents of other children, but the issue goes deeper.

The neotenous infant may have a form of inborn representation of the other that he requires, the helping other without whom he cannot live and whom he fundamentally needs in the "fundamental anthropological situation" (Laplanche, 2002).

This is probably what Bion (1962, 1963, 1965) meant with his concept of preconception. On the subject of the maternal breast, he says that the baby searches for the breast "where it is usually found".

This strange but interesting statement may not mean that the infant searches for it on the mother's body on the basis of memory traces he has of suckling, nor that it is in response to an instinctive attraction for the smell of milk; it rather means that he seeks it in that very place for which he has a sort of proto-representation. For Bion, a proto-representation can only become a stable representation by the encounter in external reality with the corresponding object, which then fixes it by way of the emotional experience of the encounter.

This is also what is envisaged by Missonnier (2009) when referring to the register of the virtual in relation to the "first chapter of life", in other words pregnancy.

He goes as far as to speak of a virtual object-relation as being what we generally mean when we consider the representations that parents can have of their unborn child, representations that can be described in part under the phrase "imagined child".

However, we may need to instate a form of symmetry and envisage that the foetus, for its part, has the ability to invest a proto-representation of the parents-to-be, a proto-representation of functions, naturally, rather than this or that static, variously figurative characteristic.

In the artistic sphere, finally, among different possible illustrations of the place of the object, we can recall Dino Buzzati's *The Tartar Steppe* of 1949, a book in which the hero spends the last years of his life surveying the horizon, focusing on a point where he thinks an improbable enemy army might come into view; or again the theft of the *Mona Lisa* from the Louvre museum in 1911, in the wake of which from 1911 to 1913 Leader (2011) tells us that there had never been more numerous visitors to contemplate the empty space of the painting, a masterpiece that nevertheless draws huge crowds; and finally the temporal place of the object in the works of Borges.

The representation of the bonds with the object forms another level of the object-relation

If we refer to bonds formed with the object, we are in fact referring to the domain of early interactions and their modes of mental representation.

There is consensus around the fact that the concept of interaction, emblematic of the general theory of systems, is today the focus of all studies and all research concerning the infant and his early development.

The investment of interactions is a theme taken into account both by researchers in the area of attachment and by those who call for early psychoanalysis.

However, the investment of interactions and the representation of the resulting bonds has nothing in itself to say about the object involved in these interactions, since only the interactive characteristics of the object are represented.

We can thus consider the example of Bretherton's "internal working models" (1990) deployed in the area of attachment and the "generalised representations of interaction" described by Stern (1989) on the subject of his model of affective tuning.

The great interest of attachment theory is that it encourages us today to consider symbolisation in the presence of the object.

Before considering this question, we can note that while the necessary encounter with an object procuring satisfaction is propounded by Freud in his article on negation (1925h) as being the *sine qua non* condition of its possible later symbolisation, conversely the "strange situation" is certainly centred on the observation of the child's behaviour on the return of his mother, but there is no doubt that there is naturally no return if there has not initially been a departure.

In other words, if we can put it in this way, there is a presence on the side of psychoanalysis, and absence on the side of attachment, and even an interesting to-and-fro, since presence precedes absence in Freud's 1925 article on negation, while the absence of the mother precedes her return and her presence in the attachment-oriented protocol of the "strange situation".

In present-day research, however, attention to this issue of presence and absence appears to be giving way, at any rate at the start of development, to the issue of gap and difference.

Indeed, everything seems to point to the idea that the child, before wondering if his mother is there or not, first wonders if she is "as usual" or not. This is one of the main phenomenological questions concerning the infant (Golse, 2006), which is in fact reminiscent of the proposal by Bion (1962, 1963, 1965), according to which the absence of the object is first of all experienced as a "hostile presence" before being experienced as absence per se.

Thus the question by the baby concerning his mother—"Is she like she usually is?"—proves in reality to be very different from the question of whether she is there or not, which means that the baby operates on small differences, or the difference between "the same" and "not the same", very well expounded by Haag an issue that she considers far more important, at least initially, than the issue of absence–presence, which will only be elaborated at a later stage.

If the mother is too different from what she usually is, the gap is too great to cope with for the baby (this can, for example, be observed in the case of maternal depression), but if the gap is not too great, it can form a stimulating "surprise" for the baby's thought processes.

This observation of the mother by the baby, and the assessment of departures from what is usual, occur in the second semester of life by way of an analysis of the mother's interactive style, or the quality of her affective tuning (Stern, 1989)—more or less unimodal or transmodal, more or less immediate or postponed, more or less attenuated or amplified (the intrapsychic interiorisation of which will occur by way of the baby's "generalised representations of interaction"). However, for the baby this process can start earlier, in the first semester of life, via observation of the responses of his mother to his attachment behaviours.

Indeed, the infant imprints in his psyche a sort of "average" of maternal response in terms of attachment, and on the occasion of each new interactive encounter with her he will measure the gap between the present maternal response and the "average" representations he has formed, which are no other than his future "internal working models" as described by Bretherton (1990).

If the mother is "not as usual" (for instance, because she is anxious or depressed) the baby finds himself confronted with a triadic situation, since it is better for him to incriminate a third party rather than himself as having caused these changes in his mother.

This issue, as we know, will, throughout life, infiltrate our love stories, since it is the question of the differences of the object of love from what is usual that will generate in us the fear of a rival third party, just as in infancy we encountered that triadic situation via this effect of the variability of the image and the functioning of our mother.

We can thus see that the attachment system, like the system of affective tuning, enables the baby to represent and to imprint on the psyche the variations in maternal responses, which is clearly a form of representation of the manifestations of the object present.

What we have here is an investment of the variations in the maternal response, rather than an investment in the mother as an object.

We can thus talk of investment of the pre-object bond, and that is precisely what we wish to highlight here.

We can add, so as to connect to the acquisitions of the neurosciences, that the notion of "representaction" proposed by Jeannerod (1983, 1993) is also equivalent to a mental representation of interaction and not of the object as such and its various characteristics.

To conclude on this level of representation of bonds with the object, it can be added that Haag often stated that in a way the baby forms a portrait of the mother in abstract manner, a rhythmic portrait based on representations of his dynamic interactions with her, before being able to form a truly figurative portrait.

According to Haag, this links to the hypotheses of Leroi-Gourhan according to which abstract art dates much further back in the evolution of humanity than figurative art as exemplified by certain figurative representations discovered in caves dating much further back than those at Lascaux, with scenes of hunting, fishing, and war.

Is modernity a return to abstract art?

The representation of the object as such

It is ultimately this level of representation of the object as such that is what we intuitively think of when speaking of object representation. It is also this level that corresponds to the concept of the mental image in the classic meaning, the image of the other, the representation of faces, places, or objects.

The idea proposed here is that this level of representation of the object could in fact occur later than the other two, as a sort of result or culmination.

In all events, it is clear that to talk of the loss of the object is, today, too imprecise.

For instance, in case of depression, what is in fact lost: the representation of the place of the object, the representation of the bonds with the object, or the representation of the object itself? And what happens with babies according to their age? What can be said about melancholy—does the loss then concern the three levels?

These are fascinating questions, arising in fact from our reflections on the early development of infants.

In favour of a third topography

Given the above, if a metapsychology of the dyad or the triad or an intersubjective topography does not appear relevant, is it possible to envisage a topography of the mental representation of the bond?

From our point of view, as already stated, we are among those who consider that it is possible to care for very young children with the legitimate claim to remain as psychoanalysts in these very specific conditions, given that it is the meta-psychological and topographical dimensions that are probably the most clearly called into question by the baby.

Indeed, how can we take account of the maternal "psychic transparency" (Bydlowski, 1991), of the perinatal neo-topography and of "the original unity" to envisage the dyad and the triad in meta-psychological terms, given the central difficulty that is clearly the passage from the interpersonal to the intrapsychic?

Can we assume that the father–mother–baby system is itself the source of the dynamic that is able to transpose the triadification into triangulation? There is certainly no guarantee that this is true, and it raises the whole question of interiorisation.

Nevertheless, the question is whether we can envisage, in contrast, that the presence of a third party is essential here, and thus the system of joint therapies that we deploy in the Necker-Enfants Malades Hospital could be liable to provide the dyad and the triad with a framework commensurate with the group psychic apparatus (Kaës, 1976)—a framework serving as an observing, participating third party within the same group topography and able to launch the movement of "psychisation" of behavioural interactions.

A setting of joint therapies, in all events, in our view provides a valuable paradigm to envisage the concept of the third topography.

It is plausible to consider that what we need here is a metapsychology of the bond (Brusset, 1988, 2006), a metapsychology possibly opening the way to a third topography that could enable the cleavage between the interpersonal and the intrapsychic to be overcome.

But what do we mean by a metapsychology of the bond?

Is it a metapsychology that is strictly intrapsychic, as described by Dejours (1986, 2002), or is it rather what one could perhaps call an intersubjective metapsychology, without however surrendering to the temptation of a fantasy of a collective apparatus, in the perspective of the work by Kaës?

We have seen above that the concept of the third topography as used by Dejours in reference to his hypothesis of an unconscious that he terms "amential" is in no way a topography of the bond as we propose here. It is on the contrary a topography of a cleavage within the unconscious, which thus relates solely to the internal objects that make it up.

Brusset's third topography does not correspond to what we are attempting to demonstrate here, in that for him it is mainly a matter of building a bridge between the interpersonal and the intrapsychic, a link between internal and external objects, a link that is not really a mental representation as such of the bond with the external object.

Concerning the stance adopted by Kaës, it extends the subject/object focus to the level of the group, so that it can indeed concern the baby (a dyad or triad can be considered as a group), but if there is a third topography it is an encompassing topography that does not solve the problems that we set out concerning the baby and his intrinsic abilities for representation of the bonds between himself and the other.

Indeed, Kaës refers to a third topography in his book *Un singulier pluriel* (2007).

Following on from his proposal for a "group psychic apparatus" (1976) and several successive elaborations (1993, 1999), he calls on the need to resort to "a third topography or a third metapsychology able to give an account of the unconscious in terms of inter-subjectivity".

For the present debate, it is important to note that Kaës does not call for an intersubjective view that could take the place of an intrapsychic topography, but for a "bi-faceted" use of psychoanalytic concepts that have "a dual, meta-psychological belonging to the singular and the plural".

He cites the example of "unconscious alliance" (1993, 2007) that merits description for a better understanding from the viewpoint of an intersubjective topography of the bond. So as to fully understand the dialectic, Kaës writes: "Unconscious alliances have specific functions in the intrapsychic space, and at the same time they support the formation and the processes underpinning inter-subjective bonds, which in turn reinforce the intrapsychic formations and processes".

Ultimately, in line with the proposals by Kaës, the opposition between these two viewpoints is not as radical as might appear.

There is indeed a way of considering the link between the intrapsychic and the interpersonal consisting in recalling that, for the baby, there is no representation of the self that is not a representation of the self in interaction with another, and no representation of the other that is not a representation of the other in interaction with the self, as can be clearly seen in the concept of "generalised representations of interaction" developed by Stern (1989).

Thus, the establishment of the psychic apparatus, which is always, whether we like it or not, a representation of the bond—in the bond and by the bond—plays out precisely at the interface between the intersubjective and the intrapsychic, where joint therapies particularly favour the dual movement of interiorisation and specularisation underpinning the transition from the interpersonal register to the intrapsychic register.

There are two remarks we would like to add here.

First, as seen earlier, the intrapsychic representation of the bond probably appears very early, since it is possible on this side of the object, that is to say, even before the object is clearly represented.

Second, this pre-object emergence of the intersubjective bond in the baby can only occur in a continuum with the prenatal epigenesis pervaded by maternal–foetal interactions, and more broadly by foetus–environment interactions.

In a setting of joint therapies, it is thus possible to envisage that it is the psychic work by the third party, that is to say the therapist or the co-therapists, that plays an essential role in opening the way towards investment of the pre-object bond, by entering into the complexity of the family group psychic apparatus in the making.

In this perspective, joint therapies could well correspond to a figuration or materialisation of the third topography that we advocate here.

Without entering further into this still evolving reflection, we however wish to point to a possible way to model joint therapies, which could gain from differentiating and refining the transference and countertransference modes and techniques in prenatal and postnatal therapeutic consultations.

While it is as yet too soon to determine whether this framework of action will provide decisive elements for reflection, it is nevertheless already plausible to state that the father–mother–baby system that is the focus of joint therapies provides an antenatal prefiguration followed by a postnatal figuration of the intrapsychic triangulation still forming in the foetus or baby concerned, and that, as a result, joint therapies can be considered "psychoanalytic", given that we interpret material that is collected at that level in reference to the trans- or inter-generational concept.

In our view, joint parent–foetus–baby psychotherapies are a genuine conquest of psychoanalysis, rather than a deviation or pitfall thereof.

The pitfalls of psychoanalysis do not always appear as such, and only an honest, strict, meta-psychological approach can ensure that we are on the side of conquest: it is indeed not written in stone that the foetus or baby will remain forever banished from psychoanalysis with the unconvincing pretext that the reconstructed child is not yet rid of the observed child.

It is only in this open perspective, in our view, that the foetus/baby can really enrich psychoanalysis in general, and even our theory of interpretation in the setting of the typical cure.

Towards a perinatal metapsychology

The issue of whether or not we can uphold the existence of a perinatal metapsychology is not a merely theoretical or academic question. In reality it opens onto the question of the demand, where the clinical challenges are considerable.

Babies have no specific demands towards us. Nor do autistic or very archaic children.

Yet people who care for infants or autistic children clearly perceive that something is addressed to them, something they need to report, return, and transform.

The pre-object investment of the bond on which we place emphasis is a sign of this movement towards the outside (an intransitive demand), even before the other is identified as such, which is quite clear in the setting of care for autistic children (Haag, 2018).

This then enables a distinction between the intransitive demand and the autistic dimension specific to psychic life, since the permanent process of construction/deconstruction of the object reflects that autistic dimension specific to psychic life.

The intransitive demand is probably not addressed to the object, but it could already reflect an investment of the pre-object bond for which we are attempting to trace an intrapsychic representation by way of the concept of a third topography.

Lending an ear to this type of demand seems to us essential with babies and autistic children, and to some extent with adolescents.

Naturally, the countertransference challenges of this type of demand are considerable, since they mean that the therapist him/herself needs to regress upstream of his/her object status so as to retrieve and hear the bond that is not addressed in object terms in the setting of archaic pathologies.

To conclude, while in development the bond predominates on both the interpersonal and intrapsychic levels, the absence of the bond is certainly not a freedom but an alienation.

Object-to-be, object that has disappeared: these are possibly the representations that the third topography can help us to envisage beyond the object once it is constituted.

The pre-objective investment of the link accounts for the outward movement (intransitive demand) even before the other is identified as such, as illustrated by the treatment of autistic children.

The intransitive demand would not be addressed to the object but it would already testify to an investment of this intersubjective pre-objective link, whose intrapsychic representation we are trying to track down through the concept of the third topic.

References

Abraham N., & Torok M. (1987). *L'écorce et le noyau*. Paris: Flammarion.

Anzieu, D. (1993). La fonction contenante de la peau, du moi et de la pensée: conteneur, contenant, contenir. In: Anzieu et al., *Les contenants de pensée*. Paris: Dunod.

Balint M. (1971). *Le défaut fundamental*. Paris: Payot, 1977.

Bergeret, J., & Houser M. (2004). *Le fœtus dans notre inconscient*. Paris: Dunod.
Bion, W. R. (1962). *Aux sources de l'expérience*. Paris: P.U.F. (Coll. "Bibliothèque de Psychanalyse", 1979, first ed.).
Bion, W. R. (1963). *Eléments de psychanalyse*. Paris: P.U.F. (Coll. "Bibliothèque de Psychanalyse", 1979, first ed.).
Bion, W. R. (1965). *Transformations—Passage de l'apprentissage à la croissance*. Paris: P.U.F. (Coll. "Bibliothèque de Psychanalyse", 1982, first ed.).
Bleger, J. (1966). Psychanalyse du cadre. In: R. Kaës et al., *Crise, rupture et dépassement*. Paris: Dunod, 1979.
Blin, D., & Soubieux, M. J. (1997). La mort prénatale: à deuil infaisable, une issue la nostalgie. *Le Carnet/PSY, 31*.
Bowlby, J. (1978). *Attachement et perte* (3 volumes). Paris: P.U.F. (Coll. "Le fil rouge" 1978, 1984, first eds.).
Bretherton, I. (1990). Communication patterns—Internal working models and the intergenerational transmission of attachment relationships. *Infant Mental Health Journal, 11*(3): 237–252.
Brusset, B. (1988). *Psychanalyse du lien (La relation d'objet)*. Paris: Editions Le Centurion.
Brusset, B. (2006). Métapsychologie des liens et troisième topique. *Revue Française de Psychanalyse, LXX*(5): 1213–1282.
Bydlowski, M. (1991). La transparence psychique de la grossesse. In: *Etudes freudiennes, 32*: 2–9.
Dejours, Ch. (1986). *Le corps entre biologie et psychanalyse*. Paris: Payot.
Dejours Ch. (2002). *Le corps d'abord*. Paris: Payot, Paris.
Diatkine, R. (1979). Le psychanalyste et l'enfant avant l'après-coup ou le vertige des origines. *Nouvelle Revue de Psychanalyse ("L'enfant")*: 49–63
Freud S. (1915b). Thoughts for the times on war and death. *S. E., 14*: 273–302. London: Hogarth.
Freud, S. (1917e). Mourning and melancholia. *S. E., 14*: 237–258. London: Hogarth.
Freud, S. (1925h). Negation. *S. E., 19*. London: Hogarth.
Golse, B. (1999). *Du corps à la pensée*. Paris: P.U.F. (Coll. "Le fil rouge", first ed.).
Golse, B. (2006). Vie fœtale, trans-générationnel et après-coup. In: *L'Être-bébé—Les questions du bébé à la théorie de l'attachement, à la psychanalyse et à la phénoménologie*. Paris: P.U.F. (Coll. "Le fil rouge").

Golse, B. (2007). Y a-t-il une psychanalyse possible des bébés? Réflexions sur les traumatismes hyperprécoces à la lumière de la théorie de l'après-coup. *La Psychiatrie de l'enfant, L, 2*: 327–364.

Golse, B., & Missonnier, S. (2005). *Récit, attachement et psychanalyse. Pour une clinique de la narrativité*. Toulouse: Érès.

Haag, G. (2018). *Le moi corporel*. Paris: P.U.F. (Coll. "Le fil rouge").

Hugues, P., Turton, P., Hopper, E., & Evans, C. D. S. (2002). Assessment of guidelines for good practice in psychosocial care of mothers after stillbirth: A cohort study. *The Lancet, 360* (13 July).

Jeannerod, M. (1983). *Le cerveau machine*. Paris: Fayard.

Kaës, R. (1976). *L'appareil psychique groupal*. Paris: Dunod.

Kaës, R. (1993). *Le groupe et le sujet du groupe*. Paris: Dunod.

Kaës, R. (1999). *Les théories psychanalytiques du groupe*. Paris: P.U.F.

Kaës, R. (2007). *Un singulier pluriel: La psychanalyse à l'épreuve du groupe*. Paris: Dunod.

Laplanche, J. (2002). À partir de la situation anthropologique fondamentale. In: C. Botella (Ed.), *Penser les limites: Écrits en l'honneur d'André Green* (pp. 280–287). Paris: Champs Psychanalytiques, Delachaux & Niestlé.

Laplanche, J., & Pontalis, J.-B. (1967). *Vocabulaire de psychanalyse*. Paris: P.U.F.

Leader, D. (2011). *Ce que l'art nous empêche de voir*. Paris: Petite Bibliothèque Payot.

Lebovici, S. (1960). La relation objectale chez l'enfant. *La Psychiatrie de l'enfant, VIII* (1): 147–226.

Missonnier, S. (2009). *Devenir parent, naître humain. La diagonale du virtuel*. Paris: P.U.F Coll. "Le fil rouge".

Missonnier, S. (2015). Le traumatisme de la naissance. In: R. Perron & S. Missonnier, *Cahier de l'Herne, Freud* (pp. 227–235). Paris: Éditions de l'Herne.

Stern, D. N. (1989). *Le monde interpersonnel du nourrisson—Une perspective psychanalytique et développementale*. Paris: P.U.F. (Coll. "Le fil rouge", first edition).

Trevarthen, C., & Aitkin, K. J. (2001). Intersubjectivity: Research, theory and clinical applications. *Journal of Child Psychology and Psychiatry, 42*: 3–48.

Widlöcher, D. (2000). Amour primaire et sexualité infantile. In: *Sexualité infantile et attachement*. Paris: P.U.F. (Coll. "Petite Bibliothèque de Psychanalyse", first edition).

CHAPTER SIX

Infantile autism: a pathology of otherness

Didier Houzel

Splitting of the containing object and psychic bisexuality

The problem of sameness and otherness is one that philosophers have long tried to solve. It gradually became a metapsychological issue, entering into that field in a way reminiscent of the plot of a detective novel, with the need to keep going back in time. It is the ultimate difference with which the mental apparatus has to deal: first came the difference between the sexes, which Freud explored in his early case studies involving the neurotic states of mind of adult patients. Gradually, the psychoanalytic study of other psychological structures and of younger patients led to other differences, until finally the original fundamental one—that between Self and Other—emerged. On this return journey the problem of qualitative differences came to the fore—the good and bad aspects of the object and of the self, their masculine and feminine qualities. All of Melanie Klein's work involved the exploration of these qualitative differences, and the solution to that kind of problem must indeed be found before the sexes can be clearly differentiated within a whole-object relationship. In the Kleinian universe, objects are defined above all by their physical and psychological qualities and are represented by organs which symbolise these properties: breast, penis, etc. Though this part-object world is already highly differentiated, it does not have the overall stability and organisation that would confer a clear and lasting meaning on what is experienced therein. The judgement of existence is settled: there are objects on the one hand and a self on the other. Judgement of attribution, however, remains an open question. What are these objects I am dealing with? Are they good or bad? Masculine or feminine? Nourishing, seductive, controlling, persecutory, destructive?

One more step—still going back in time—and we find ourselves in the world of autism in which no objects, not even part-objects, can exist. The question here is that of the judgement of existence—the great philosophical question about the nature of being. At the moment of our psychic birth, each of us is faced with the question: "Can there *be* anything? An object?" In the autistic world, the answer to that question is "no": nothing separate can exist, no object can ever possess a shape that lasts, only fleeting and shapeless sensations have currency here.

I intend to examine the reasons behind—or, rather, the meaning of—that impossibility. My starting point will be the hypothesis that, as the continuity between a need and its satisfaction is interrupted, a *caesura* as Bion (2005) stated, the nascent self already possesses embryonic shapes seeking out the object but unable to stabilise and develop unless they encounter the appropriate object. There may well be, in fact, several caesurae all through one's life, thereby creating a multi-layered universe in which each level corresponds to the space between any two discrete events. Every time we go through a caesura, we have to reformulate these fundamental questions as to sameness and otherness, as to the judgement of existence and of attribution.

Let us suppose, then, that we are on the threshold of the initial caesura, on the *locus* of original singularity, in other words just as the Big Bang of mental life is about to occur. What is going to happen? Is it possible for us to describe these first moments in a manner similar to that in which Steven Weinberg (1977) offered us such a fascinating description of the initial moments of our material universe? I would argue in favour of the creation of a dynamic system that is extremely powerful. The widening gap between self and object is not simply geographical—distance—but also temporal, in that it is defined by the time that elapses between the emergence of a need and its satisfaction; it is therefore a temporal *and* spatial gap. But it is also—and above all—a dynamic gap, the field in which mental forces are deployed. This hypothesis leads me to argue that a dynamic system is created between the self and its objects; the question then becomes one of discovering how this dynamic system will develop—towards a stable form of organisation or, on the contrary, to instability and chaos? In my view this is a fundamental issue, because the primary cause of mental suffering seems to me to be turbulence, instability, and chaos. In order to avoid this chaotic experience, the mind automatically sets up a certain number of defence mechanisms. Rather than confront too powerful a turbulence, it tries to do away with the dynamic system that created such a situation in the first place. This is exactly what occurs in the purest form of infantile autism.

I imagine that waiting for the object is experienced as a very powerful, not to say overwhelming, attraction within a force field that is initially represented as essentially spatial, before, later, being felt to be temporal in nature. I have previously suggested the term "precipitation anxiety" (Houzel, 1995) to describe the initial emotional responses to this dynamic experience. The attractor field generates a representation of a bottomless pit or precipice into which the self is dragged down so irresistibly that it is threatened with destruction. This kind of precipitation anxiety, to my mind, lies at the root of the autistic experience.

Going a step further, I would want to differentiate between *relation* (or relationship) and *communication*. *Relation* corresponds to the classic concept of object relation; there are forces which suck the self into the object's gravitational field, following certain spatial and temporal curves. *Communication* is quite different. Here, the situation is not one in which an attractor-object pulls towards itself (attracts) a self, but a reciprocal movement in which each draws closer to the other. Many of those who have made a detailed study of infant development have emphasised the need for such reciprocity. Emde (1980) writes of "emotional dialogue", Trevarthen (1979) of "primary intersubjectivity", Stern (1985) of "affect attunement". Psychoanalysts who have worked with children with autism have also emphasised—each with his or her own metapsychological vocabulary—the need for this mutual coming together of self and object. Tustin (1986) wrote of "flowing-over at-oneness", Meltzer of "aesthetic reciprocity" (1988). In my opinion, all of these concepts refer to the same thing, and are another way of putting what Bion (1962) called "realisation": the encounter between a preconception and the corresponding object.

If there is reciprocity—or, rather, a feeling of reciprocity—there is no irreversible pull into a field of destructive forces. It is as though the encounter between preconception and object created a level of *stability* in the dynamic system which was generated simultaneously with the caesura of birth. Some psychic shape or other can become stabilised and a representation created which can support the nascent self and help it gradually to separate out from its surroundings; this will prevent the self from feeling carried away in an endless whirlwind movement or from sliding down a precipice that knows no end. As a kind of visual illustration of what I mean, I would say that it is as though the *realisation* in Bion's sense of the term hacks out a platform somewhere in the wall of this precipice, much as a mountaineer uses his ice-axe to hack out a handhold or a foothold that will allow him to continue climbing. From handhold to handhold, from platform to platform, a whole new world opens up, one in which the object is no longer a destructive attractor; it is more of a rugged landscape with its hills and dales, enchanting, yes, but not without mystery and risk—the kind of picture that the lover paints of the loved object.

These encounters with the object—successive realisations—lie at the heart of what André Green (1995) calls the "work of representation". Psychoanalytic studies of infantile autism, together with baby observation according to Esther Bick's method, have enabled Geneviève Haag (2018) to show that the work of representation begins at the level of bodily experience, leading gradually to the construction of a global and coherent body image. Haag has shown in particular that the two sagittal halves of the body represent, respectively, the child's self and his or her maternal object; the quality of their combination is underpinned by the more paternal aspects of the primary object relation. Children with autism make a very early and massive split between the maternal and paternal aspects of their objects; as a result, they find it impossible to build up a stable and coherent body image. In particular, they are very anxious about the possible falling apart of the two halves of the body—as though their body were a walnut shell that could be split in two.

The work of representation continues to develop in somewhat mysterious ways over the whole range of sense-data, though gradually it comes to focus more and more on visual material—in human beings, sight is the most highly developed and discriminating of all the senses. Freud (1900a) wrote of "considerations of representability" in the use of visual material, one of the principal aspects of the work of the dream. Bion's notes, edited by his wife Francesca and published after his death (1992), show that the model for what he called the "mother's capacity for reverie" was based on Freud's ideas concerning dream-work. The mother's capacity for reverie enables her to understand intuitively the messages her baby sends out to her—initially in a way that is essentially projective. The meaning of the restlessness and turbulence shown by an infant who feels the need to be fed has to be deciphered by the mother if her response is to be appropriate—not only has she to satisfy her baby's physical need, she must also communicate the sense-data and emotional experience that the infant requires for continuing the work of representation—in other words, building the levels of stability that give shape to the mind and people it with objects that are stable and identifiable.

Having reached this point in developing my hypotheses, I would like to give some idea of the questions that remain to be discussed, even though I may not be able to go into them in any great detail. The first concerns the type of stability to which I refer when I say that drive-related and emotional turbulence has to be stabilised if a self is to be constructed and the universe of the mind to be properly organised. The second is closely related to this: the psychic bisexuality of the container.

Psychic stability

The term "stability" may give rise to confusion if it is not clearly defined from the outset. On several occasions, in fact, people have raised the objection that, in talking of stability, I am simply referring to an inorganic state, to the return to a minimal level of energy—the outcome of the death drive, in other words, quite the opposite of mental life. It all depends on what type of stability is being discussed. The scientific literature identifies three types: simple stability, periodic stability, and structural stability.

Simple stability corresponds to the common-sense idea of something that is stable, that is, a body remains in the same place over time as long as no sufficiently powerful external force makes it change place. In a dynamic system such as gravity, a stable object in the sense of simple stability consumes at least some of the energy available to the system. If we imagine a spatial representation of energy levels, the body in question would be at the bottom of a valley, surrounded by higher strata of energy; if the force field is too weak to lift it up over the summit or crest of the mountains and into a neighbouring valley, the body will tend to return to its original position. If we take as an example a golf ball at the bottom of a hole, the fixed place of the ball is the lowest point of the hole. The ball and the hole together constitute a system governed by simple stability. This is the type of stability to which Freud referred when he introduced the principle of constancy in *Beyond the Pleasure Principle* (1920g). It is the kind of stability that autistic children are compulsively looking for; it fits the description of *sameness* by Leo Kanner (1943): everything must remain at the same place where the child perceived it for the first time.

Periodic stability is characterised by the repetition of the same sequence at regular intervals, always in the same way. There is a difference between each of the sequences and its situation in time, but each is identical with the one before. One of my adult patients told me that he experiences the time between two sessions as an "interval", a "waiting for", but as soon as there is an irregularity in this rhythm it becomes a rupture. I underline that Frances Tustin (1972) insisted on the fact that it is important for autistic children to have a regular and predictable setting and recommended that sessions take place at the same time each day.

Structural stability is dynamic, in that it is the dynamics of a given system, not the initial position of the object, that generate stable shapes that can be seen as such. Here, as before, stability refers to the fact that a phenomenon returns to its original state as long as the parameters that govern it vary only within certain defined limits; this is not, however, a static position but a dynamically determined state of the given event. In other words, even if the object moves from one position to another or is subjected to acceleration/deceleration, its state or shape remains constant. An intuitive representation of this type of stability is given by the nowadays well-documented fact that a dynamic system can generate states or shapes featuring this kind of structural stability. The shape an object may take on is no longer to be looked upon as preconceived or predetermined independently of the forces to which it is subjected, but as the actual consequence of those forces, which are the only constants in a system subjected to continual change. It is this kind of stability that I find helpful for understanding mental growth and in particular the work of representation that I mentioned earlier.

In my opinion, the workings of the autistic child's mind do not possess the attribute of structural stability. Anything that changes place implies, for the child with autism, a catastrophic change in his or her representations of self and surrounding world. The immutability described by Leo Kanner in his seminal article of 1943 is the clinical manifestation of the inability to construct a structurally stable universe. The consequence is exceptional dependence on the concrete environment, hence the adhesiveness and two-dimensionality described by Bick (1987) and by Meltzer (1975). It is as though the stability of the autistic child's universe depended not on dynamic mental processes which would guarantee the on-going identity of self and object but on the *locus* in space occupied by the child—hence the child's excessive sensitivity to changes of place and the actual localisation of material objects, the preoccupation with immutability and permanence of sensory experience, clinging and other sensory phenomena described by Frances Tustin: autistic shapes, autistic objects.

Psychic bisexuality and the container

In my view, containment is not the exclusive prerogative of the maternal figure; it must also involve paternal components, the task of which is to lend support to the maternal aspects of the container. This is a necessary function—it guarantees the resilience of the container, and it prevents its being torn by the infant's projections or deformed and pulled completely out of shape under the impact of these projections. The bisexuality of the containing object draws support in the first place from the mother's internal objects: her own maternal and paternal objects, united in a sufficiently harmonious and productive relationship. Later, the containing function will be relayed by the support it receives from the parental couple.

The child's integration of otherness seems to me to be closely related to the bisexual qualities of the containing object. If the container does not possess maternal/feminine attributes, it will not be able to take in the infant's projections and bring them together in one space; if it does not have paternal/masculine qualities, it will be unable to limit the distortions to which it is subjected and it will either become engulfing or be destroyed by the sheer violence of the projections aimed at it. The weaving together of masculine and feminine components is necessary if the container is to be both receptive towards and able to transform the primal somato-psychic experiences which the child projects into it—only thus will the container be able to send these back to the infant after having detoxified them and made them meaningful.

In addition to the role of buttress for the maternal container, the presence of paternal elements in the containing object gives the child the opportunity to experience a kind of dynamic relationship with his/her partner characterised by the so-called scale invariance which allows the emergence of structurally stable objects. The basic idea of dynamic systems theory is to liken every change in the state of the system to a phase shift in physics. It is not possible to know what is happening for each of the molecules in a phase change, but we can calculate the trajectories of the curves by means of the parameters on which these phase shifts depend. These curves are located in a phase space. The evolving trajectories of a dynamic system governed by a form of stability converge towards a stable part of the phase space, which is called an attractor. The form of the attractor depends on the type of stability that governs the system: in the case of simple stability, the attractor is a point that always attracts towards the same immutable state: in that of periodic stability, the attractor is a closed curve, each point of which represents a moment of the period rhythm in the evolution of the system; in the case of structural stability, it is a strange attractor that is defined by its fractal structure characterised by scale invariance.

Scale invariance means that whatever the scale of perception of an object in a spatial reference or a sequence in a temporal reference, the shape of the object or the course of the sequence seem similar. Benoit Mandelbrot (1984), the inventor of fractals, has given as an example of a fractal object the coast of Brittany: on whatever scale this coast is represented, it always has the same form. My hypothesis is that, in the different experiences that the baby has with his/her mother, he/she is seeking a *scale invariance*. Mummy is never always exactly the same:

sometimes she is joyful, available, and attentive, and sometimes concerned, preoccupied, and distracted; one day she is elegant, dressed up, and wearing make-up, the next day she is undressed on getting out of bed, has not brushed her hair, and has no make-up on, etc. In spite of these constant changes, the infant must identify his/her mother as one and the same person. He/she must form a unified and structurally stable representation of his/her mother. To do this he/she needs to discover a scale invariance in his/her relational experience with her: sometimes very close, achieving what Donald Meltzer (1994) has called a "relationship of intimacy", sometimes more or less distant. To this end, he/she must have an experience of *psychic bisexuality* within this dyadic relationship, that is, a double maternal and paternal polarity. I would add that the patient in analysis must also find this double polarity in his/her relationship with his/her analyst. It is the experience of this bisexual polarity that allows the infant to sail along an axis from intimacy to distance, escaping both merging with the object and losing it.

Without this maternal and paternal polarity, the infant cannot form structurally stable forms; he/she is in danger of living in an unpredictable and formless world, with ill-defined frontiers, and in order to protect him/herself against this, returns to a more elementary form of stability, to an autism with a simple stability: the sameness evoked by Leo Kanner (1943), and the self-generated sensory experiences described by Frances Tustin (1986) under the terms "autistic sensation shapes".

My experience of treating psychoanalytically autistic children makes me think that in autism there is an active splitting of psychic bisexuality inasmuch as the paternal pole is felt to be persecuting and, consequently, excluded from the autistic capsule into which the infant withdraws.

As far as children with autism are concerned, bringing together the masculine/paternal qualities and the feminine/maternal ones seems to be experienced as mutually destructive: maternal softness threatens to engulf the paternal components, while paternal hardness threatens to tear apart and rip to shreds the maternal container. Instead of there being conflict dynamics seeking to establish some kind of balance between these two aspects, a destructive system of gradient dynamics is set up between them as soon as they are in relation. The only way to survive is to separate them completely and keep them as far away as possible from each other. However, this deficiency in integrating the bisexuality of the container is an obstacle to developing conflict dynamics—the very kind that is required for the work of representation. Without such integration, the process of individuation cannot begin to operate.

Clinical illustration[1]

Alan was an autistic boy I began treating when he was four years old. In his case, the overflow was expressed as fireworks. That material appeared in a session some two and a half years into the therapy, which at that point was being carried out on a four-times-per-week basis. The session took place shortly after the summer vacation, and just before a scheduled session that had had to be cancelled. Some sessions previously, Alan, to my surprise, had asked: "How do you get ready for being born?" I understood the question to mean being born psychically, that is, as Tustin (1986, p. 235) put it, getting "the sense of being an 'I'", which entails the sense of "Otherness" as well. It was only later that I realised that, for a child coming out of autism, that kind of birth was inevitably explosive.

In November 1993, he did a very talented imitation of an organist playing low and high notes—taken together, it was very pleasant-sounding. Alan has a fine ear for music, he is a talented pianist, and in his imitation of organ-playing, I had no difficulty in recognising a Bach fugue. He drew on the floor a set of organ pipes and explained how, when air passed through them, musical notes came out. I encouraged him to draw them on a sheet of paper, and he agreed.

I could then see the resemblance between these pipes and the diagram I drew of what I called "our days", which little by little were transformed into musical notes. This musical metaphor brought to mind a paper by Suzanne Maiello on "The sound-object: A hypothesis about prenatal auditory experience and memory" (1995). Alan seemed to be telling me that the envelope of our sessions needed to have both

---

[1] The reader will find a more detailed account of Alan's treatment either in a French version (*Journal de la psychanalyse de l'enfant*, 32, 2003: 75–96), or in an English one (D. Houzel & M. Rhode, eds., *Invisible Boundaries: Psychosis and Autism in Children and Adolescents* (pp. 75–95). London: Karnac, 2005).

maternal-feminine tones (the high-pitched notes coming from the organ) and paternal-masculine ones (the low notes) in order to produce a pleasant-sounding melody that would promise him an opening onto psychic birth and onto the world as a whole. This interpretation of high-pitched and low-pitched notes was, as it were, forced on me by Alan himself, who compared the low notes made by musical instruments to the voices of the menfolk in his family and in particular to that of his paternal grandfather.

Without attempting to define categories too narrowly, I would say that qualities such as receptivity and flexibility belong to the maternal-feminine side of the container, while those such as consistency and orienting belong to the paternal-masculine one. From the point of view of the mind, these correspond to the mother's maternal and paternal identifications, united in a harmonious relationship. To my way of thinking, it is essential to remember this double polarity: male or female, we all have maternal and paternal objects in our minds in a more or less harmonious relationship. The infant has thus first to process the psychic bisexuality of the container; it is on this that any possibility of integrating psychic bisexuality at the most primitive of levels depends. It was some six and a half years into his therapy that Alan taught me this, as he recalled a memory from his very early childhood in which his grandfather gave support to a weakened maternal container.

3 September 1996

Alan reminded me that some time before I had warned him not to spit at me; in fact, I had once threatened to end the session if he carried on doing so. He asked question after question about what would have happened had I in fact put an end to that session: would the taxi that brings him here for his sessions have taken him back home? Would he have had to wait in the waiting room? Then he spoke about the various occasions on which a session had had to be cancelled. After that, he mentioned the fact that, according to legend, church bells fall silent at Easter because everyone is saddened by Jesus' death; but on Easter Sunday they all come back from Rome because Jesus rises from the dead. Then he came close to me and tried to tickle me, telling me about the rotating lamps at the pig fair.

I replied that we felt sad every time we could not meet, like when sessions had to be cancelled or during the holiday period we had just had; maybe this was like feeling sad at Jesus' death. Then we were glad to be back together again, like when church bells begin ringing again on Easter Sunday. I added that perhaps he was trying to get rid of all the sadness by tickling me or in switching on inside me the rotating lamps he had seen at the pig fair.

Then he spoke of things he said were disgusting and not very nice. Once, when saying hello to his aunt Marie-Claire, he had smelled her armpits; his mother had smacked him for that. On another occasion he had demanded a biscuit from another of his aunts, and his mother had reprimanded him for doing so. He spoke of pony droppings, a pony that had diarrhoea; Alan soaked a sheet of paper in water to make balls representing pony droppings and threw them against the wall.

I said that all this reminded me of something his parents had told me. For professional reasons to do with his father, they had lived abroad when Alan was about one year old. He had suffered from chronic diarrhoea that had lasted eleven months, and no doctor had been able to discover the cause. I added that perhaps he was wondering whether I was going to be like a mummy thinking all that was disgusting, or on the contrary a mummy ready to accept everything that came from her little boy. Since he had spoken about bad smells, and especially about odours from armpits, I added that it was very hot in the country they had stayed in abroad, he had perspired a lot and maybe that had made a bad smell (his parents had told me that he had suffered also from a skin infection that had been attributed to excessive perspiration).

Alan went on to tell me about something that had taken place when, according to him, he was about two and a half years old. He was out sailing with his grandfather in his boat, and had vomited. His mother smacked him, saying: "Why did you vomit?" Alan told me that the sea was so rough that he had felt sea-sick. He explained that he had noticed a lot of marker buoys indicating places that boats should steer clear of in case they ran aground on the rocks.

I spoke of his desire that I should be like a mummy, who was both able to accept whatever came out of him without feeling disgust—diarrhoea, vomit, "not nice" things, etc.—and who had a "grand-daddy" figure with her who would be able to navigate properly and prevent the boat breaking up on the rocks.

Alan listened carefully and calmly to me—in fact, I had never seen him so calm before.

I think that this session is a good illustration of how important it is for the maternal container to have the internal support of a paternal object (the "grand-daddy") that makes it solid enough to weather any storms (the boat that did not run aground) and gives it some idea of where it is heading (grandfather's skilful manoeuvres). The death of Jesus probably refers to the mother's depression—while she was expecting Alan, her own mother had died.

There is one very important technical consequence entailed by the bisexual nature of the psychic container. Psychotherapists have to be in contact with their own parental identifications and constantly work over the links between the maternal and paternal objects that inhabit their internal world. The autistic process tends to make a very deep and very early split between the elements of psychic bisexuality. Therapists are therefore subjected to splitting projections that tend to dissociate the elements of their own bisexuality, hence the need for meticulous and ongoing processing of the countertransference in order to reintegrate the dispersed elements of their own psychic bisexuality.

Conclusion

Whether we are referring to childhood autism *stricto sensu* or to the autistic enclaves described by Tustin in other pathological syndromes, the psychoanalytic exploration of this pathology leads me to suggest that there is an initial level at which psychic bisexuality becomes integrated: that of the container. Any defect in integration at this level leads to a pathology of otherness, given that one of the essential functions of the container is to enable the construction of a psychic envelope that can differentiate between the inside and the outside of the mind, between "me" and "not-me" (Tustin, 1972), "I-ness" and "Otherness".

References

Bick, E. (1987). The experience of the skin in early object-relations [1968]. In: *Collected Papers of Martha Harris and Esther Bick* (pp. 114–118). Perthshire: The Clunie Press.

Bion, W. R. (1962). *Learning from Experience*. London: Heinemann.
Bion, W. R. (1992). *Cogitations*. London: Karnac.
Bion, W. R. (2005). *Tavistock Seminars*. London: Karnac.
Emde, R. (1980). Toward a psychoanalytic theory of affect: Part 2. Emerging models of emotional development in infancy. In: S. I. Greenspan & G. H. Pollock (Eds.), *The Course of Life: Infancy and Early Childhood* (pp. 85–112). Washington, DC: DHSS.
Freud, S. (1900a). *The Interpretation of Dreams. S. E.*, 5: 339–627. London: Hogarth.
Freud, S. (1920g). *Beyond the Pleasure Principle. S. E.*, 18: 7–64. London: Hogarth.
Green, A. (1995). La représentation de chose entre pulsion et langage. In: *Propédeutique* (pp. 109–125). Seyssel: Champ Vallon.
Haag, G. (2018). *Le moi corporel*. Paris: P.U.F. (Coll. "Le fil rouge").
Houzel, D. (1995). Precipitation anxiety. *Journal of Child Psychotherapy, 21*: 65–78.
Kanner, L. (1943). Autistic disturbances of affective contact. *Nervous Child, 2*: 217–250.
Maiello, S. (1995). The sound-object: A hypothesis about prenatal auditory experience and memory. *Journal of Child Psychotherapy, 2*: 23–41.
Mandelbrot, B. (1984). *Les objets fractals* (2nd edition). Paris: Flammarion.
Meltzer, D. (1975). Dimensionality in mental functioning. In: D. Melzer, J. Bremner, S. Hoxter, D. Weddell, & I. Wittenberg, *Explorations in Autism: A Psychoanalytic Study* (pp. 223–238). Perthshire: The Clunie Press.
Meltzer, D. (1988). *The Apprehension of Beauty*. Perthshire: The Clunie Press.
Meltzer, D. (1994). *Sincerity and Other Works*. London: Karnac.
Stern, D. (1985). *The Interpersonal World of the Infant*. New York: Basic Books.
Trevarthen, C. (1979). Communication and cooperation in early infancy: A description of primary intersubjectivity. In: M. M. Bullows (Ed.), *Before Speech: The Beginning of Interpersonal Communication*. New York: Cambridge University Press.
Tustin, F. (1972). *Autism and Childhood Psychosis*. London: The Hogarth Press.
Tustin, F. (1986). *Autistic Barriers in Neurotic Patients*. London: Karnac.
Weinberg, S. (1977). *The First Three Minutes: A Modern View of the Origin of the Universe*. New York: Basic Books.

CHAPTER SEVEN

Multi two-dimensional: on autistic thinking

Marganit Ofer

In this chapter, I wish to portray the extreme manifestations of autistic two-dimensional thinking and discuss their theoretical and clinical consequences.

Klein has demonstrated that internalisation and projection processes are active from the very beginning of life and that the baby is capable, from birth, of internalising experiences, learning from them, and ejecting harmful material. Bion, embracing the "psychic digestion system" model, added the role of the containing mother. Klein, followed by Bion, Meltzer, Bick, Tustin, Alvarez, and others, made the ostensibly unquestionable assumption concerning the existence of two psychic spaces/containers—that of the mother and that of the baby—in which psychic activity and, in fact, thinking, takes place.

Psychoanalysis enables the two-directional transition of projected, contained, worked-through, and internalised material. But what happens when the patient's container function is severely impaired? Do internalisation and projection take place in such cases? Where and in what way? Is thinking possible? If the patient indeed lacks the capacity for projection, identification, projective identification, a (non-sensory) experience of togetherness and symbolisation, can such treatment be considered psychoanalysis?

Bick (1968) argues that the primitive parts of the personality are separated in the infant and that it thus requires the feeling of a skin/sack that is holding it together in order to sustain the boundary between inside and outside. However, achieving this feeling requires the infant to internalise the function of an external object which provides it for them. She claims that this state precedes splitting and idealisation. This depiction is a milestone in our understanding of primary mental states and in distinguishing them from other pathological conditions (Symington, 1985). It is conjectured that the infant needs its own container in order to contain the containing function; the development of a container requires it to already exist.

Meltzer elaborates on this further, stating that autistic children are unable to form three-dimensional concepts of objects that contain spaces. They are incapable of identification, either by projection or by internalisation. They perceive the object as having no interior space. The alternative identification they engage in consists of skin-to-skin contact, which Bick termed "adhesive identification" (Meltzer, 1975; Meltzer, Bremner, Hoxter, Weddell, & Wittenberg, 1975). Meltzer argues that autistic children have lost—or have never had—an adequate psychic skin. His depiction of the impaired psychic skin these children possess differs from that offered by Bick, as he believes it to be a result of an impaired capacity for creating concepts rather than insufficient containing.

Meltzer claims that, normally, the experience of being (having) a container involves the ability to control the sphincter rather than incorporate/eat. In my work with autistic children, I have noticed that the late onset of speech is often accompanied by constipation, encopresis, or a preoccupation with faeces. This awareness of one's sphincter and the onset of speech appear in close proximity in normal development as well. These are two states of being aware of one's control over what is "coming out".

Meltzer notices that autistic children experience objects using only one sense at a time. This allows them to employ a defence mechanism against painful or powerful emotions that precedes splitting, a mechanism that he terms "dismantling". These children allow their mental organisation to passively be dismantled, resulting in a state of mindlessness that bears destructive consequences for their development (Harris Williams, 2010). Alvarez (1992), quoting Bruner (1968), demonstrates that the baby's ability to be fed and to look at the mother simultaneously emerges over time and that, initially, one action suppresses the other. This means that the healthy baby has a certain capacity for regulation from the moment of birth. In my understanding, such sensory regulation enables control and development. The pre-existing container develops gradually and is equipped with an organising function that can make use of the mother's container and its organising/containing function. In contrast, the autistic baby lacks this primary organising function and is therefore bombarded with stimuli, which it is forced to block. This will eventually result in dismantling or "collapse" to a single sense, as depicted by Meltzer and later on Ogden (1989), as well. The newborn baby which either feeds or looks—performing a single action—will later be able to avoid the collapse to a single sense.

Anzieu emphasises the neglect of that which links inside and outside—the skin. The baby's contact with the mother's skin facilitates the establishment of a sense of safety concerning the integrity of its physical envelope and, later on, a sense of safety about the function of its orifices, which entails a vague sensation of area and volume. Much like Tustin, he argues that when the containing function of the skin-ego is lacking, it evokes the anxiety of a "shell-less kernel" seeking an alternative shell or the experience of perforated skin and the terror of emptying out. Like a deflated ball, such emptying out will lead to a state of "two-dimensionality" (Anzieu, 1985). Tustin states that the two-dimensional child will enter a container or envelope, but not because they picture themselves within a three-dimensional structure; rather, they will do so to distinguish themselves from the "not-me". Rosenfeld (1981) proposes the image of the body as a system of pipes containing bodily fluids, arguing that this image precedes Bick's notion of the body as a sack. Rosenfeld's proposed body image also requires the recognition of interiority. Segal (1957, 1978) notes that difficulties in the development of symbolisation and the creation of "symbolic equations" stem from excessive use of projective identification. In other words, even in a state where part of the ego is seen as identical to the object, where symbol and symbolised are the same, we witness the operation of a projection and identification mechanism that presupposes the existence of two containers, one in the object and one in the subject.

Psychoanalytic literature discusses the subject of *interrelations* between the emotional and cognitive aspects, between mother, infant, and the interactions shaping their relationships, between congenital impairments and impairments resulting from faulty relationships. Throughout their career, many theoreticians move (and change) along these axes. Towards the end of her career, Tustin (1994) wrote that she had been mistaken in assuming the existence of a normal autistic state. She did so with the kind help of Anne Alvarez. Alvarez herself, in the papers she wrote about Robbie (1977, 1992), the well-known patient whom she had been treating virtually throughout her entire career, depicts how her theoretical understanding has changed over the years. She describes her shift from the almost automatic interpretation of projections to searching for Robbie and trying to bring him back to life and relatedness, suggesting the notion of "reclamation". Alvarez has been deeply aware of observational and biological research, while still leaving ample room for a dynamic understanding of the development facilitated by relationships, either parental or therapeutic ones. Mahler too, following Stern, has retracted her notion of a normal autistic state.

While it is understood that children who eventually develop autism suffer from some fundamental congenital impairment, the nature of this impairment remains unclear. There have been many attempts to explain it as well as attempts to integrate different kinds of explanations into a more profound and comprehensive understanding of these phenomena. Adherents of psychoanalytic theories who also take into account the existence of congenital impairments are required to demonstrate how such impairments dictate observed abnormal development. Consider, for example, Tustin's (1981, 1994) "premature awareness of separation". One may ask, what causes the baby to attain such premature awareness. Since the nature of the impairment is unclear, we have to continue to rely on the descriptions of autistic children in our attempts to grasp primary mental states.

Theoretically speaking, there are states in which the external container either precludes the baby from developing its innate container or fails to support this development. It is also possible, however, that the primary innate container of the autistic child is itself impaired, lacking an organising function that could enable containment. In certain cases, external containment (either parental or therapeutic) may facilitate the rehabilitation of the container. Because having an impaired internal "organising function" affects the baby's ability to utilise its mother's organising function, potentially affecting the mother's capacity as well, early intervention both enhances the baby's neurological/psychic development to some extent and deepens the mother's capacity for containment (whether her capacity had suffered from some primary problem or had been affected by an "unresponsive child"). The accumulated clinical experience of the relevant psychoanalytic literature indicates the crucial significance of early and intensive therapeutic intervention (Acquarone, 2007).

I wish to argue that autism per se is a (probably neurological disorder) which has no equivalents in the non-autistic personality (unlike, for example, psychotic cores). Autism entails the curtailment of any development of thinking or perception beyond two dimensions. This fact explains the autistic inability to take into account the mind of the other (Frith, 1989) as well as concrete thinking. The autistic subject has no container or no experience of a container, either for themselves or for others. There may exist a state of (proto-mental) notation, thus enabling language but bereft of symbolisation, imagination, dreams, and empathy. There may be a wish for the closeness of others, but not for their interior. There may exist a state void of projection, internalisation, and displays of envy or aggression.[1] In such a state, the autistic subject may strive for understanding while simultaneously being detached from the experience of being understood.

The matter at hand is not solely the existence of mental representation or the lack thereof, which had been thoroughly discussed (Bion, 1977; Bergstein, 2010), but rather its confinement to two-dimensional

---

[1] Klein (1952) argues that the child's aggressive libidinal preoccupation with the body of the mother and later that of the parents leads to anxiety and guilt which compel the child to displace this preoccupation to the external world and to symbolic development. This happens alongside the development of the superego. Furthermore, the intensity of these sadistic impulses is closely linked, in terms of development, to symbolic development. I believe that this is not the only point of interface between aggression and autism but, given the scope of this chapter, other such examples will be discussed elsewhere.

perception. I would like to emphasise the link between the vocabulary of images, including container, space, skin, and sack, as models of "places" where processes occur and the unifying, organising function which enables, for example, symbolic development. Symbolic capacity enables one to contain difficult mental states, and containment, in turn, facilitates symbolic development. In other words, the absence of the container is not merely the absence of a sack or a skin, but also an impairment of the potential for integration, for referring to several parameters and thereby to a triangular and three-dimensional state.[2] Two-dimensional thinking precludes the potential for being "autistic with normal intelligence", since the absence of three-dimensional thinking manifests itself as a difficult lack of understanding, a kind of intellectual disability.

Two-dimensional thinking includes concepts such as "opposites", "odd one out", "big and small", "allowed and not allowed", "positive and negative". In its higher instances, this type of thinking includes many overlapping two-dimensional "surfaces". These are accumulated and retrieved from their storage for use (each surface has its own particular use), but there is no interactive motion (as no third dimension exists) and they are not forgotten (not repressed). A state in which the meaning of one surface contradicts another leads to a catastrophic experience.

This claim has two consequences:

1. It limits one's ability to use autistic states (with their two-dimensional perception) to provide the substrate for conclusions about more developed states (psychotic, borderline, and neurotic ones).
2. It has certain implications regarding the psychoanalytic treatment of such children.

Psychoanalytic literature is rife with case studies of autistic children. Nevertheless, even those cases that served as the clinical foundation for the conceptualisations of Meltzer et al., Tustin, Bick, and, later,

---

[2] I would like to thank Bat-sheva Adler for her comments on the link between three-dimensionality and triangular perception, by which the child may refer to several parameters at once (depending on their symbolic capacity) and integrate them. See also Britton (1989).

Alvarez about two-dimensional experience, perception, and thinking, present moments in which motion towards three-dimensionality is already emerging. Alvarez criticises the tendency of certain therapists to conclude that cases in which autistic children were able to use the therapy and "escape their autism" indicated that they were not autistic to begin with, rather than attesting to the efficacy of the therapy.

To a considerable degree, "escaping autism" involves the extent to which three-dimensional thinking may develop. Many autistic children become psychotic during this transition, in which the child must "deal with the 'destructive fire' of his impulses" (Tustin, 1981, p. 148) or the unconscious phantasy which is the representation of these impulses (Isaacs, 1948), which had remained invisible for the autistic child prior to this development. However, there are certain states in which we may witness development and improvement in autistic patients, while they nevertheless remain within the "two-dimensional" domain. Instead of the development of three-dimensionality, they create a structure which I term "multi two-dimensions".

Eden's analysis, which sparked my interest in this subject, is highly unusual. In other autistic children, one could immediately notice the cracks in their two-dimensional thinking and their growing capacity for three-dimensional thinking, including the ability to project and contain thoughts and, in fact, the ability to think. The various case studies documented in psychoanalytic literature accompanied me, helping me understand parts of Eden's being. Nevertheless, over the years I came to realise that none of these case studies depicts such rigid two-dimensional thinking. After being treated with psychoanalysis and other para-medical treatments and with the help of his attentive parents and supportive environment, Eden showed improvement across the board. Eden was happy; he spoke, wrote, read, made normal eye contact, and exhibited a willingness to experience new things. Still, he had not surmounted the obstacles on his way to three-dimensional thinking. Thus, in a more profound sense, he was incapable of thinking and finding his place in the world. Similarly, he also did not dream.

I have been treating Eden for twelve years. I first examined him at eighteen months old and, despite many signs of autism, I also saw encouraging indications of the development of a container and the ability to seek out the psyche of others. I referred him to a colleague in his area of residence. When he was five years old, this colleague had to terminate the therapy and his parents approached me once again. At six, he started talking and at fourteen he began to talk about himself in the first person. In contrast to autistic children who do not speak and lack this notational capacity, Eden's language allowed me to trace his way of thinking.[3] I will now describe his thinking and how it challenged my understanding.

For several years, we have been writing books; one book each session. Written words serve as something that exists. We had our communication as we talked and wrote, and I used verbal and written means for interpretation. Eden tends to make lists and I tend to comment upon and thereby "open up" these lists and endow them with meaning. He takes the book with him and, on his way home, reads it to his mother or father. During a certain period of time, he used to read the book out loud at the family's Friday dinner. This enabled his parents and his family to form a deeper understanding of his way of thinking.

From a young age, Eden would collect video tapes. He did not watch them, as he was unable to understand the story and the events. Rather, he was preoccupied by the external appearance of the covers, the stickers, the reels, and the tape. He never explored their internal contents, not even concretely speaking (for example, by taking the tape apart). His collection grew to include hundreds of tapes. At some point, his parents told him that it was getting too big and that he should get rid of the tapes that were for babies. Eden is very capable of distinguishing a baby from a child and even "wants to grow up". However, he does not understand the essential difference between tapes for little babies and tapes for older children, beyond the text or the images on their covers. He does understand that being little is "bad" and being big is "good": two two-dimensional understandings with a two-dimensional link, which do not add up to a three-dimensional structure. When several people in his environment passed away, he told me: "First, you're in your mother's tummy, then you're a baby, then you're a boy, then you're a teenager, then you're a man, then it's the nursing home, then you die, then you start all over again. You get back the tapes that you gave to

---

[3] In this chapter, I will not discuss whether the incapacity for language is a congenital impairment or an ability that failed to develop.

the Ethiopians!"[4] While Eden did not express any noticeable sadness or unease, I witnessed the impaired sense of time that stemmed from his failure to grasp ongoing change. Time was circular (Meltzer, 1975).

At fourteen, he started going to the cinema and "collecting" movies and movie theatres. He read the list of what was showing online, made an appointment with one of the adults in his family, caring just as much about the venue as he did about the movie they went to see. He prefers the Glilot Cinema City: "They have twenty-three screens"; "Rishon leZion has twenty-five screens"; "Glilot has a catalogue with more stripes". He is unable to recount the plot of the movie he watched. With considerable effort, he can list several things that appeared in the movie: "the dog ate from the bowl". He is preoccupied with externalities—the theatre, the date, the popcorn, etc. In our sessions, he asks to make lists of the movies he will watch. He wonders which movies and which theatres he could attend. A sense of unease emerges alongside an endless repetition of phrases spoken to him, which he was left unable to comprehend: "you don't go to a far-away theatre", "that movie is for babies", "that one is for grown-ups", "grown-ups like cartoons too". Something is bothering him. This "something" (in my opinion) is comprised of his misunderstanding of what is happening in the movie and his parents forbidding him from watching certain movies. He is trying to organise this in his two-dimensional way: sorting movies by age or by genre, declaring that he is grown-up. I understand that, at this stage, his alarm is caused by the contradiction between two two-dimensional structures: positive and negative, big and small. As far as Eden is concerned, as someone who is encouraged to "act like a grown-up" (even though his understanding falls short of that of a child), the fact that he is big is a positive thing. If he watched movies "for little kids" (as he is not allowed to watch "grown-up" movies), something negative happens. This discrepancy creates restlessness.

In recent years, I began talking to him about his autism very openly. I told him that he really wants to be grown up and that there are certain things that he does not understand because of his autism and not

---

[4] Several years prior to this analysis, there was a massive immigration of Ethiopian Jews to Israel. "Donating to Ethiopians" became a common expression of giving away the unnecessary belongings one did not need.

because he is a baby, that he is worried that he is a baby (this is where his restlessness reaches its peak). I write down:

Non-Autistic Child
Non-Autistic Grown-up
Autistic Child
Autistic Grown-up

I tell him that he is an autistic grown-up, not a child. This definition calms him down. He flaps his hands[5] joyfully and says that he is excited.

Eden found out that a theatre in Afula (a distant town) is screening a movie that is not offered in theatres closer to where he lives and wanted to "accumulate" it as well. He was told that Afula was far away and that it is an hour and a half by car. Eden asks: "Is an hour and a half far?"

When I mentioned that going to the cinema is similar to collecting videotapes, he replied: "It's different. I watch the movies at the cinema". This is factually true. His binary thinking has the concepts of "similar" and "different". This is different, by a single variable: watch *vs.* not watch. The fact that in both cases he does not understand the question of what enables him now, despite not being able to understand, to sit through a movie—all these cannot be thought.

After two years in which we talked about movies in every session, Eden says: "Everyone sees the movies that are right for them"; "*To Rome with Love* is for old people"; "Some movies are not suitable for my age". He repeats such phrases over and over again. I understand that he is bothered by the fact that he is still unable to understand why he is not allowed to watch any movie he chooses. Once again, he musters up all the reasons and the explanations—which amount to a dichotomous distinction—but remains unsatisfied. I say to him: "Your parents think that you won't be able to understand certain movies because of your autism. Some things are hard for you to understand. What's hard for you to understand?" "Talking," he replies. He is awfully stressed, pressing his hands against his mouth, making noises, looking as if he is trying to pull something out and squeeze it in at the same time.

---

[5] The flapping abated some time ago and reappears only rarely. Still, excitement and anxiety are expressed motorically.

"It's not very nice to be autistic. I think you would rather not be autistic." "Like Danny" (his brother), he replies. His movement subsides. "You can't change your name," he says. "Would you have liked to?" "No!!" His notion of identity is two-dimensional. If something is impossible then he will not want it because that would be negative. "And if you could play pretend and change it, what other name would you want?" Eden usually does not respond to such questions, offering only a blank stare. He knows that "pretend" means "something not true which is not negative", but this knowledge does not facilitate any playful motion. This time, he answers: "Yotam. You can't change your date of birth." One could wonder whether this "Yotam" is the beginning of a representation of something, but Eden keeps at it, bothered by what could not be changed. "You can't change your name and you can't change your date of birth and you can't change the fact that you're autistic, but you are learning more things all the time and you keep growing." Is the impossibility of change soothing or distressing? In my view, it is difficult for him to perceive change on a three-dimensional level.

Now that he is watching movies, I asked him again if he had any dreams. I knew from his parents that he was never woken up by a dream or gave any other indication of having dreams. He asks: "What's a dream?" I say: "At night, when you sleep, you see a pretend movie in your head." "No!" He answers in the tone which I recognise as expressing his need to stop the questioning, because he is noticing something negative. I believe that had he been aware of dreaming, he would have been able to report it, just as he can communicate to me other complex and misunderstood things, such as his masturbation. "Masturbating is making your penis feel nice." He takes a jar of mayonnaise—only the Hellmann's brand, only on Mondays—to his room, makes a rectangular hole in the mayonnaise and looks at it. Then he presses the jar between his legs, looking at the shape, until he ejaculates. He finds the taste of mayonnaise disgusting. If mayonnaise is not available, the procedure may be undergone with a jar of peanut butter (which he loves). I do not understand the meaning of this ritual. I have various assumptions regarding the colour of milk or faeces, about the hole, but for now they only rely on my associations and my theoretical knowledge, rather than Eden himself. I am attentive to the way he positions himself between what is allowed (in his room) and what is not allowed (instructions he received at school). He does not understand why it is not allowed or why he does what he does. The fixed order organises his experience and, step by step, enables sexual release. "First the penis is hard and then he takes the mayo", "then he showers." There is a special look on his face when he tells me this. He is neither ashamed, nor is he interested in hearing what I think about it, unless I am forbidding or allowing something.

The sound of crying is heard from outside. "Marganit, the noise is bothering me." "Me too," I replied. Eden tried to say, "We're both bothered by the noise", but could not form the proper syntax for this sentence. I cannot retrace exactly why. He took his time, he exerted himself like someone who is just learning a language and found it difficult to say "both of us", a phrase he never uses because he lacks a sense of "both of us sharing the same experience". He understands that he and I are "both", in the same sense that the green marker and the yellow marker, are both made by the same company. However, in order for this shared experience to have meaning, each of us must have an internal container that could take in the other's material and compare it to other internal material (common sense). Eden also had trouble choosing the proper tense for "bothered". "We were bothered", in the past tense, notes (lists) what had happened. A present-tense formulation implies a shared experience. After I had said that both he and I were hearing the same thing (somebody crying) and that it was hard for him to think that I, too, was hearing that same crying, he asked who was crying. I said that we cannot see and do not know who it is, but that we can guess according to their voice. "It doesn't sound like a baby crying to me, more like a boy." Eden replies, "It's not a baby and it's not a cat." His sorting technique is two-dimensional. "Maybe you're worried about what could have happened to the crying boy," I add.

Can we nevertheless think that this entailed a glimpse or a crack that indicated the existence of a container? His identification with the crying? His shared experience with me? One could try and tackle this question by regarding my immediate reaction: "Me too." For Eden, it is far from obvious that hearing something means that I am hearing it as well or that him being bothered means that I am also bothered. When I point this out, he has received validation that enables him to think about what is bothering him. I knew that he was incapable of answering a question like "What's bothering you?" and I had no idea about how and what he was thinking at that moment. Was he bothered by the noise? Was he capable, through some manner of identification, of feeling concern at another person crying? If so, this implies the existence of a container. I believe that my automatic "Me too" response preserves the possibility that this was an unsettling experience shared by two people: Eden and the crying boy or Eden and me or me and the crying boy. I am offering myself to him so that he could think through me, use my mental apparatus. In my understanding, I am taking into account his two-dimensional understanding and the limitations it imposes on his grasp of the world, helping him establish a "different understanding".

Memory and forgetfulness: Eden remembers everything. As a collector and accumulator of his own knowledge and actions, he also catalogues things according to date. He can name the exact date of each time he went to get a haircut or watch a movie in the past several years. He can say which day of the week will correspond to any date in recent years and several years to come. He does not rely on calculations; he simply remembers calendars he had seen on an "iPhone".

One time, I informed him that one of our sessions was to be cancelled. We wrote about the cancellation in the session-books of the previous sessions and I also informed his parents of it. His parents nevertheless forgot and brought him to see me on that day. The following day, his father told me that he had only realised his error when they arrived at my door. He was surprised that Eden, possessing such remarkable memory, had said nothing when they left the house. Eden told me, "No need to get all stressed up" and "It happens to everybody" (again and again). I understood how nervous he was. My reaction was gradual: I made room for the experience that something stressful had happened. Once we are both able to stay with it, I started to find out what happened. This investigation includes the precise tracing of events and potential thoughts (what I had thought when I wrote things down, what his father thought when he drove him over, what he had thought when he left the house with his father, etc.).[6] I mention that Eden did remember

---

[6] The handling of this event is potentially reminiscent of the "Mentalization Based Treatment" approach, developed by Fonagy. However, the foundation in which this approach is grounded is not applicable for treating conditions marked by two-dimensional thinking.

the cancellation, but did not think it was relevant to the fact that his father was driving him over and that he did not think that his father was wrong (nor did he think that he was wrong). The relevance was only discovered at the door to my office. I can assume that Eden really wanted to come or that he thought that coming to my office meant that I would be there. I can imagine that I would say right away, if another child had done the same: "Maybe you really wanted to come, really wanted me to be there." But knowing how Eden thinks, I once again came up against "two surfaces": one was the fact that we had written in our book that Marganit will be away; the other was "dad is taking me to see Marganit". There is no imagined conflict that could keep them from leaving the house. There is only an ongoing present and the contradiction is revealed at my doorstep. As a first response, telling him that he had really wanted to come might have further exacerbated his emotional turmoil—as well as the forces suppressing it—because wanting something "wrong" (coming to see Marganit when "there is no Marganit") = "he is bad" = "Marganit is angry". This set of equations led to my attempt not to hide the stressful element but stay with it, perform our investigation through "two-dimensional" language, and only finally address his wish for me to be there, his disappointment and emotion.

In the context of Eden's split between positive and negative, negative elements are not projected but must be terminated. When faced with two contradictory two-dimensional structures, Eden is left with a negative element that cannot be terminated. This situation is catastrophic, explosive, frustrating; not a conflict. This is evident in Eden's physical movements, the way he crams his fingers into his mouth and shakes them. He looks as if he were simultaneously pushing and shaking an explosion, without any projection, internalisation, or repression. Once he manages to make it stop, an equilibrium is restored—an equilibrium that comes at the cost of halting the development.

Thinking that is based on the concepts of container–contained, two and three dimensions, adhesive identification, and the ability for symbolic thinking is grounded in the assumptions that these are tantamount to human development (from life *in utero* or early infancy), that development is mutually affected by the infant's relationship with their caretaker and that impaired development is a defensive reaction. The extent to which this defence becomes a structural feature affects the flow of development (forwards or towards regression) and the therapeutic intervention. In the development of psychoanalytic thinking, these assumptions have opened up the broad and rich world of treating patients with severe disorders, regressive states, children, autistic patients, psychosomatic conditions, Holocaust survivor reactions, and more. In his contribution to the tribute to Tustin volume, David Rosenfeld (1997) compares Tustin's thinking to that of Galileo, who invited us to peer through the telescope and realise that we are not the centre of the universe; a revolutionary new perspective.

In this chapter, I sought to propose a state in which two-dimensional thinking has been structural and virtually exclusive from an early stage and development is not aimed towards three-dimensional thinking but rather towards *"multi two-dimensionality"*. Contradictions between two two-dimensional structures lead not to conflict and creative solutions but to a catastrophe which is suppressed by one of the stronger structures.

Cases and states which require structuration instead of interpretation have been discussed before (Anzieu, 1985; Keinan, 2009). Other theoreticians have proposed a change in technique, such as an active stance or an increase of physical contact. Many have explored the attempt to understand that which cannot be represented verbally, to "hunt" the thought that has no thinker. I would like to propose a discourse between a therapist who thinks three-dimensionally and a patient with "multi two-dimensional" thinking. As the sole part of the dyad who (potentially) speaks both languages, the therapist can serve as an interpreter of mental states, endowing anxiety with meaning and enabling the patient to understand and to have the experience of understanding and even of being understandable.

A review of the severe autistic cases documented in psychoanalytic literature demonstrates that all these authors presuppose the existence of three-dimensional capabilities, however minimal, in the patient. The patient's developmental prognosis depends, in fact, on the maturation of this capability. In her conclusion of her treatment of Robbie, Alvarez mentions his tendency to enter autistic states in order to avoid situations he does not like, such as acknowledging the prices he pays because of his condition. She describes this as a tyrannical, exasperating act of communication which, in my view, nevertheless entails a significant element of three-dimensional reflection. In the case presented here, Eden *felt* that he did not understand; but this experience cannot be discussed in terms of acknowledging costs but of frustration/restlessness/catastrophe.

"Multi two-dimensional" children are "forsaken" in two opposite ways:

1. In psychoanalytic therapy, when the therapist presupposes the existence of three-dimensional thinking and is thus less able to understand the catastrophic experience of not being able to understand.
2. By being left outside the psychoanalytic field and handed over to behaviouristic educational and therapeutic methods (Piontelli 2001[7]) (e.g., ABA[8]).

In my understanding, the psychoanalytic treatment of these children does not "address" the unconscious, the pre-conscious, and the unconscious phantasy in the conventional manner. Because of the fundamental difference in projection, the use of transference and countertransference in this treatment is different. The therapist is not only a "hunter" of thoughts that cannot be thought; she also treats thoughts that are trapped in two-dimensional understanding and are not projected into her. Such thoughts will often be expressed in a repetitive (but not necessarily ritualised) or physical manner. The therapist understands these on a three-dimensional level, but is able to offer them back to the patient in two-dimensional terms so that they are understandable. I would like to emphasise that I am not referring here to reclamation, but to states in which the patient is present and completely with the therapist, seeking her help in their attempts to understand. Is the patient asking us to understand their experience of misunderstanding? Is this the sense of being understood by another? I am afraid that this is not always the case.

---

[7] In her addition to the Hebrew translation of her book, *From Fetus to Child*, Piontelli (2001) notes that due to new findings in the neurological field, she now thinks that autism isn't purely psychogenic. Over the years, she had changed her mind and now she thinks that psychoanalytic psychotherapy is not applicable to autistic children, and is not the treatment of choice.

[8] ABA—Applied Behavioural Analysis—is a behavioural treatment developed by O. Lovaas that is widely used today in treating autistic children.

I believe it is a sense of order. One more two-dimensional "surface" can be set down, until some internal or external trigger causes a discrepancy in the "pile" of surfaces, bringing about the next bout of unease and turmoil.

This turmoil may be the optimistic aspect of this description, as it requires a space in which to exist. This turmoil is a psychic catastrophe which seeks suppression through previous and potent two-dimensional phrases or understandings or removal from the body via motoric activity. The therapist's insistence on being with the child in the turmoil of misunderstanding may facilitate the elaboration of the capacity to tolerate this turmoil.

The kind of work I am proposing entails the identification of the two particular two-dimensional surfaces which are incongruent at a particular moment, thus causing a potentially catastrophic turmoil; the elaboration of the capacity to remain in this catastrophic three-dimensional state; and interventions which include reference to emotion and an "explanation" or "solution" which, while in itself two-dimensional, does not conform to the formula by which the more powerful two-dimensional structure erases the structure that is incongruent with it and suppresses the turmoil at the cost of negating emotion and thinking (which are, in any case, problematic).

Eden goes out of the consultation room to use the restroom. He sees my partner Robby sitting in his room with the door open and proceeds to close it. Robby asks him to leave it open. Terrified, Eden asks: "Is closing right or wrong?" For him, there exist "closed–open" and "good–bad". Closed is good. I say that he thinks that closed is good but that is not his room, so he should ask permission if he wants to close the door. "Is closing right or wrong?" I tell him that he is worried that he had done something wrong and that it is a "small wrong". "Closing is right or wrong? Closing is grown-up or not grown-up?" I tell him it was a small wrong situation, a mistake. One learns from mistakes and he has learned that when he wants to close something that belongs to someone else, he needs to ask first. "I love learning. Is a mistake one time? Is closing violence or not violence? I want to tell Robby about Neri". Neri is a violent boy from Eden's school and Eden had just told me that Neri came into his classroom, took his glasses, and broke them. "That's violence," he said. I tell him that he would like to know whether closing Robby's door is violent. "Yes." Then he starts laughing. His laughter starts out strange but becomes more pleasant. "You're enjoying the fact that Neri is violent and you're not violent." "Yes!" Eden was afraid that he was being violent; the equation of violent and wrong did not add up with "closed is good". It is hard for him to understand that closed can be either good or bad in different situations. We thus added a new surface: "you need to ask about someone else's door"; but "you learn from mistakes (made one time)". That might be a little more complicated.

As mentioned, if we view these moments of misunderstanding as a turmoil in a three-dimensional space, my capacity to tolerate them together with Eden and jointly seek an adequate understanding—although in two-dimensional language—facilitates a certain augmentation of his container and the development of three-dimensional thoughts. Indeed, something is starting to happen, moments in which I think I notice something that is three-dimensional and an understanding of "interior". I "lie in wait" for these moments. Because "closed is good", Eden wants to close my letters as I write. I chuckle and tell him that because it is so important to him that everything is closed, he can go ahead and close them. One day, as he is fixing and closing my letters, he asks, "What does silly mean?" "What does silly mean?" I asked him back. "It's silly not to close the letters." "Maybe you don't know whether it's silly not to close the letters, or to close them all the time." He looks into my eyes and laughs a new laughter, one that I understood as meaning: "You know how I love closing letters, I know it's unusual, I know that closing letters doesn't matter to you, but that you won't get in my way, you'll let me do it." He knows something about me and he knows that I know something about him.

In conclusion, I view the essence of autism as the absence of three-dimensional thinking. Naturally, this absence corresponds to concrete thinking and a disinterest in the other's interiority. The accumulated literature and insights regarding the experience, thinking, and development of autistic children has two branches: (1) children (and adults) who are "on the autistic spectrum"; (2) the understanding of primary, unrepresented, and unsymbolised mental states as similar to those experienced by autistic patients. (It is interesting to note that psychoanalytic literature almost always depicts infants or adults in analysis and seldom features children, unless they are autistic. In my view, this results from the fact that children play—and if they play, then they are not autistic.)

My understanding of two-dimensional thinking in non-autistic patients suggests that this is a different phenomenon. Therefore, our intervention (interpretative or otherwise) will always aim towards the three-dimensional. The three-dimensional is that which we can call the patient's container or organising function, it is the element with which we enter into alliance, with which we "discuss" two-dimensional phenomena. Patients suffering from different degrees of autism exhibit different extents of two-dimensional thinking as well as a capacity for three-dimensional thinking and for communication that involves identification, projection, and internalisation. However, when autistic two-dimensional thinking is at the fore, our intervention (and I will not be surprised to discover that we react this way intuitively and without theoretical conceptualisations) will be *with the two-dimensional* rather than *towards the three-dimensional*. Even in the most autistic child, we may be able to trace three-dimensional cracks, never giving up hope of finding them, joining them, and working with them. Therefore, I believe it is important for autistic children to receive therapy which is not exclusively behavioral. Nevertheless, we must be careful not to be tricked, not to proclaim as three-dimensional what is solely the result of our own projection (which we will always recognise only in retrospect) or of "multi two-dimensionality". On the other hand, autistic two-dimensional thinking or the phenomenon of "multi two-dimensional" thinking are characteristic only of autistic disorders of varying severity and are not the same as unthought or unsymbolised instinctual or sensory materials.

Does this amount to psychoanalysis? I believe that this work ought to be performed by psychoanalysts, who are able to identify the fracture between two contradictory two-dimensional understandings, to stay with the catastrophic experience, to translate emotional states into two-dimensional language, and to lie in wait for moments, glimpses, of three-dimensional thinking. In addition, I would like to call to mind that one sometimes has to spend a very long time uncertain about whether three-dimensional thinking will even develop. Undoubtedly, giving up on it in advance does little to facilitate its development.

As depicted in the literature and according to my own very similar experiences, in situations where the patient is withdrawing from an existing three-dimensional capacity, the therapist will feel immense boredom. I have noticed that in cases where such capacity is altogether absent, the quality of listening is different. The therapist's attention to "how this is being experienced and understood by the 'two-dimensional' speaker in the room with me" is mesmerising. The attempt to translate the two languages into each other and to trace any clues for the understanding or misunderstanding of these translations is challenging and stimulating. While it appears to be a more "cerebral" course of action, after one is comfortably situated in both languages, one finds oneself in that "lively looseness" (reverie?), a state that allows one to be in the room with a person who speaks that different language, engaged in a shared intimacy—the intimacy of labourers, fixing surface after surface, occasionally examining their order.

References

Acquarone, S. (2007). *Signs of Autism in Infants: Recognition and Early Intervention*. London: Karnac.

Alvarez, A. (1977). Problems of dependence and development in an excessively passive autistic boy. *Journal of Child Psychotherapy, 4*: 25–46.

Alvarez, A. (1992). *Live Company: Psychoanalytic Psychotherapy with Autistic, Borderline, Deprived and Abused Children*. London: Routledge.

Anzieu, D. (1985). The notion of a Skin-Ego. In: *The Skin-Ego* (pp. 39–48). London: Karnac, 2016.

Bergstein, A. (2010). On the possibility of knowing the other's mind: Reverie, dreaming and counter-dreaming. Lecture given at the Israel Psychoanalytic Society, 28 December 2000.

Bick, E. (1968). The experience of the skin in early object-relations. *International Journal of Psychoanalysis, 49*: 484–486.

Bion, W. R. (1977). *Two Papers: The Grid and Caesura*. Rio de Janeiro: Imago Editora.

Britton, R. (1989). The missing link: Parental sexuality and the Oedipus complex. In: J. Steiner (Ed.), *The Oedipus Complex Today: Clinical Implications*. London: Karnac.

Bruner, J. S. (1968). *Processes of Cognitive Growth: Infancy.* Worcester, MA: Clark University Press.

Frith, U. (1989). *Autism: Explaining the Enigma.* Oxford: Basil Blackwell.

Harris Williams, M. (2010). *A Meltzer Reader: Selections from the Writings of Donald Meltzer.* London: Karnac.

Isaacs, S. (1948). On the nature and function of phantasy. *International Journal of Psycho-analysis, 29*: 73–97.

Keinan, N. (2009). The perforated envelope—therapeutic work with psychic holes. *Sichot, 23*(2): 138–151. [Hebrew]

Klein, M. (1952). Some theoretical conclusions regarding the emotional life of the infant. In: M. Klein, P. Heimann, S. Isaacs, & J. Riviere, *Developments in Psychoanalysis.* London: Hogarth.

Meltzer, D. (1975). Adhesive identification. *Contemporary Psychoanalysis, 11*: 289–310.

Meltzer, D., Bremner, J., Hoxter, S., Weddell, D., & Wittenberg, I., (1975). *Explorations in Autism: A Psycho-Analytical Study.* Perthshire: Clunie Press.

Ogden, T. H. (1989). The autistic-contiguous position. In: *The Primitive Edge of Experience* (pp. 47–82). New York: Jason Aaronson.

Piontelli, A. (2001). *From Fetus to Child: An Observational and Psychoanalytic Study.* Tel Aviv: Modan. [Hebrew]

Rosenfeld, D. (1997). Understanding varieties of autistic encapsulations: A homage to Frances Tustin. In: *Encounters with Autistic States: A Memorial Tribute to Frances Tustin.* Northvale, NJ: Jason Aronson.

Rosenfeld, H. (1981). On the psychopathology and treatment of psychotic patients. In: J. Grotstein (Ed.), *Do I Dare Disturb the Universe?* London: Karnac.

Segal, H. (1957). Notes on symbol formation. In: *The Works of Hanna Segal.* Northvale, NJ: Jason Aronson, 1981.

Segal, H. (1978). On symbolism. *International Journal of Psychoanalysis, 59*: 315–319.

Symington, J. (1985). The survival function of primitive omnipotence. *International Journal of Psychoanalysis, 66*: 481–487.

Tustin, F. (1981). *Autistic States in Children.* London: Routledge.

Tustin, F. (1994). The perpetuation of an error. *Journal of Child Psychotherapy, 20*(1): 3–23.

CHAPTER EIGHT

From screaming to dreaming: notes on anxiety and its transformation

Jeffrey L. Eaton

Introduction

Psychotherapy with children diagnosed on the autism spectrum forces an analyst to reconsider his conceptual frameworks. Over the past few decades, building on the seminal work of Frances Tustin, important contributions in extending an analytic paradigm have been made by many analysts from around the world. Among the people I am inspired by are Anne Alvarez, Joshua Durban, Didier Houzel, and Suzanne Maiello. Building on aspects of their work, I have come to question, and even tried to expand, the models that orient me. In what follows I will make particular use of ideas advanced by Durban and Maiello to help sketch out my own evolving "scheme of understanding" (Maiello, 1997, p. 2).

Maiello has written (2001, p. 180):

> Recent formulations, both of psychoanalysts and developmentalists, show a shared need to create new conceptual containers for the primary levels of proto-mental experiences.

I will describe how Maiello's work sheds light on how the earliest experiences of life, especially prenatal experience, contribute to the formation of what I call *a floor for emotional experience*. Durban's work helps to map the deepest anxieties, below or before the paranoid–schizoid position, which can constitute what I call *a background of emotional catastrophe*.

The presence of primitive anxieties can stimulate omnipotent survival defences (Symington, 1985). These defences can become entrenched through the ongoing impact generated by a background of emotional catastrophe. My interest is in thinking through some of the complexity of early experience and the possible relationship between the creation of a floor for emotional experience and its interruption by overwhelming anxieties.

Pre-object relatedness

Ivri Kumin, MD, was a psychoanalyst in Seattle, Washington. He was a keen, sensitive, creative analyst whose life was tragically cut short by brain cancer. In 1996 he authored a book titled *Pre-Object Relatedness: Early Attachment and the Psychoanalytic Situation*. When combined, the work of Durban and Maiello contribute to the description of what might be called "pre-object relatedness" (Kumin, 1996). I will offer here a brief sketch of a pre-object territory, linking Kumin's ideas with the work of Maiello and Durban.

Kumin (1996, p. 20) notes that it was René Spitz who first used the term "pre-object". Following Kumin, the idea of pre-object relations, in the way I am using the term, does not imply an objectless state. Instead, it emphasises the complexity of a process of experience-dependent realisation and the construction of the first part-object relations. Kumin (1996, p. 21) uses the term "pre-object relatedness" to describe:

> a variety of archaic forms of relatedness that are present at birth but persist throughout life. Pre-object relatedness, so conceived, persists in the background as the core of primary relatedness, the sense of "being there" and "being with" which accompanies all … human experience.

It is not my intention to survey the many writers who have evoked similar kinds of concerns. I do, however, want to indicate awareness of some of the many people exploring this area. I find ideas relevant to pre-object relatedness in Winnicott, Balint, and Tustin; in Ogden's (1989) work on "the autistic contiguous position"; in Didier Anzieu's (2016) work on "the skin ego"; and in René Roussillon's (2011) work on symbolisation and primitive agony. Pre-object relatedness evokes what Christopher Bollas (1987) calls "the unthought known"; what James Grotstein (2000) calls "the background object of primary identification"; and what Michael Eigen (1993) explores as a "union-distinction paradigm". Aulangier, Bleger, Eshel, Gaddini, Houzel, Mitrani, and Tracey all have ideas relevant to this area. The list could be enlarged with still more names.

Kumin (1996, p. 21) explains:

> I postulate that pre-object relatedness is not vestigial … but is ongoing and continually structures all human relationships. Pre-object relatedness does not fade from existence with the advent of the capacity for differentiated object relationships but accompanies all object relationships as the affective autonomic "core" that renders one's experience of self and others uniquely one's own.

Building a floor for emotional experience

In her book *The Thinking Heart*, in a chapter titled "Some emotional conditions for the development of two-tracked thinking: The sense of agency and the sense of abundance", Anne Alvarez (2012, p. 29) writes:

> The normal infant is, in many ways, helpless and dependent; but he is also competent, thoughtful, alert, and, when conditions allow, full of passionate curiosity about his world.

Alvarez continues (2012, p. 29):

> Developmental researchers have spent decades attempting to analyse the separate elements in the conditions essential for healthy cognitive/emotional development. The sense of efficacy—or agency—is one such element … this sense of efficacy—and the pleasure associated with it—are the foundations of self-feeling.

When does a sense of self begin? We might ask, differently, what are some of the feelings of what it is like to be a foetus? Additionally, what kinds of conditions sponsor the unfolding of self-experience even before birth? How can we imagine such primitive experiences and find language for our conjectures?

Maiello (2000, p. 69) has much to say on these topics. For example, she writes:

> I suggest that mental development grows on the ground of a basic trust in an ongoing rhythmical object, which can, once it is securely internalized, also be playfully varied.

Maiello (2000, p. 69) describes how the foetus has a variety of forms of experience, including its own movements "accompanied by the song of the mother's voice" that contributes to the development of a rhythmical object. She describes (2000, p. 69):

> the mother's voice ... reaches the unborn child in the amniotic bath, immersed in the ongoing rhythmical pulsating sound of her breathing and heartbeat ...
> I suggest that the perception of the rhythmical sounds of the maternal organism during prenatal life may constitute the base that prepares the fetus to receive the sound and rhythm of the mother's voice, with its infinitely more complex articulations in terms of pitch, loudness, timbre, and rhythm.

Describing her concept of a sound-object, Maiello (2001, p. 180) writes:

> With this term, I describe an early, possibly prenatal precursor of the later maternal object, whose qualities may result from the earliest auditory experiences of the maternal voice. The most basic rhythmical qualities of the sound-object may be rooted in the foetus's perception of the maternal heartbeat, the pulsations of her blood-flow and the respiratory rhythm. In developmental terms, I would place the rhythmical aspects of prenatal reality at the primordial end of auditory, and in part, vibratory, experiences. Intertwined with kinesthetic and tactile

levels of experience, they may constitute the foetus's, and later the infant's, most basic awareness of pulsating life, and therefore be at the core of "basic trust" (Erikson, 1950).

Finally, Maiello (2000, pp. 69–70) poetically explains:

> The rhythmic prenatal "song-and-dance" experience is reproduced after birth every time the mother rocks the baby and sings a lullaby. But it is most significantly transformed and recreated at the breast, where the baby takes part actively in shaping the quality of the new relationship. When things go well, the baby's sucking and mother's milk-flow adjust to each other and find a rhythm of cooperation and reciprocity. Mouth and nipple could be described as dancing to the rhythmical sounds of swallowing, together with the little guttural vocal sounds many babies produce as they suck.

At this primitive level, I am interested in the influence of a process that the foetus is immersed within and how perception is gradually transformed after birth.

Early self-experience is rudimentary and sensational. Sensation becomes patterned rhythmically, that is, the earliest form of self is probably a temporal experience. This is not a reflective experience, but a felt sense of primary awareness, an experience of registration of sensation and movement in relationship to environmental conditions.

Sensation events gradually accrue primitive shapes and patterns (Maiello, 2001) which, over time, become part of a floor for emotional experience. I want to abstract two patterns or shapes from these observations of prenatal life. I suggest that not only is prenatal experience important in creating a floor for emotional experience but that a floor for emotional experience has a dynamic structure. The earliest self-experiences which become part of pre-object relatedness may have a double or "dual track" (Grotstein, 2000) structure.

The first track of experience can be called the self as object (SAO). The second track can be named the self as agent (SAA). I emphasise, again, that despite this language, the challenge is to imagine a developing shape of experience, something unfolding in time, rather than discrete separate object relations. To add to the complexity, there will be an oscillating influence between two kinds of developing shapes that can be noted: self as object ←→ self as agent. This is a structure of a floor for emotional experience (FEE) that is co-created with coping with greater or lesser degrees of impingement from a background of emotional catastrophe (BEC):

SAA ←→ SAO

FEE ←→ BEC

This structure, in turn, influences the unfolding of the relationship between the paranoid–schizoid position and the depressive position:

PS ←→ D

FEE ←→ BEC

The implications of this complexity exceed the scope of this communication. However, one of the most important aspects of this model is that it may shed light on whether the paranoid–schizoid phantasies function to organise the nascent self and create a developmental momentum, or, conversely, whether the paranoid–schizoid phantasies either fail to develop (inadequate splitting and communicative projective identification) or over-function, creating a pathological momentum (excessive projective identification and splitting leading to fragmentation and attacks on links).

Building on the idea of a sound-object, Maiello has observed that hearing begins around four months of intrauterine life. She notes that low frequencies are associated with the sounds of the mother as environment or organism (her heartbeat, breathing, and digestive noises). Higher frequencies, which are unpredictably present and then absent, are how the mother's voice is gradually recognised and emotionally invested. This higher-frequency auditory register can be imagined as calling forth an enigmatic elsewhere world, an unreachable place. This aspect of voice may stimulate the foetus's preconception for seeking; it may activate the shape of proto-agency.

Here, in the primordial relationship to sound, can be glimpsed the shape of the self as object (immersed in the low frequencies of the background of the womb environment). It may also be the origin of moments of seeking and discovery that create proto-patterns of the self as agent (the spontaneous movements that enliven the foetus when registering the higher frequencies of mother's voice).

What happens, then, when the construction of a floor for emotional experience is interrupted by the presence of overwhelming primitive anxieties, sometimes even before birth?

A background of emotional catastrophe

Freud's ideas about anxiety provide a starting point to briefly consider some views on the nature of distress in earliest life. Freud discovered that anxiety might function as a signal to help prepare the ego to cope with potential danger situations. His ideas evolved over several years and can be briefly summarised as involving five kinds of potential danger.

At the deepest level there is a danger of traumatic overstimulation which Freud equated with an experience of helplessness. This is the level that is most important when considering pre-object relatedness. Next, there is the danger of the loss of the object, and, later, the loss of the object's love. Then there is the danger of castration and of superego disapproval or judgement. Finally, there are realistic perceptions of external dangers, what might be called awareness of existential circumstances.

The work of Melanie Klein and many who followed her, including Bion, Winnicott, Meltzer, and Tustin, expanded appreciation for even more primitive sources of anxiety. In these formulations, anxiety does not evolve to function as a signal. Instead, it can be felt as the concrete experience of overwhelming threat to the self or even to existence.

Durban (2019), in his valuable paper "'Making a person': clinical considerations regarding the interpretation of anxieties in the analyses of children on the autisto-psychotic spectrum", offers an intricately detailed description of the variety and complexity of primitive anxieties and how they can coexist and combine to create what I call a background of emotional catastrophe. Such a background often interferes with the construction and realisation of a floor for emotional experience.

Drawing on the recent work of English and French psychoanalysts immersed in the psychoanalytic treatment of autism, Durban proposes what he calls an "autisto-psychotic spectrum". It is extremely important to consider anxieties before or below the paranoid–schizoid position. Durban (2019, p. 926) describes primitive anxieties-of-being as including experiences such as:

> liquefying, dissolving, having no skin or a skin full of holes, freezing, burning, losing a sense of time and space and existing in a bi-dimensional world.

Durban (2019, p. 926) writes:

> When analysing a child on the autisto-psychotic spectrum, we experience constant fluctuations between different levels of anxieties, defenses, and of self-object differentiation and integration. Thus we may encounter in the same child, and often in the same session, anxiety states ranging from archaic anxieties-of-being to more clearly defined anxieties concerning object relationships of the paranoid–schizoid and depressive kind … Psychotic anxieties might cover up and bind primitive anxieties-of-being, while the latter might serve as a retreat from psychotic anxieties. These dynamics are embodied in the unconscious phantasies characteristic of early malformed mental states.

I want to highlight the complexity in Durban's model of the non-linear relationships between psychotic, non-psychotic, narcissistic, and autistic processes that can simultaneously coexist and influence a child's developing picture of the world.

I suggest that in addition to tracking the movement in and out of autistic and narcissistic retreats, we should consider the structure of the most primitive self-experience, looking again at its oscillation between the self as object and the self as agent.

Drawing on Durban's observations we can see how at the deepest level of anxieties-of-being, a primitive self (what if feels like to be me at the level of sensation and shape) can feel like being the object of annihilating forces. At the pre-object level of experience, these forces are not easily organised, personified, or differentiated. They feel environmental, nonhuman, energetic, even cosmic. In my experience, a primitive sense of self as object does not experience a link to an overwhelming other. Instead, the experience is one of *immersion* in a toxic or violent environment. What happens in the environment happens to the self. That is why we can perhaps learn so much from trying to imagine prenatal experience. The earliest forms of link arise from and are differentiated out of an experience of immersion which either supports an experience of going on being or thwarts it.

I'm trying to evoke an experience that is neither objectless nor involving stable clearly differentiated part-object relations. In a pre-object register, the background of catastrophe implies immersion within an annihilating process. And, to the extent that the patient recognises the analyst as separate at all, the analyst is felt to exist within, and be subjected to, the same annihilating forces.

This intimidating subjective reality generates real interpersonal pressures, related to the evocation of a nameless dread that saturates the analytic field. This kind of experience is beyond the dyadic formulations more familiar at the part-object or paranoid–schizoid level of interpretation. The terror of annihilation is felt to be immediate, concrete, and saturating. It thus resists description and symbolisation and tends to overwhelm the analyst too. As Bion (1977) has indicated, attention must shift to the link, the caesura, the experience that arises between. Or, as I like to say, attention must focus on what the moment itself calls forth.

It is no wonder then that the sense of the self as agent can become caught up in omnipotent survival functions, seeking refuge in autistic or narcissistic retreats. Agency is captured in a desperate attempt to create conditions of survival, which foreclose awareness of dependent object relationships, and rid the self of awareness of its helpless exposed states.

It is a significant challenge to the analyst to realise that the patient has little or no sense of the value of co-operating with the analyst in his treatment. Instead, the patient's sense of agency is captured and organised by trying to escape the presence of the object or to survive overwhelming annihilating forces that he often feels the analyst is subjecting him to.

Nevertheless, in my experience, a hidden part of the personality, a lost, helpless, dependent, and traumatised part, often in the shape of the self as object, can be sometimes detected. This aspect of the self is somehow desperately trying to signal its distress at the pre-object level. Its signals of hope are faint and the ability to initiate contact with the analyst fleeting.

The following two tables (Tables 8.1 and Table 8.2) summarise some of these ideas:

Table 8.1 Dual track 1

	Self	*Other*	*Link*	*Anxiety*
Pre-object relatedness	Self as object	Environment background presence	Immersion	Annihilation Primitive agonies Nameless dread
	Self as agent	Enigmatic proto-object	Fleeting awareness of presence/absence	
Paranoid-schizoid	Self as object	Part object + or −	Influence	Threat to self through presence of bad object or loss of the good object
	Self as agent		Control	

Table 8.2 Dual track 2

	Floor for emotional experience	*Background of emotional catastrophe*
Self as agent	Patterned by shared contingent interactions Affect regulating dyadic experience	Captured by primitive omnipotent survival functions; withdrawn from dependent object relations
	Realisation of container–contained relationship	Living "elsewhere" in omnipotent "one-person solutions" Fear of emergence
Self as object	Unintegration Relaxation Distress → comfort Faith in going-on-being	Primitive agonies Nameless dread Annihilation of being

Case vignette

I met Sandy (as I shall call her) when she was four years old. She is an attractive intelligent child. Her parents sought psychotherapy for her because she was too disruptive to remain in pre-school. Her frequent tantrums involved screaming, kicking, hitting, biting, and pushing teachers and children. Sandy's parents described the emotional intensity and violence of her behaviour as uncontrollable.

Sandy was born four weeks prematurely and spent the first month of her life in a neonatal intensive care unit (NICU). Like many such children, Sandy exhibits several kinds of sensory hypersensitivity, the most severe being terror at loud noises.

In our first sessions Sandy moved frantically around the consulting room. She would sit down on the floor and begin to talk and then suddenly jump up and run around. She would take out all the toys from the toy box without looking at them and then go look out the window and narrate what she saw. She would climb on the couch, then roll on the floor, then kick and squeal.

Sandy would start to draw and then immediately abandon what she was doing. She was in constant motion during her sessions. Sometimes, especially if a loud noise impinged, she would scream and seem to panic.

The impact of her fragility coupled with her relentless motion left me exhausted. I felt bewildered and disoriented. There was no way to track any themes in her activities. She was never actually playing. Things seemed to break off as soon as they started.

I gradually recognised that the meaning of her behavior was not in the content of her actions but in their quality, in their very rapidity and fragmented nature. I determined to try to welcome the chaos of her activity without trying to change it.

I said descriptive things like: "You are moving so fast", "You are moving from one thing and now to another", "I wonder if you are choosing what you are doing?", "You seem pushed from one thing to another thing by something, or some feeling without a name."

Slowly, a sense of a relationship began to develop. At first, this was not between us, but a sense *within me* that I was becoming better able to be with her. I became able to say things like, "It must feel strange to be here with me. I feel like you and I are in the middle of an emotional storm."

I was surprised when in the next session Sandy remembered the phrase "emotional storm". She said, "I'm in a storm again."

For the first time, she showed an interest in the large white board I kept with the toys. She asked me if she could draw. I gave her a set of coloured markers and an eraser. She started to make giant black swirling circles.

Sandy said, "Do you know what it is?"
I said, "I bet it's the storm."
She said, "What kind of storm is it?"
I said, "It's a storm made out of very intense feelings."
Sandy said, "It's a tornado. It can destroy anything."

I said, "You must feel like you are a tornado, and you are wondering if I am afraid of being destroyed by your tornado feelings." She looked at me closely but did not say anything. She said she had finished drawing and moved to create a violent game with puppets.

In the sessions that followed, Sandy was noticeably calmer. She was better able to sustain her play activities for longer durations before breaking them off. Sandy continued to draw tornados for many sessions.

"Do you remember the tornado," she would ask. "I do," I said. One day Sandy said, "I'm going to draw a tornado. Do you want to see?" "Yes," I said, "I want to see whatever you want to show me." She said, "I want you to go to sleep." I was sitting on the floor next to her with the white board between us. Sandy said, "Lie down and close your eyes and go to sleep." I said, "This seems important to you. I will close my eyes and pretend to sleep." She said, "No, you have to lie down."

I decided to comply with Sandy's instructions. It was an intuitive choice that I was uncertain about. I was aware of feeling controlled, but, at the same time, I did not want to interrupt something that felt like it was evolving. I thought Sandy was trying to express something that felt potentially significant.

I stretched out on the floor. "Don't open your eyes until I say so," she said. "Are you asleep now?" she asked. "Yes," I said.

While I was pretending to sleep, I was trying to pay attention to my experience in case I might glean some clues about the meaning of this evolving scene. Suddenly, to my surprise, Sandy yelled "Wake up now!"

I was authentically startled, which Sandy observed. My shock made her gleeful.

"Look!" she said. She had drawn another black tornado which covered the entire white board.

I said, "You laughed when you saw how startled I was when you yelled wake up. You were excited by this," I said.

Then I said, "I wonder if you wanted me to pretend to be asleep so that you could have a feeling you could control me. I think this might be another way of trying to control the feelings of the being trapped inside the tornado storm."

Sandy said, immediately, "I wanted you to have a dream."

In the following sessions Sandy returned to this game, repeating the instruction for me to go to sleep so she could startle me awake again. I said I wondered if she often felt startled by how suddenly tornado feelings could appear in her. I said it must feel like those feelings get put inside her by others or events and she desperately wanted to find a way to control what upset her.

She said, "I know what to do." She took an eraser and started to make what she called "tiny cuts" in the tornado. She said that she would control what she called "a cutting machine". The purpose of the cuts in the tornado seemed to be to make the storm's energy dissipate.

I linked this to how she had interrupted her own experience in the early sessions, moving from one thing to another. I said that I thought that when she moved from one thing to another, she might be feeling interrupted by the intensity of the stormy emotions inside her. I said, now the tiny cuts are a way of showing, with my help, how to interrupt the tornado feelings and to not feel so taken over by them.

In the next session Sandy drew her first picture of herself. It was a very primitive stick figure, like something a toddler might draw. She said, simply, "This is me."

Discussion

Sandy's history suggests exposure to a very deep level of anxiety. I speculate that Sandy's nascent sense of self felt overwhelmed from the beginning of her life. For Sandy, anxiety could not operate as a signal. Instead, whenever anxiety began to arise, it overwhelmed and interrupted her, becoming a catastrophe that she was never able to prepare for.

According to Winnicott, distress at the level of environmental failure gives rise to anxiety that is felt as annihilation of the feeling of "going on being". Winnicott described what he called "primitive agonies" which he listed as going to pieces, falling forever, having no relation to the body, and having no orientation. According to Jan Abram:

> For Winnicott, the primitive anxieties constitute *impingement*. The result in the infant of too much impingement is that the sense of self is annihilated. This is the opposite of being; it is the trauma of *annihilation*, which violated the very core of the self.
> (Abram, p. 161)

When faced with anxieties like this, a child will be concretely dependent on the environment to provide the alpha function needed to help to contain, organise, and process distress. Without this provision, there is no way to move from screaming to dreaming.

At a cognitive level, Sandy was clearly aware of separate people, including her mother, father, me, her sibling, and her grandparents. But, at an emotional level, I think Sandy often felt immersed in an unnamed and unshared emotional catastrophe.

According to Alvarez (2012) there are three levels of interpretation. The first level is explanatory and helps a child to recognise additional or alternative meanings for her experience. This requires a capacity to share attention and to take in another's different point of view. A second level of interpretation, one that Alvarez feels is appropriate for borderline, psychotic, and autistic children, involves what she calls descriptive interpretations. These are designed to name and lend meaning to the child's experience helping to bring something into focus so that it can be recognised and contained.

Alvarez (2012) says that this second level deals more with a feeling of being, and what she calls "thinking on a single track".

I associate impingement with a background of emotional catastrophe at a pre-object related level and feel that Alvarez's strategy of thinking on a single track is most appropriate in trying to establish a container–contained relationship. This level helps articulate a child's experience and give verbal shape to a picture of the world.

The third level, what Alvarez calls a vitalising interpretation, involves harnessing the child's attention that has been captured and trapped in some form of severe alienation. This level of interpretation may be necessary when the primitive experience of the self as an object feels trapped within a background of emotional catastrophe. This may give rise not only to reclaiming a child's attention, but also to use of interpretations in action, that Durban has recently described and can be seen in my play experience with Sandy.

My descriptive interpretations to Sandy were an attempt to orient and organise us. At the level of annihilation anxiety, I believe that, subjectively, the threat is felt not just to the self but to everything. Making contact, or making a link, can be felt as evoking catastrophe. One needs to make a link to find help to feel, think, and express experience. But it is this very act of connecting or linking that is felt to bring awareness of catastrophe. This seems like the place where Sandy and I started.

Reflecting on Sandy's early experience in the NICU, one can imagine that she had a primordial perception that her very existence was in jeopardy. How is such an awareness to be registered, tolerated, explored, and expressed?

Regarding the game of waking me up, I'm much more in touch now with the possibility that Sandy might have been unconsciously trying to make a scene about a newborn baby in a NICU who could be terribly startled by sudden happenings that seem to come from out of nowhere. Her innovation of the game of making "tiny cuts" in the swirling storm seemed to be a discovery of reclaiming her omnipotence to master something traumatic.

I believe that the first picture of herself emerged because together we had created a process that could register, tolerate, explore, and express, some of the tornado experience. This meant that everything was in less danger of being destroyed and there was space for a connection to develop and be elaborated. Instead of being an overwhelmed object of a tornado storm, Sandy began to find her own agency, and to be able to explore, express, and share experience with me. At a deep intuitive level Sandy recognised we were engaged in creating a shared dreaming process to register, tolerate, and transform the tornado scene which represented an early pre-object experience.

References

Abram, J. (1996). *The Language of Winnicott: A Dictionary of Winnicott's Use of Words*. London: Karnac.

Alvarez, A. (2012). *The Thinking Heart: Three Levels of Psychoanalytic Therapy with Disturbed Children*. London: Routledge.

Anzieu, D. (2016). *The Skin Ego*. London: Karnac.

Bion, W. R. (1977). *Two Papers: The Grid and Caesura*. Brazil: Imago Editora.

Bollas, C. (1987). *The Shadow of the Object: Psychoanalysis of the Unthought Known*. London: Free Association Books.

Durban, J. (2019). "Making a person": Clinical considerations regarding the interpretation of anxieties in the analyses of children on the autisto-psychotic spectrum. *International Journal of Psycho-Analysis, 100*(5): 921–939.

Eigen, M. (1993). *The Electrified Tightrope*. Northvale, NJ: Jason Aronson.

Grotstein, J. (2000). Autochthony and alterity: Psychic reality in counterpoint. In: *Who Is the Dreamer, Who Dreams the Dream? A Study in Psychic Presences*. Hillsdale NJ: The Analytic Press.

Kumin, I. (1996). *Pre-Object Relatedness: Early Attachment and the Psychoanalytic Situation*. New York: Guilford Press.

Maiello, S. (1997). Going beyond: Notes on the beginning of object relations in the light of "the perpetuation of an error". In: T. Mitrani & J. Mitrani (Eds.), *Encounters with Autistic States: A Memorial Tribute to Frances Tustin*. Northvale, NJ: Jason Aronson.

Maiello, S. (2000). "Song-and-dance" and its developments: The function of rhythm in the learning process of oral and written language. In: M. Cohen & A. Hahn (Eds.), *Exploring the Work of Donald Meltzer: A Festschrift*. London: Karnac.

Maiello, S. (2001). On temporal shapes: the relation between primary rhythmical experience and the quality of mental links. In: J. Edwards (Ed.), *Being Alive: Building on the Work of Anne Alvarez*. London: Routledge.

Ogden, T. (1989). *The Primitive Edge of Experience*. Northvale, NJ: Jason Aronson.

Roussillon, R. (2011). *Primitive Agony and Symbolization*. London: Karnac.

Symington, J. (1985). The survival function of primitive omnipotence. *International Journal of Psycho-Analysis, 66*: 481–488.

CHAPTER NINE

A "felt-self": aspects of symbolising through psychotherapy

Jeffrey L. Eaton

This chapter explores what Frances Tustin called "the development of I-ness" in the context of an analytic process. Attention will focus on primitive experiences of a "felt-self" and the role of autistic defences against awareness of primal vulnerability. Establishing a psychoanalytic situation can sometimes make possible emergence from autistic states and the growth of emotional aliveness and expression. Clinical vignettes from the treatment of a child diagnosed on the autism spectrum will be presented to illustrate the development of symbolisation.

Frances Tustin (1986, p. 235) writes:

> Studying the stiff and halting development of the body image and the sense of being an "I" of the ... autistic child cannot but impress us with the complexity of the task achieved by normal infants without their ever being aware that it is taking place.

My work in psychoanalytic psychotherapy with several children who were diagnosed on the autism spectrum has convinced me of the complexity of each child's unique personality. To understand a child's picture of the world, it is helpful to try to imagine and observe primitive dimensions of experience generated by unconscious aspects of a primitive body image.

I want to explore the role of sensations in creating what Tustin calls "a felt-self" (1986, p. 222–223). Tustin states that "Autistic children 'rubber-stamp' the outside world in terms of their body image—their 'felt-self'" (1986, p. 222–223).

I will emphasise the complexity and importance of the role of sensation in the formation of a primitive body image and of a developing sense of identity. I believe that by attending to the level of the "felt-self" a sensitive therapist is sometimes able to establish good enough conditions for promoting meaningful emotional contact with difficult-to-reach children. From this contact, communication can develop and deepen. By attending to the implications of a "felt-self" in the child's experience an analyst can help sponsor the realisation of a containing process upon which a symbolising capacity can develop, allowing a child a wider range of expression and shared opportunity for meaning-making.

The development of I-ness

Most likely you experience yourself, without reflecting upon it, as a whole body with boundaries defined by your skin. Your mind and body can communicate seamlessly and are felt to be somehow united. You feel separate, oriented, and able to act in the world. Your co-ordinated senses contribute to an unconscious background feeling of coherence. An unconscious floor for emotional experience (Eaton, 2014) allows you to selectively deploy attention, imagine expectations, and make predictions about your actions. Your actions "make sense".

A sense of orientation, with all its complexity and dimensionality, often cannot be realised in autistic states. Imagine, instead, a "felt-self" that is sloshy like a liquid; or floppy, without a backbone; or hardened like a shell; or oozing like colours that spread and blend into one another. In such primitive experiences, objects cannot be reliably differentiated or interacted with, much less explored, trusted, or understood.

According to Tustin, the earliest body sensations involve a "felt-self" experienced in terms of "fluids and gases". "This is not surprising," Tustin writes (1986, p. 223), "since the newly born infant has emerged from a fluid medium and his early food and excretions are associated with fluids and gases".

Tustin believes that "primordial states of sensation are of basic significance in the development of the body image and of the sense of self" (Tustin, 1986, p. 235). Sensation both shapes the developing sense of self and the dawning perception of connection or link to another. In a good-enough mother and baby relationship *sensuousness* becomes patterned through affect-regulating interactions.

Tustin also explores the role of what she calls auto-sensuous activity. According to her, in a healthy scenario, auto-sensuous activity takes place within the context of developing relationship and in oscillation with the dawning tolerance for the awareness of separation from another.

Sensuousness is differentiated from auto-sensuousness. Tustin writes:

> I would suggest that in *normal* early infantile development, there is an awareness of separateness which is made bearable by auto-sensuous activities such as sucking and bodily interactions with other people, particularly the mother.
> (Tustin, 1986, p. 43, emphasis in original)

We can speak, then, of two kinds of "felt-self" experience. One kind is sensuous and patterned through relationship to another caring and mindful object. This "felt-self" gradually realises "a floor for emotional experience" (Eaton, 2014) that helps to build tolerance for moments of awareness of separation. In this scenario, there is a rhythm of union and differentiation unfolding in relationship to another. Auto-sensuous activity is used to help modulate anxiety but does not become a dominate or primary mode of organising experience.

By contrast, the second kind of "felt-self" relies heavily on auto-sensuous activity and creates what Tustin called "a taboo on tenderness" (Tustin, 1986, p. 290), blocking out awareness not only of separation from another but ultimately of contact with the other altogether. In this scenario, auto-sensuousness is unconsciously used as a defence against the awareness of separation or, equally important, of the awareness of the presence of the object. According to Tustin, (1981) this can be done by using sensation to create barriers to the awareness of the other, or, by using sensation to fuse or entangle with the other so that the other is experienced as an extension and organiser of the "felt-self".

In health, sensation is a bridge to both self-experience and connection with another and is patterned through interaction. Auto-sensual activity is a strand of this evolving relational and emotional experience. Sensuousness becomes a shared experience, taking place within a context of deepening reciprocity, contingent communication, and playful to and fro. Sensation is a part of a floor for emotional experience, a factor in what becomes a symbolising function.

In pathological situations, auto-sensuous activity, the manipulation of sensation for various omnipotent defensive purposes, comes to predominate and define experience with many downstream developmental implications. The reliance on rigid and repetitive sensation-dominated activities leads to an increasing sense of isolation and aversion to contact with others. This form of manipulated sensation becomes a barrier to realising links with others and obstructs the realisation of a symbolising function.

Often children diagnosed on the autism spectrum experience some form of agonising sensory hypersensitivity. Each child I have treated had some idiosyncratic element of sensory processing difficulty. The inability to coherently modulate and organise sensations contributes to a profound sense of disorientation and vulnerability at the level of a "felt-self". Often, there are neurodevelopmental factors that exacerbate the perception that contact and separation can involve an insult to the senses. This can lead to a background of intense shame, frustration, and withdrawal for both the child and the family.

Tustin (1986, p. 217) gives a description of the "felt-self" in agony when describing a patient named Jean:

> Jean said that … she felt as if "deep down" she were a "waterfall"; "falling and falling out of control" into a bottomless abyss, into boundless space, into nothingness. She emphasized that it was the feeling of being out of control, as much as the falling, which was so frightening. Significantly, she added, "I'm afraid I shall lose myself".

The importance of the image of a waterfall conveys a concrete sensation-dominated intensity characteristic of the experience of a primitive "felt-self". The patient, Jean, is trying to convey something before or beyond or without words. Her images and language are poetic. But here there is a paradox. Her words must be taken literally to appreciate the intensity of the experience that they seek to represent.

A "felt-self" experience only gradually enters representation through the mediation of another's caring reverie and attention. Jean's image of the waterfall points to a profound concreteness. Her experience is not like a waterfall. Her experience *is* a waterfall. Psychic reality is not a category that is automatically realised as real. It is gradually discovered as raw experiences at the level of a "felt-self" become registered, tolerated, explored, elaborated, and expressed through relationship. For this process to occur, emotional contact must become possible as autistic defences soften and wane.

The pathological "fate of sensation" has many possible trajectories. Without skilled and caring intervention, in cases involving a chronic feeling of insult to the senses, the consequences seem to include a progression of increasing alienation. This sequence unfolds as (1) fear of ongoing connection to others, (2) fear of any contact with others, (3) determined withdrawal from others, (4) the erasure of any awareness of the links to others, and (5) erasure of any awareness of links to one's own experience through retreat into auto-sensuality.

The chronic experience of insult to the senses can lead to an over reliance on auto-sensuous activities as organisers for sensory barriers, walls, and other omnipotent isolating manoeuvres. An ultimate outcome is that the child not only creates a barrier to contact with others but, perhaps even more profoundly, gradually loses contact with his or her own bodily experience, becoming, instead, immersed in rigid repetitive one-dimensional sensory shapes or objects.

I want to ground Tustin's ideas and my use of them in clinical work and to offer a taste of an analytic experience with a child diagnosed as on the autism spectrum. To illustrate the theme of a "felt-self" and its transformations I will share some glimpses into the treatment of a boy I will call Martin.

Martin's experience

I met Martin when he was nine. He was diagnosed with autism at age six at the University of Washington Autism Center. Martin is a good-looking, sensitive, intelligent boy. He was described at nine as self-absorbed, obsessive, easily frustrated, and subject to violent tantrums. His use of language involved much repetition about his favourite subjects, especially cartoons and video games. He began speech and language therapy after his diagnosis at age seven. His parents sought psychotherapy because Martin bluntly said that he wanted to die and that he was evil.

According to his teachers, Martin would wander around the school room without any clear intention. He did not "hear" instructions from his teacher. He would sing loudly to himself, unaware of how disruptive this was to his classmates. He needed repeated reminders to focus and became easily frustrated, even violently agitated, by what he perceived as "criticism".

Martin exhibited repetitive hand movements and auto-sensuous gestures, such as constantly twirling his long curly hair. Sometimes, when highly aroused, he flapped his hands and arms or hit himself in the face. He had no friends and was unable to develop peer relationships. Many of these behaviours were observable in his early sessions with me.

It is not my intention to provide a thorough developmental history. Martin's mother had a long history of significant trauma and abuse. She and Martin's father were very devoted to Martin's care. It is important to note, however, that the pregnancy was unplanned. Martin's mother was anxious about becoming pregnant and found her entire pregnancy difficult both physically and emotionally. Martin was born prematurely and spent six weeks in an incubator before being brought home.

Three of Martin's early drawings represent, I think, an experience of a "felt-self" moving from unsymbolised distress to primitive organisation. When Martin drew a picture, it was usually at my suggestion. I would get the paper and pens out and ask him if he would try to draw something. Martin would sit for a long time staring at the empty page. He might repeat lines from an episode of *Sponge Bob* or some other cartoon. He might hum and look out the window. He might take all the caps off the pens and then replace them. Or, he might organise the pens according to colours. Eventually he would say something like "Now I'm ready". It was important that I be very patient. I tried not to pressure or interrupt whatever time he needed to "get ready".

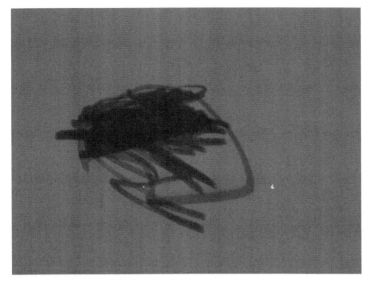

Figure 9.1 Untitled

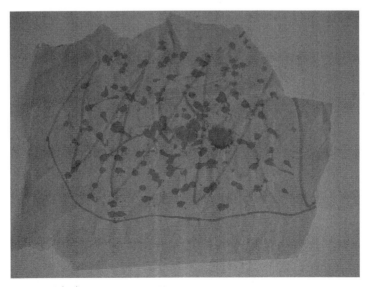

Figure 9.2 Untitled

174   AUTISTIC PHENOMENA AND UNREPRESENTED STATES

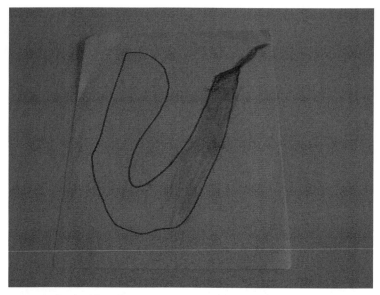

Figure 9.3 Animal with tail

Martin produced these images over the first year of twice weekly sessions.

The first image (Figure 9.1) was quickly abandoned after its creation. The second (Figure 9.2) was crinkled up then partially torn but not destroyed. Martin was disturbed by producing the drawing. The third image (Figure 9.3) was abandoned midway through. He called it "animal with tail". This involved one of the first "characters" to emerge in his sessions. This character had no story.

I think these drawings show a progression of the representation of a primitive body image, or "felt-self". One thing I realised witnessing the creation of these drawings is the difficulty not only of representing experience, but of tolerating "touching" experience at the level of a "felt-self."

Each of these early drawings represents a sense of the "too much-ness" of experience. Ask yourself what it would be like to experience the channels of your senses bringing disorganising, disorienting, and disturbing experience into awareness. You would naturally turn away from almost everything because it feels too new, too confusing, too dangerous, too unpredictable, or even too beautiful, too exciting, or too enigmatic. In other words, awareness of experience creates a chronic situation of "too muchness". An important imperative would be to try to control the experience of "too muchness".

One way of coping with too muchness is to communicate about it. But this requires that a child trust contact with another to organise and modulate experience. When there is no trust in the reliability of transformation from distress to comfort, some children seem to settle on idiosyncratic omnipotent methods of control, based on the manipulation of sensation. Over time they come to trust their own omnipotent behaviours more than contact with separate people.

Over time Martin began to communicate more with me. Three years into treatment Martin (then age twelve) produced a drawing that was able to *represent* his self-experience as a special kind a machine (unfortunately I did not prevent him from destroying this drawing at the end of one of his sessions).

I will describe, in detail, the drawing and what Martin told me about it. This description is condensed and does not convey the important developing rhythm of exploration between us. Our conversations about this drawing extended over several sessions until Martin finally destroyed it. My feeling is that the drawing represents Martin's unconscious creative attempt to cope with the problem of the "too muchness" of his experience of a primitive background "felt-self".

Martin's drawing pictures a robot-like machine. The main details of the image emphasise the function of the senses. The eyes are represented as "powerful search lights". The ears are "giant radio receivers". The nose is "a giant vacuum that sucks up smells". There is no representation of skin or touch. The mouth is missing, but there is a hole with "giant crushers" for the food and "a valve" to separate "the air passage from the food passage".

These ideas offer precision in dramatising Martin's unconscious "felt-self" and his relationship to his senses. One is immediately impressed with the fact of intensity. Each sense is a channel of intensity.

Of particular interest is the absence of a mouth. If, as Tustin believed, the fit between the infant's mouth and the mother's nipple is a primordial template for the first realisation of coupling, Martin's image shows a profound challenge of relating to another being through an unconscious phantasy of the mediating organ of "a hole with giant crushers".

It is important to imagine that not only is this how Martin unconsciously experiences himself, but, at the same time, that this is his view of others as well. Emotional contact, then, raises an implicit question of who will crush and who will be crushed.

The complexity and creativity of Martin's psychic reality is further elaborated by his descriptions of his picture. Senses flow into the "Central Command and Control". Thoughts are stored in the "Library of Thoughts". Feelings are "churned up" in "the Feeling Mixer". There is a "Dream Deposit Box" where dreams are delivered from the Library of Thoughts and the Feeling Mixer.

The emotional impact of this dream-like interchange left me in awe at Martin's unconscious creativity. I was particularly interested in the creation and development of a "dream deposit box" as a symbol for the construction of a container–contained relationship happening through the transference.

The ability to begin to share experience was crucial in freeing Martin's captured attention and making it available for interaction. It was through this shared interaction in sessions that Martin began to discover ways of tolerating and expressing his anxieties, emotions, and the mysterious capacity to transform experience.

Returning to my conversation with Martin about his drawing, I will summarise what I learned from him. He told me that: conflict between feelings and thoughts, or, between two kinds of feelings is to be avoided, at all costs, if possible; there should be only one feeling at a time or "the system will crash"; conflict between feelings and thoughts can negatively impact the stomach, the lungs, and the heart; the stomach processes fear, the lungs process sadness, and the heart processes joy. There is also a representation of an anal passage to eliminate waste, which can include bad thoughts, feelings, and dreams, but not sensations; sensations remain "stuck in the machine".

Over time I tried to imagine and to observe some of the consequences of sensations becoming "stuck in the machine". In *Learning from Experience*, Bion (1962) theorised that what he called "beta elements" impinge upon awareness. Beta elements, without transformation through alpha function, cannot be made unconscious. Beta elements are experiences of raw sensation that are not yet meaningful by themselves. The key point is, however, that beta elements are experienced.

An important distinction between being aware of an experience and making meaning of experience must be recognised by the analyst. Martin was showing me, I think, that sensations "stuck in the machine" were painful experiences that impinged upon his awareness but that he could not make meaning of by himself.

The problem of awareness of disturbing sensation creates a situation of "too muchness" that constantly jeopardises a "felt-self". There are many possible fates of this "too muchness". Tustin (1981) described auto-sensual activities and the creation of autistic shapes, objects, and barriers. Meltzer (1990), following Klein, described the role of intrusive projective identification, amplified by the manipulation of sensation, as in anal masturbation. Joan Symington (1985) described primitive omnipotent survival functions and Mitrani (1996) elaborated what she called adhesive pseudo-object relations and their relationship to unmetallized experience. All these ideas may have a role in describing how a primitive "felt-self" copes with the problem of "too muchness" registered as raw experience prior to entering a space of meaning or symbolisation.

It is quite possible to be aware of an experience at the level of sensation without being about to reflect upon it. Nonetheless, some meaning does accrue, unconsciously, at the level of primitive value systems. Alpha function is never absent absolutely. Unconscious phantasy seems to operate as a background process that gathers a portion of painful experience into a symbolising process while leaving an excess unmetabolised.

Some of the primitive values that form rudimentary patterns in how a "felt-self" relates to self and other can be notated:

Avoid ←→ Approach
Pain ←→ Pleasure
Alone ←→ Together
Torn ←→ Woven
Here ←→ Gone
Hard ←→ Soft

By focusing on awareness, I am emphasising that in autistic states there is experience at the level of the "felt-self" that must be closely attended to. This experience is complex. It is often profoundly sensation dominated.

That is why I want to introduce the question "what is the fate of sensation?" As we get to know each child in an analytic process, we begin to appreciate the complexity of states of mind that each child is living through. There are many small moments when transformation is possible if we can witness and describe them in the relationship between contact with others and the experience of a "felt-self".

I imagine that sensations that cannot be processed and remain "stuck", create pain and frustration. When pain is too great attacks on one's own capacity to register experience can take place. This amplifies feelings of disorientation and confusion. Often the only way to cope is to withdraw into a kind of psychic numbness or deadness or to return to familiar auto-sensuous activities.

It seems that emergence from autistic states can be complicated by the problem of a violent *sensory* superego. This primitive *sensory* superego seems, at least sometimes, to be the personification of pain that has become "stuck in the machine". This pain is amplified by the hatred, frustration, and shame of helplessness and vulnerability that greets an unprotected "felt-self" as it risks making emotional contact with another.

Clinical experience suggests a link between the presence of a "wilfully misunderstanding" ego destructive internal object (what Bion calls an Obstructive Object (Eaton, 2011)) and its possible origins as an outgrowth of a primitive sensory superego. The Obstructive Object relentlessly threatens to amplify the pain if it is not immediately extinguished. This is also linked to a scenario of ego-destructive shame (Eaton, 2021).

A sensory superego's imperative to minimise or extinguish pain leads to an unconscious value system that ranges from refusal of all experience to adherence to power, perfectionism, and control. There is a hair-trigger hatred of vulnerability and of shame which is felt to be ego destructive. This violent organising attitude tries to substitute for the absent realisation of maternal and paternal reverie and for a real container–contained relationship by dominating experience to create order, predictability, and sensory equilibrium.

Some of Martin's use of language demonstrates the need to control sensation and rid himself of awareness of experiences of pain. Martin had a concrete sensation-dominated use of language that he deployed almost adhesively, repeating favourite narratives over and over.

For example, early in our work Martin would want to tell me about a cartoon episode he had watched. He did not summarise the content. Instead, he recreated, line by line, the episode so that his narration would take twenty or thirty minutes to perform. If I interrupted him, he would become angry and start over from the beginning.

There was a significant communication of distress which I received in my countertransference through projective identification. I understood his repeated narrative as erasing his awareness of my presence as a potential predator. Only after he had erected a wall of sensation-dominated words and images could he allow himself to be fleetingly curious about me.

I gradually came to understand that I needed to tolerate this way of being together and not try to modify it until much later when Martin began to seek my contributions. The sensation-dominated use of words and images seemed to protect him, organise him, and even gratify Martin. It provided a sensory barrier to the anticipation of impingement from others or the outside world. As Martin developed trust in me, this kind of use of language waned, but was always available to return to under stress.

In addition to using language to create autistic barriers, at other times Martin used language as a way of escaping into or intruding into concrete sensory-dominated images. This kind of escape or intrusion involved intrusive projective identification but was still highly sensory-dominated. Martin also had a competent and compliant way of using language when he decided to co-operate at home, at school, or with me. All these different uses of language could be detected as constantly shifting at different times within a single session according to the unconscious level of threat Martin seemed to detect.

Martin's concrete sensation-dominated set of images and words gradually began to transform and develop as he allowed more interaction with me. In one session, I commented on Martin's use of language. I said, "There are times, Martin, when you speak to me and I feel like a person. I feel there is something you want me to know and understand about you. In those moments, I feel you are using words to build a bridge to me. At other times, I feel you are using words to build a wall between us, to keep me out. And, sometimes I feel like I don't even exist, that you are using words to create a cozy sensation that makes you forget that either one of us is really a person."

Martin was quiet. He looked directly into my eyes and held my gaze for an extended time. Later in the week Martin's mother left me a voice mail saying, "Whatever you talked about really impacted him. He has been telling his father and me about words and how they can be used as walls or bridges. He really feels like he has discovered something. It is exciting to see. He can't stop talking about it."

With the expansion of his language use Martin slowly began to discover the capacity to feel his own feelings more deeply and to communicate about them with me and his parents. The next two pictures (year five of therapy) show first the explosiveness of his feelings and then the complexity of his experience. The first drawing (Figure 9.4) is called "Someone swallowed a bomb!" and the second (Figure 9.5) is untitled.

Figure 9.4 "Someone swallowed a bomb!"

As Martin began to get in touch with his emotions, he went through a few months of violent meltdowns both in his sessions and at home. I had several emergency phone calls from his parents saying that he would only talk to me. He would get on the phone and scream "Jeff, help me, please, I'm dying." These were terribly difficult interchanges. Martin's emotions were literally raw screams of pain. Though I was not sure, I thought this movement was part of a breakthrough, rather than a breakdown.

Martin was now *feeling* his "felt-self", that which was before, below, or beyond language. I believe that Martin was becoming embodied and feeling his emotions and anxieties in completely new ways. These were emergences from the level of the "felt-self" that needed to be recognised, tolerated, welcomed, patterned, imagined, felt, and described together.

Martin's parents were heroic in their ability to tolerate and work with him during this period. Martin's mother recognised that something important was happening and that he was coming alive emotionally. She had the idea to tape giant pieces of blank paper on Martin's bedroom walls so that he could draw the flood of feelings that were emerging from him.

Martin spent many hours making murals on his bedroom walls. Sometimes his mother would call or email me because she was disturbed by the violent images Martin was creating. My attitude was to receive this information to "hold" mother's anxiety so that she could remain curious and supportive about what was emerging for Martin. Martin knew that I was learning about some of these images and he felt free to tell me about what he was drawing. Eventually there were even a handful of family sessions to help process of the violence of the images as a group.

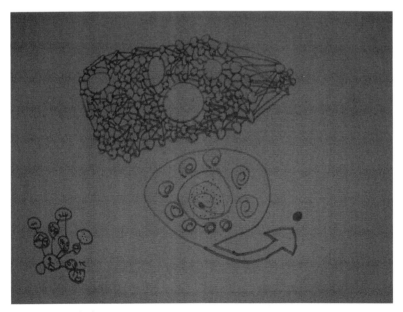

Figure 9.5 Untitled

Though this drawing was untitled, it could be called "from a point to the universe". Martin explained that the point represents himself. Here is how his narrative about the drawing unfolded. Martin explained that he gets sucked into a portal and is taken through multiple universes and does not know when or how he will get out. He also said that he does not know where he will end up when he is out. This gives a sense of the profound disorientation that can be experienced when emerging into a shared relational field.

In the corner of the drawing, an image of a person who is connected to various objects can be seen. Martin said this represents his new perceptions of himself after emerging from the portal. In his own words, the structure at the top represents his discovery of the connections between his thoughts, memories, feelings, wishes, and desires. He calls this long phase of emerging "my awakening". Clearly one of the most important themes is that emerging into a field of persons, emotions, and links is a journey of enormous complexity.

After I had emotionally comprehended something about Martin's communication, then I could try and to describe, from the inside out, some of my own experience of the meaning or significance of the drawing and its impact. So, for example, regarding the previous drawing, I said things like "It's so immense. It is like discovering one universe after another. They are all so full of feelings and emotions. It's almost more than one person can stand. It's an extraordinary journey." This way of speaking emphasised a shared experience and an unfolding process.

In the sixth year of therapy (age fifteen) Martin began to report dreams. Here is one of the dreams he brought: "There is a giant caterpillar inside an engine trying to find its way out. I shrink down to its same size so I can help it out. There's lots of dried blood on the sidewalk so I become like a detective in order to find out what's happened." He explained, upon waking: "I had a funny sensation, it was tingling, and it lasted all day."

I asked Martin what he thought about the dream. He said, "It was interesting." I said I thought that he was like the caterpillar looking for a way out and that he appreciates how I can shrink down to a size that allows me to have caterpillar thoughts to help him out. I said that I thought he was afraid something terrible had happened to leave all the blood on the ground. I said that instead of being afraid of the blood on the ground, we could find out together what it might mean.

Martin had tears in his eyes. I waited for a while and finally I said, "I can see you are feeling a lot. I wonder what you are feeling?"

Martin said, "I'm thinking about Tinkerbell."

I said, "From Peter Pan."

He said, "Yes."

Now he had tears running down his face.

I waited.

Finally, he said, "When Tinkerbell is hurt, you have to *believe* in order for her to get help."

Now he was silent for a long time. I have learned to allow children a lot of time to gather, process, and express their experience. Often, though they are not saying anything, they are using the time and space, "trying to think".

Finally, Martin said "I didn't know how to believe."

After a moment, I said, "Now you are finding your way out, and discovering a new kind of world. It's painful, but here you can feel connected and you can learn with others, like with me."

"That's right," says Martin.

In subsequent sessions a new theme emerged about confusion and connection. In one meeting Martin became goofy, smiling and shivering. I asked him what was going on. He sang a nonsense song about a cow named Lula Bell. I said I thought that his silliness showed how excited he was about something, but it also created a strong distraction from being able to communicate about his feelings. I said I wondered if he used silliness sometimes as an escape route from feelings, especially when he was in the presence of another person.

Martin told me that some cartoons are made to hypnotise the viewer. I said that we had talked a lot about how lost he could become in silly cartoons. But, I said, I have another idea now. I wondered if Martin was worried about me and whether I was trying to hypnotise him. It might be, I said, that when he feels I understand him, that I can somehow see directly into his mind, and this would give me a scary amount of power over him if it was true.

Martin quickly admitted that in his imagination he wanted to be able to control other people, especially other's minds. He said, "I know it's not real, but I still think it should be." He said, "Ever since I was little, I have wanted to do things my way, like I was a king who could do anything he wanted to anyone." I said that he probably wanted unlimited power and that whenever he approached a limit this made him enormously frustrated. This, I said, was an important source of why he often said things felt so unfair to him.

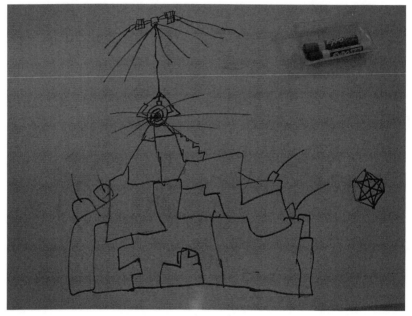

Figure 9.6 Untitled

Martin explained that there was a satellite in the sky that sends signals to a machine to control everyone in a town (Figure 9.6). It takes a lot of power to run this machine, Martin said. It has lots of gears and wires. I told Martin that I thought that the machine was like a part of his mind. I said that the actions that control things are his thoughts. I said that he was worried about who was controlling whom and that being in a relationship felt like it was a battle for control.

What followed were a series of productive sessions where Martin was able to talk much more realistically about his worries at home and in school. He was able to make links between living too much in his imagination and having to face his anxieties about homework, about his mother and father and their "influencing feelings", and about how his worries can spoil things for him.

Martin and I made a list of his worries together:

1. the pain of not being able to always have things your way
2. the feeling that frustration will make you shatter
3. the constant temptation to distraction
4. the fear of competition
5. shame at feeling a lack of confidence
6. envy of other kids who know how to "socialise" easily
7. the problem of getting lost in your imagination
8. feeling out of control when your body goes crazy
9. fear and guilt over wanting to hurt others and make them feel pain
10. feeling trapped in obsessive thinking
11. embarrassment when you can't think of anything to say
12. shame at being focused only on things you know that you like
13. shame at not really being interested in what other people think
14. aggravation that you have so little patience
15. sadness and fear about having to grow up and leave the past behind
16. worry that the world is unsafe and you are not prepared to be in it
17. terror and disgust over emerging sexuality.

Now Martin began to earnestly symbolise a background catastrophe that I think had origins in a primitive infantile "felt-self." The problem of forming and sustaining relationships was documented in a drawing that he named "The 100 obstacles" (Figure 9.7).

This drawing emerged after some emotional sessions where Martin was consciously reflecting upon the pain of feeling alienated from his peers. He was frustrated and sad that he did not feel able to naturally talk to others. He felt other teens were not interested in the same things he liked. I took his report up both as information about the transference, but also as testimony of real pain about his actual interpersonal desires and challenges.

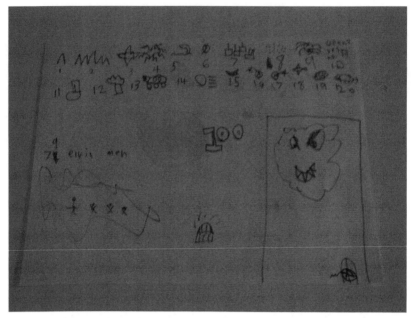

Figure 9.7 The 100 obstacles

A key to "the 100 obstacles"

1 spike, 2 pit of spikes, 3 block of spikes, 4 thunder cloud of doom, 5 giant wave, 6 evil eye that shoots lasers, 7 pounders of doom, 8 mob of mosquitoes, 9 giant tarantula, 10 the door of questions, 11 giant foot, 12 giant hand, 13 army tank, 14 rolling boulder, 15 mouth that wants to eat you, 16 atomic bomb, 17 hydrogen bomb, 18 fighter plane, 19 poisonous gas, 20 poisonous lizard + 79 evil men + your worst nightmare

"What is your worst nightmare?" I asked Martin.

He replied, "An evil cloud of dust. You must face your worst fear. A door opens, and you can't get away. The door leads you … to home."

I feel that the evil cloud of dust represents the bodily feeling of an "insult to the senses".

There is an open door to experience, but it involves the risk of having to tolerate an "insult to the senses" at the unconscious background level of a "felt-self". The question of what home means is complicated by the level of a fragile bodily self.

Martin said, "I wish I didn't have autism." I said, "I wonder if you are going through a door right now and facing your worst fear. You are afraid that if we talk about this it is like inviting a disaster to happen." After being quiet for some time, Martin said he was thinking about a colour map and how if you can mix certain colours together then you can change them.

Look at the variety of "the 100 obstacles" that Martin portrays. They all involve sensations at the level of the "felt-self". All the sensory modalities are represented: skin and body (spikes and mosquitoes); hearing (thunder cloud of doom); vision (lasers); affective intensities (bombs); smell (poison gas). Here is a remarkable unconscious attempt to symbolise a sensory floor for experience at the level of an unconscious "felt-self" that always is active in the background of experience.

Concluding thoughts

A child's unconscious use of sensation can be a way of avoiding the intimidating challenge of learning how to think, feel, and communicate with others. But, additionally, it seems important to appreciate how for some children sensation can be disorganising and part of a background of unprocessed emotional catastrophe at the level of a "felt-self".

I have tried to offer a glimpse of one boy's progress, as well as introduce an evolving model that helps to organise some of the data of experience at the level of what Tustin called a "felt-self". In trying to understand an insult to the senses at the level of a "felt-self", I suggest we investigate the experience of primitive awareness rather than consciousness. Beta elements *are* experiences registered by awareness. They are not felt as having psychical qualities or meanings and they cannot be repressed. They are experiences of "too muchness" at the level of awareness that require access to the containing attention and reverie of another.

By focusing on awareness, I am emphasising that even in autistic states there is experience at the level of the "felt-self" that must be closely attended to. This experience is complex. It is often profoundly sensation dominated. That is why I want to introduce the question "what is the fate of sensation?" As we get to know each child in the analytic process, we begin to appreciate the complexity of states of mind that each child is living through. There are many small moments when transformation is possible if we can witness and describe them.

References

Bion, W. R. (1962). *Learning from Experience*. London: Heinemann.

Eaton, J. L. (2011). The obstructive object. In: *A Fruitful Harvest: Essays after Bion*. Seattle: The Alliance Press.

Eaton, J. L. (2014). Building a floor for experience: a model for thinking about children's experience. In: N. Tracey (Ed.), *Transgenerational Trauma and the Aboriginal Preschool Child: Healing Through Intervention*. New York: Rowan & Littlefield.

Eaton, J. L. (2021). On caesura, temporality, and ego destructive shame: Ominous transitions in everyday life. In: L. Hinton & H. Willemsen (Eds.), *Temporality, Shame, and Social Crisis: Ominous Transitions*. London: Routledge.

Meltzer, D. (1990). *The Claustrum: An Investigation of Claustrophobic Phenomena*. London: Karnac.

Mitrani, J. (1996). *A Framework for the Imaginary: Clinical Explorations in Primitive States of Being*. Northvale, NJ: Jason Aronson.

Symington, J. (1985). The survival function of primitive omnipotence. *International Journal of Psychoanalysis*, 66: 481–487.

Tustin, F. (1981). *Autistic States in Children*. London: Routledge.

Tustin, F. (1986). *Autistic Barriers in Neurotic Patients*. New Haven, CT: Yale University Press.

CHAPTER TEN

The mute voice: autistic enclaves and transgenerational transmission

Suzanne Maiello

The Austrian author, Ingeborg Bachmann, ends her novel, *Malina* (1971), with a lucid description of an irresistible pull towards autistic isolation, accompanied by the breakdown of senses, one after the other, and the ultimate loss of the very basis of relatedness, the preconception of linking:

> I look at Malina fixedly, but he does not look up. ... I have moved to the wall,[1] I move into the wall, I hold my breath. ... The wall opens up. I am inside the wall, and Malina will see nothing but a crack, the crack that we have seen for a long time. He will think that I have left the room. ... Something is in the wall, it can no longer scream, and yet it screams. Malina looks

---

[1] The German language uses two different words for "wall": "Mauer" mostly designates the external wall of a building; "Wand" refers to an internal wall which separates two rooms. The original German text refers to a "Wand". It is likely that the end of Bachmann's novel was inspired by another Austrian writer, Marlen Haushofer, whose novel *Die Wand* describes the experience of a woman who is unexpectedly trapped behind and, at the same time, protected by a glass wall.

around meticulously, he sees everything, but he no longer hears … Footsteps, Malina's incessant steps, fading, disappearing. Standstill. No alarm, no sirens. Nobody coming to rescue. … It is a very old wall, a very solid wall, from which nobody can fall, and which nobody can break open. No sound will come from it ever again.

At the beginning of this last scene, the "I", a woman, tries desperately to remain hooked with her eyes on the man, Malina. He does not look up. The visual connection is lost. The woman seems to move backwards towards the wall, in a last attempt to see, to be seen and called back. Malina does not hold her back. She disappears in the wall and stops breathing: the basic rhythm of life, inspiration and expiration, is gone. This is psychic death. Malina does not notice any change. He checks the inanimate objects in the room. She, the alive other, disappeared, but remains unnoticed. The formerly needy "I", the *somebody* with her desperate need to cling to a relationship, to be seen and heard, turns into an inanimate *something*. She and the crack have become one. Malina does not hear the mute cries from inside the wall. He is deaf. Both the visual and the auditory connections are lost. Finally, Malina's footsteps become weaker and weaker until they disappear altogether. As if a heart stopped beating. The last witness of pulsating life is gone.

Introduction: a phenomenology of autistic states

Autistic states are characterised by the absence or loss of the inborn capacity of all living beings to create links, at both the interpersonal and intrapsychic level. Some infants seem to be autistic already at birth. They do not actively search for new connections with the unknown external world, into which they have just been catapulted. Birth is the most radical caesura of our lives. It involves the transition from the primary intrauterine container with its characteristics of continuity of nutrition and temperature with its rhythmical background of mother's heartbeat, into a potentially limitless world of unknown light, noises, and unforeseeable ruptures. Mother's breasts, her holding arms, her eyes, and her voice represent the first objects needed by the newborn baby for his psycho-physical survival. When the normal infant latches onto the nipple and sucks, it contributes actively to the first co-operative act of reconnection after being thrown out into postnatal space. The very act of sucking brings about a rhythmical experience of *con-centration*, which counteracts the potential panic of dispersion in the vastness of the new environment. Sucking implies not only a firm circular organisation of the infant's lips, tongue, and palate around the nipple, but is an intrinsically three-dimensional act, a pulling *inside*, followed by swallowing, and finally by letting go at the end of the feed. Incorporation constitutes the ground plan of a dynamic connection between container and contained, with its mental counterpart of internalisation and introjection.

The encounter between mouth and nipple may be seen as the first postnatal realisation of the preconception of linking. This means that experiencing and tolerating two-ness, even for brief moments, represents a powerful motivation for the reconstitution of the primary experience of containment. Mouth and nipple, container and contained, united in a co-operative relationship, reinforce the experience of the external/internal restoration of the primal unity at a dynamic interpersonal level. By definition, container and contained need three-dimensional space to exist. This is true not only at a concrete level of bodily reality, but has become a creative metaphor for psychic functioning and mental activity.

Being held in mother's arms and sucking at the breast reconstitutes temporarily not only the state of containment at the level of tactile experience of contiguity. At the same time, the baby's distal senses of seeing and hearing take in mother's mobile facial expressions, the light of her eyes as well as her voice, which was the prenatal infant's intermittent companion and primary messenger of otherness long before birth (Maiello, 1995). In normal development, connections and reconnections, repetitions and variations occur at all sensuous levels and represent the indispensable nourishment for the development of a mental container able to create, combine, and weave emotional links, thus building the capacity to think thoughts in evermore complex combinations of memory and anticipation.

An infant who is autistic from birth may have shown signs of withdrawal already during prenatal life (Maiello, 2001). In autistic states, all channels of communication between the external and the internal world are severed. The senses of seeing and hearing are neutralised, because, by bridging an undeniable physical distance, they inevitably evoke the gap between me and not-me. Autistic children, as well as adults, avoid eye contact, and young children are often thought to be deaf, because they do not respond to another person's call. The sense of smell is likened to the proximal senses of touch and taste, which require direct contact, thus by-passing any perception of discontinuity as well as any need for bridging a distance. In autism, distance is experienced as a fathomless abyss, into which the fragile self would precipitate. If containment is not continuous, it is dangerous. The container might not be reliably tight and might have openings, orifices, doors, windows, through which the fragile self could fall endlessly and die. Annihilation anxieties are unbearable. They are the catastrophic version of normal separation anxieties.

The most radical way of escaping the danger of precipitating into nothingness is to flatten the psychic life-space by eliminating the third dimension of psycho-physical functioning and experience altogether. In a two-dimensional world, there is no space for anxieties, but at a high price: projective and introjective processes need a three-dimensional psychic reality to operate. If they are eliminated, all emotional and cognitive experiences are frozen. With the elimination of all that is *not me*, that is, of all manifestations of otherness, the perception of an existing me, of "I"-ness, is eliminated as well. This is why thinking of autistic functioning in terms of the attempt to assimilate any "not-me"-object to a "me"-object does not fully reach the fathomless abyss of autistic states. In fact, by eliminating the other's otherness, my own potential "I"-ness is automatically erased as well.

In *Malina*, the *somebody* who disappeared in the wall becomes a *something*, an inanimate object, and ultimately a *no-thing*. Malina thought that the woman had left the room, implying that she had gone into *another* room. Rooms are by definition three-dimensional, and Ingeborg Bachmann still refers to three-dimensional space when she writes that *somebody* is *inside* the wall. But when the *somebody* has become a *something* and coincides with the crack itself, it dawns upon the reader that there is no *other* room, no container *into* which the former "I" could have escaped. A similar move occurs in the temporal dimension. At the beginning of psycho-physical life, the basic experience of time is structured by rhythmic events, which, if safely introjected, will make the exploration of variations and of linear time not only possible, but enjoyable. In *Malina*, the former "I" holds her breath, as Malina's footsteps become weaker and weaker until they disappear altogether. The rhythmic ground plan of all that is living, the act of breathing and the heartbeat, are gone. No space, no time. What is left is *nothingness*, and a muted cry.

Meltzer (1975) introduced the notion of what he described as two- and one-dimensional mental functioning in autistic states. Tustin (1990) further explored the consequences of the breakdown of any dynamic relation between *container* and *contained*, which, in Bion's terms, represents the prerequisite for the development of the capacity for thinking thoughts and experiencing emotional links between thinkable elements (1962). How can psychoanalytic theory deepen our understanding of mental states which have collapsed into two-dimensional flatness, which excludes by definition any experience of dynamic movement in space and time? How can the two systems communicate? "The potential of three-dimensional functioning … is the *conditio sine qua non* both for the experience of separation and separateness, with its wide range of emotions, and for the development of symbolic thinking (Maiello, 2017). We need three-dimensional mental functioning for the exploration of the two- and one-dimensional world of autism. This is the challenge of working with autistic patients.

The *crack* that results from the collapse of relatedness is unable to produce and communicate any experience or thought. The final result of *Malina*'s woman who had gone *into* the wall and disappeared *in* the wall is that, ultimately, she and the wall and the crack have become one and the same meaningless inanimate two-dimensional shape. Without the patients' fantasies, their projective and introjective identifications, the corollary of persecutory anxieties, analysts are deprived of one of the main sources for understanding patients' mental states, and for nourishing their countertransferential response. This is true not only for patients in deep autistic states, but also for autistic parts in the personalities of non-autistic patients. In psychoanalytic literature these inaccessible parts are described as autistic barriers, autistic pockets, autistic encapsulations, autistic enclaves, or autistic shells (Tustin, 1986, 1990). All these notions evoke three-dimensional shapes:

the barrier delimitates two separate areas in space; the other concepts describe three-dimensional objects which contain contents that have been locked away from the patient's awareness. It seems that we do need three-dimensional metaphors for thinking and exchanging images and thoughts. A two-dimensional mind can neither think nor feel nor communicate. This is the challenge when working with, and exchanging among colleagues, clinical experiences with autistic patients or patients with autistic enclaves.

Prisoner in an autistic enclave:[2] Joe

A mute voice

Joe was thirty-seven years old when he came for analysis, shortly after leaving his wife and four-year-old daughter. He was unable to give any precise reason for abandoning his family. He was a slim, smart-looking, and very tall man. When I opened the door to let him in for the first time, I looked up at him, but our eyes did not meet as he walked past me swiftly, following my indications to the room. It felt as if his eyes were the headlights of a fast-running car. During the exploratory sessions, he managed to shun any encounter of our eyes. There did not seem to be any active avoidance of eye contact, nor any looking "through me". He was simply tall enough to look straight at the wall above my head as he spoke swiftly.

What struck me was the contrast between his precise biographical information, formulated in articulated sequences, and the tone of his voice. The voice is the carrier of a speaking person's oral communication, but its tone, its variation in volume, pitch, and rhythm, communicates more about the emotional state of the speaker than the semantic content of the verbal communication itself. Joe's language was articulate, but it was as if his words were not carried by his voice, which was not hollow, nor did it come from far away. If it had conveyed a feeling of distance, it could at least have communicated the patient's fear of emotional closeness. But his voice felt as if it was on its own, with nobody

---

[2] The title of the history of this adult patient's analysis once more bears witness to the impossibility of thinking, speaking, and writing in a two-dimensional mental state: a prisoner is inside a prison, and an enclave is placed inside a given territory.

to produce it: toneless, shapeless, bodyless. I was haunted by my association with Spitz' description of institutionalised infants who stopped crying in their state of primary anaclitic depression, having lost any hope ever to be heard and rescued. Some of those babies ultimately died of emotional starvation (1945).

During the thirteen years of Joe's analysis, I had often to lean forward to catch his words, as they seemed to dissolve in the air the very moment they were pronounced. Joe thought that, like most people, I was hard of hearing. Malina no longer hears the no-voice of the woman who can no longer cry out. It felt as if Joe's *no-voice* did not actively cancel his words the moment they were uttered, they were just dropped and disappeared. Nothing seemed to be left in the end, and his sophisticated verbal formulations ultimately became *no-things*, which arrived from *no-where*.

Joe was convinced that he had been born prematurely and had spent the first part of his life in an incubator. His mother, however, denied this. Her story was that he had been born only three weeks before term, with a natural, though difficult forceps delivery, but she confirmed that when he was two months old, she had to go back to work and left the baby in her mother's care until he was two years old. Whatever the biographical facts of the beginning of Joe's life were, I was left to think about the abysmal solitude of pre-term infants in their incubators. Infant observation in intensive care units has shown how they move their tiny arms and legs, as if searching for a containing boundary. There are moments when their mouths are wide open as if they are crying, but no voice reaches the observer. Do the glass walls prevent their weak cries from reaching the distant human being on the other side of the divide, or do these almost skinless babies not yet have the strength to voice their distress? Joe's mental state of isolation and not-belonging seemed to be connected with an experience of "premature mental birth" (Tustin, 1986) and with the ensuing impossibility of filling the gap of the caesura of birth. There had been an event in Joe's family history which needs to be mentioned here, although it came to the fore much later in the patient's analysis: Joe's mother spent the first nine years of her life in an orphanage. The mother's mother was only sixteen when the baby was born. The shameful event had to be hidden and silenced, together with the identity of the baby's father, Joe's biological grandfather, who was to remain a persecutory ghost throughout the patient's analysis.

In later years, when Joe had become capable of projecting his mute despair into the transference relationship, I occasionally felt an almost irresistible impulse to urge him to shout or to scream, because, together with his hopelessness around the possibility of being heard and of bridging the distance in the transference relationship, I felt that he also kept at bay any risk of betraying the silenced traumatic family secret.

Rotatory language and the loss of the basic rhythm of life

In seeming opposition to his mute voice, the structure of Joe's verbal language was elaborate and sophisticated, and there was often a complacent and seductive quality to it. He was very successful in his writing profession. However, not having completed his university studies—much to his own surprise, since he had been a top student throughout primary and secondary school—he could not proceed any further in his professional career. It became clear over time that the interruption of his academic studies was connected with an unresolved conflict with his father who had come from a modest family and had to earn his living from a young age.

Joe felt that throughout his life, he had been running at high speed, but he had no idea of any goal that he would have wanted to reach, nor of any fearful experience from which he might need to escape. Neither desire nor persecutory anxieties seemed to be the driving forces of his hectic activity. Its ruminating quality was expressed by the circular use of verbal language. He used to put in sequence several almost synonymous substantives or adjectives to describe one and the same thing. His seeming intention was to get as closely as possible to some central meaning of any thought that he apparently tried to formulate, but his unconscious aim was not communication, but control over his own and the analyst's thoughts and words. The goal of his verbal wrapping was the wrapping itself, which ultimately led to the risk of "pseudo-insight, pseudo-communication, pseudo-analysis (Tustin, 1990, p. 210). There was no *nutshell*. If there had seemed to be one, it was empty. Meltzer connects this use of language with a cryptic masturbatory activity (1965), in which excitement replaces emotions and controls anxiety. At the level of autistic functioning, Joe's rotatory language was the result of what Resnik describes in terms of "rotatory thinking, which preserves autistic circularity" (2004, 2006, p. 7).

Over time, it became clear that the ultimate goal of Joe's defensive use of language was the need to hide the abyss of *nothingness* from his own and others' awareness. Tustin describes the analyst's difficulties when we try to reach hidden encapsulated parts of the personality of adult patients: "It seems as if a terror-stricken, frozen bit of them had been left behind and covered over in their struggle to grow up and to cope with life" (1990, p. 146). She referred to Winnicott's statement that "the clinical fear of breakdown is the fear of a breakdown that has already been experienced. It is the fear of the original agony which caused the defence organisation" (1974, p. 176). "The breakdown", Tustin adds, "is experienced by an infant who, in an immature state of neuromental development, becomes aware of his bodily separateness (1990, p. 146). This is where Joe's belief that he had been a prematurely born infant originated.

Much later in his analysis, Joe was to tell me that since his childhood he had needed to monitor that his heart continued to beat, because if he forgot to check, it would stand still and he would die. His internal maternal object seemed to be too weak to watch over and guarantee the continuity of her infant's basic rhythms of life. The prenatal infant's auditory and vibratory experience of mother's heartbeat forms the archaic part of the *sound object*, the prenatal precursor of the infant's postnatal maternal internal object (Maiello, 1995). In autistic states, this very foundation of the basic trust in living life seems to have broken down. Tustin describes her "heartbroken" patients by saying that "their 'heartbreak' goes beyond what we usually mean by the term. The feeling of brokenness goes into the very fabric of their being ... For these patients bodily awareness of their separateness had been experienced as an interruption to the pulsing rhythm of their 'going-on-being'" (1990, p. 156).

Malina's footsteps became weaker and weaker until they disappeared altogether, as if a heart had stopped beating. The last witness of pulsating life was gone.

In Joe's analysis, I felt "captured and prevented from working by the patient's encapsulating manoeuvres" (Tustin, 1990, p. 210), which were to prevent the breakdown of the basic rhythms of life. My countertransference sensations were of saturation and suffocation, accompanied by the paralysing idea that at the centre of the patient's spider web there was no prey that he could at least have fed on, but just *nothing*, the autistic void. The combination of Joe's mute voice and his endless circular ruminations provoked an almost irresistible sleepiness. However, although his words tried to cover and hide rather than to communicate, the high descriptive precision of his verbal language did allow us gradually to get a glimpse of his mental state of unexpressed despair. The analyst's ears must try to capture the harmonics above and below the autistic patients' protective formulations. With Joe, I had to reach out beyond both the flatness of his voice and the seductive fireworks of his verbal language in the endeavour to get closer to the core of his silenced despair.

Absence of dream life

During the first five years of his analysis, Joe not only never brought a dream to his sessions, but it seemed that he actually did not dream, or that any access to the realm of ongoing unconscious "dream-work" (Bion, 1992) was barred. Tustin writes: "In such patients, cognitive and affective development seems to have taken place by bypassing a 'blind spot' of arrested development which then becomes a capsule of autism in the depths of their personality" (1986, p. 216). Tustin also uses the term "autistic enclave"[3] to describe the radicality with which emotional contents are sealed off, locked away and rendered inaccessible to self and others.

In Meltzer's terms (1975), autistic two-dimensional or even one-dimensional psychic states result from the breakdown of a containing mental space, in which both conscious and unconscious memories, including dreams, are stored in normal mental development. There is no longer any *other* room, *into* which, as Malina imagined, the woman who disappeared could have gone. She and the wall coincide in a two-dimensional psychic state which results from an existential emotional breakdown.

---

[3] The French term *enclave* describes a territory, which is entirely enclosed, literally locked away with a key.

However, in the course of our long analytic journey, the day came when Joe began to wonder why he never had any dreams like other people. At first, his interest in his own potential to produce dreams seemed triggered more by envious curiosity than by genuine interest in his own nocturnal mental activity. One day he bought a tiny notebook, which, as he told me, he placed on the side table near his bed, together with a pen, in case he woke up from a dream. He did in fact begin to dream and wrote what his memory had retained, in the middle of the night, before falling asleep again. He had noticed with surprise that he dreamt only when his young daughter spent the night at his home or when one of his rapidly changing woman lovers shared his bed. It seemed that even for dreaming he needed to feed on the unconscious psychic life of other human beings. Yet, he had begun to be interested in himself and motivated to observe his mental doings.

When he came to his sessions in that period, his hand reached for the notebook in his pocket already on his way to the analytic couch. He used to lie down, search for the right page, and immediately try to decipher his nocturnal scribbles, spelling syllable by syllable of the handwritten text with his toneless voice, in the attempt to find some meaning in the graphic signs. He never revisited the dreams in his notebook before the session, and, most of the time, his efforts to read his own handwriting were in vain. He might recognise a few words, but these only rarely awakened any memory or association, and he was unable to connect them in a meaning-giving or meaning-retrieving way. He tried hard to put together a few pieces of the puzzle which could have led him to a dream narrative, but the signs in his notebook mostly remained alien to himself and felt like despairingly shapeless heaps of non-sense, rather than the result of potentially meaningful nocturnal dream-thoughts (Bion, 1959, 1992). His strenuous, but useless efforts often left me in a state of hopelessness, but at the same time in awe of his endurance.

When young children learn to read, they will proudly pronounce a word or sentence which, after the effort of uniting letters, makes sense. They will discover, at deep unconscious levels, that they are learning to complete the prodigious cycle of which the human mind is capable: dreaming, seeing, hearing, storing images and sounds, combining them, thinking thoughts, learning the signs of the alphabet for their transformation into words and into a written text, and finally reading and recognising the initial dream, enriched by their mental creativity, in a continuous cycle of discovery of new worlds and enrichment of earlier experiences.

When Joe abandoned his efforts to decipher his dream notes, it was because they had not brought back any echo or memory. His scribbles remained scribbles even to himself and lay in his notebook like inanimate objects which would not come to life again. This highly educated patient's alienation from himself was immensely painful to witness, but he insisted on scribbling and reading, session after session. It may have dawned on him at that point that he could bring the lifeless debris of his dreams to the analytic "toilet breast" (Meltzer, 1965) and leave them with me, although, and maybe even *because*, they were felt to be rubbish. From the point of view of psychic functioning, it meant that three-dimensionality was on the way and that projective and introjective processes had begun. From Joe's point of view, it dawned on him that the analytic space could be used in ways which he had not anticipated.

Running in circles—the desperate search for containment

In the fifth year of analysis, Joe had started bringing dreams to his sessions without necessarily consulting his notebook anymore, although he took it out of his pocket before lying down, holding it tight and putting it back only at the end of the session. It had become a sort of transitional object, the guarantee of his capacity to remember. This is one of his first remembered dreams:

> He was at a gym and ran in circles, anti-clockwise, holding a little boy's hand. It was a running competition with many participants. He and the little boy ran very fast, skilfully overtaking other runners. In the middle of the gym space there was a large hole in the floor. On the external side of the running track, there were two stalls, an infirmary and a food-and-drink stall. His two paternal aunts were in charge of them. However, he could not afford to stop, because he needed to win the race. But in passing he asked the aunts whether they knew the child's name. They said: "Angelo", but on a later passage, they corrected themselves and said: "Angela".

The dream was an important turning point in Joe's analysis. In the dimension of space, time, and movement, the dreamer was no longer totally isolated from his split-off infantile self, but held a little boy's hand. He was still running and highly competitive, but for the first time he saw the hole in the middle of the floor, the empty core of his mental life. Tustin's little autistic patient John's terror or the black hole (1972) appeared in the dream, and I was reminded of the tremendous attracting energy of astronomic black holes, which suck into nothingness any celestial body that comes too close to their orbit. Running in circles allowed Joe defensively to continue competing with his rivals and confirming his narcissistic superiority. But now that the central hole had become visible, running also meant counteracting the terror of precipitating into the abyss of three-dimensional mental space. The other side of the coin was that the need to continue to run did not allow him to receive nourishment and care from the two maternal figures who were waiting outside the circular running track.

In the dream, Joe not only created a connection with another human being by holding a little boy's hand, but asked his aunts for the child's name, which he himself did not know. Omniscience, which had been an important part of his defensive organisation, was beginning to leak. Curiosity around someone's identity was awakening, and his dream aunts gave him not only one, but two clues: two keys, which gave him access to unknown territory, his own and his mother's early histories. In fact, Angela was his mother's name. In those early years, newborn babies who were abandoned at an orphanage were given the name of Angelo or Angela, little angels who had fallen from heaven and were looked after by nuns. He knew about his mother's abandonment at birth, but the aunts seemed to have recognised that he had been an "Angelo" child himself, abandoned, as he continued to believe, in an incubator and then left in his grandmother's care for the first two years of his life.

Joe's uncontained-infant part, his internal Angelo, began to search for experiences of containment which were not self-produced like his exhausting autistic running in circles.

One day he came to his session puzzled by what had happened the day before. He had visited an art exhibition with works by Henri Matisse and had been fascinated by one of his paintings: *La danse*. There was something more than fascination, he said. He had felt a physical pull and was literally sucked into that famous piece of art. He went into great detail describing his feeling of utter bliss at being *inside* not only one, but two frames—the solid external rectangular frame of the painting *and* the mobile circle of the dancing figures who moved in freedom, yet holding each other's hands. In his ecstasy, he had lost the sense of time. When he became aware of his state, he felt unable to get out of the painting. He was stuck, utterly helpless and invaded by increasing anxiety. The bell rang to announce the closure of the gallery. Its sound, together with the preoccupied eyes of the guard, a young woman in uniform, ultimately pulled him out of his imprisonment in the painting.

Joe was in desperate search of a different kind of containment, both strong and solid, and rhythmically alive. This twofold primary existential need is described by Houzel with his notion of the bisexuality of the original container, with its firm paternal strength, and its soft maternal receptiveness (2005, 2007). For the first time, the patient had chosen an external object to contain him, although it was not yet a person but a reliable painting. He seemed to have been guided by the reawakening, at deep unconscious levels, of the preconception of a container in search of a positive realisation (Bion, 1962). The powerful unconscious attraction that had sucked him into the dancers' circle may be seen in relation with his traumatic early deprivation rather than in terms of an intrusion into his internal maternal object. In fact, his deeply aesthetic experience (Meltzer, 1988) was permeated by an unknown emotional intensity.

However, in the end the blissful feeling of containment inside the living dancers' circle, which may well have evoked unconscious memory traces of prenatal life, had turned into the anxiety of remaining trapped in what had become an encircling prison. He had needed the help of another person, the guardian, who had performed some sort of a midwife's job by accompanying him and sustaining the process of separation from the mother's body. Joe's unexpected experience of entering *into* a space and coming *out* of it again, with another human being's help, showed that, in terms of his mental functioning, projective identification had begun. This was reflected in the emergence of unknown overwhelming emotions connected with both primary containment and its loss, and accompanied by anxieties related to imprisonment and abandonment, separation, and solitude.

Malina had neither seen nor heard the woman who had disappeared in the wall. No trace of her was left except for the crack, which had always been there. In Joe's story, a *guardian* had heard his mute cry, seen his helplessness, had freed him from his prison and brought him back into a world of emotionally receptive and understanding human beings.

Emerging from the autistic enclave—desperate loneliness and disorientation

A dream of the same period revealed Joe's growing capacity to face desolate emotional states of loneliness, which he could now face for brief moments:

> He was in a sports palace, a huge arena surrounded by seats for thousands of people. There should have been a basketball match, but his team had left, and so had the audience. He was standing in the middle of the arena under a glass cupola, alone. The concrete walls all around were grey. There seemed to be no entrances nor exits, except for one small side door, which was half open. He went out. The landscape was barren.

Joe was now where the black hole had been in his earlier dream. No defensive running in circles any more. He had met and faced the desolate loneliness of his life in the prison of his autistic enclave. No team, no family, no fans, no competition, no victory, no defeat. Only the desolate reality of primary depression. Could the dream image be connected with a premature birth? The empty palace with the glass cupola and the concrete walls does evoke the image of an incubator with a tiny baby isolated in an inanimate container. His own lonely childhood may have resonated, as well as other elements of his earlier family history. Now, there was a way out, but the world outside was just as desolate as the internal space of the empty palace. Linear motion had become thinkable, but it involved facing distance and absence, feelings of existential despair, unbridgeable gaps between me and not me, and the discovery of the fragility of his sense of identity, as shown in another dream:

He was travelling on a train, but had forgotten the name of the railway station where his mother and his daughter were waiting for him. He was expected to contribute to giving them directions concerning his itinerary, but had no idea where he was, and his map did not correspond to where he seemed to be. He woke up in anguish.

In those months, Joe often came late to his sessions, because he did not remember where he had parked his car and wandered aimlessly in the streets of his neighbourhood in search of it.

However, both dreams represented another turning point in Joe's analysis. His autistic retreat, which had involved the breakdown of three-dimensional mental functioning, was no longer indispensable for his survival. As opposed to *Malina*'s prisoner, Joe was no longer flattened and at-one with a two-dimensional wall lacking any internal space, but had in fact gone into another room, not only surviving, but having the courage to face his barren emotional state. This was the time when the actual transference relationship started coming to life and Joe was able to accept nourishment and care, which was no longer produced by his own grandiosity or his parasitic narcissism. He had abandoned his earlier hectic promiscuous sexual life, which now felt repetitive and empty. His search for experiences of containment became central, and he dared to look for it in the transference relationship. At the beginning of his analysis, he had come to his sessions with meticulous punctuality, but now, after the period of loss of orientation when he arrived late, he tended to come ahead of his time and had to wait at the gate with feelings of hostility and intense jealousy towards the young woman who occupied the analytic space before him.

Family secrets—collusion with the conspiracy of silence

Joe had felt isolated and not belonging to anyone throughout his childhood. At school, his mind went blank when he should have written an essay. The empty whiteness of the sheet of paper in front of him gave him a feeling of inexplicable anguish. In the years of puberty, being already very tall, he had become a successful basketball player, but he recalled his distress during the endless coach trips to distant playing fields. While the other boys were chatting and joking, he was on his own. Throughout his adolescence, he spent his time at home in his room, reading and listening to music, isolated by his headphones. He hardly ever mentioned his two-year younger brother, nor his father.

Joe was twenty years old when his mother unloaded part of the family secret onto him, her firstborn son, a secret which she had never shared with anybody, not even his father, because she had feared at the time that, had she told him the truth about her infancy and childhood in the orphanage, he might have refused to marry her. When Joe's grandmother had married, her husband adopted her illegitimate daughter who was then released from the orphanage, changed her surname, and moved in with her mother and stepfather. Joe's wider family had been left to think that grandmother's husband was his mother's biological father. Nobody had ever questioned the nine-year gap between his mother's birth and grandmother's marriage, and enquired about the reason why the child should have been hidden for all those years. The blind spot of Joe's biological grandfather's identity remained blind, and he was expected to collude with the family *omertà*, the Mafia law which imposes silence and secrecy around its members' criminal enterprises. He complied.

Over time, it had become clear that part of his complex pathological defence organisation (Steiner, 1988, 1993) was in connection with the family secret. His rotatory thinking and language had not only protected himself from his internal autistic void, but was also used to prevent himself and others from the temptation to penetrate unnameable and unthinkable ghosts of his family history. He described his defence organisation lucidly as his "survival code", which included the implicit prohibition to explore the motives of the transgenerational silence of his maternal family. When his autistic enclave did not feel secure enough and annihilation anxieties threatened to submerge him, he used to escape into his omnipotent intellectual superiority or else into an overtly autistic state of immaterial lightness. He then felt like a helium balloon which hovered high above the ground and was in admiration of Virginia Woolf's capacity to "desubstantiate reality".

However, over time, it dawned on him that the conspiracy of silence exposed him to the risk of disappearing through what had seemed his safety valve. Pathological organisations, originally set up to avoid catastrophe, turn out to become a chronic catastrophe themselves (Segal, 1972). Joe's early experiences of emotional neglect and deprivation had undoubtedly contributed to his withdrawal into his autistic-like refuge, which was to protect him from the most primitive terrors of precipitating, but his autistic retreat was also connected with the cancelled pages of his family history, of which he had been a victim, just like his mother and his adolescent grandmother. In his adult years, he had chosen not only to comply with the family's *omertà*, but to collude with their secrecy. At this point in his analysis, Joe represented his ambiguous position in two dreams:

> He took part in a family celebration. It was a birthday party or a marriage. They were all together, sitting at a large lunch table in a pleasant place in the country-side. But underneath, in a cellar-room, there was a conspiratory meeting of dark men. They belonged to a gang, maybe the *Mafia*. They were putting together a criminal enterprise. The family was still banqueting upstairs, unaware of the presence of those men who at some point left unseen through a secret exit. Joe might have joined them.

* * *

> He was walking behind his mother and his grandmother in the street of his childhood home. A man in black was hidden behind the shutters of a window on an upper floor of the building behind him. The man who was a member of a gang of criminals pointed his gun and shot his mother and his grandmother in the back. The two women collapsed to the ground, but got to their feet again and continued to walk. They were ghost-like figures without real bodies. He wondered whether he should call the police, but the dream ended before he had made up his mind.

Throughout Joe's analysis, the family secret around his biological maternal grandfather's identity had been present in the background, but continued to be left unaddressed. He hated his family for their conspiracy of silence, but at the same time colluded with it. This was his dilemma: if he dared to search for the truth, he would be seen as a criminal who ruined pleasant family celebrations or shot his mother and grandmother in the back. If he didn't, he continued to comply with the Mafia law of *omertà* and remained part of the ghost-like figures without real bodies whose common endeavour was to suppress and bury the unnameable truth around the author of his grandmother's puberal pregnancy. Joe was both jailor *and* prisoner of the conspiracy of silence.

Grandmother's death—emerging from the tomb of the family secret

Joe's grandmother died, well over ninety, during an analytic holiday. She was gone before he had had the courage to ask the crucial question of his grandfather's identity. He came back to his sessions feeling "frozen, like ice, or like cement, and empty". There was, he said, an "anonymous hole" inside him, which he was unable to describe in more detail. Bion's concept of nameless dread is connected with the impossibility to think, speak, and therefore name. Grandmother's secret had not been revealed, and grandfather remained nameless. However, Joe "knew" that grandmother's puberal pregnancy had been more than just the unforeseen result of a flirtation with a village boy, and that another more embarrassing family secret had been buried together with the baby who was to become his mother.

Since his grandmother's death, the patient said, he was sleeping "like a tombstone", at one with grandmother's cold deadness and her silenced truth. Upon my question whether he really felt to *be* a tombstone, he changed his formulation and said that actually he was *under* the tombstone. This was a meaningful shift. He *was* buried, but alive, and indirectly asked to be seen and heard and rescued from the cold weight of his prison. In Bachmann's novel, Malina's prisoner had turned from a *somebody* to a *something*. Joe could now dare to reverse the process and come to life, to look, observe and see, listen, hear and use his voice, hoping to be heard, and receiving emotional clues from his formerly buried distal senses.

He reported that since his grandmother's death he had observed his mother closely and noticed that what he called her "wall", was crumbling. She had panic attacks and felt that her own death was approaching. The day came when Joe decided to ask her to tell him more about her childhood in the orphanage, which she had mentioned to him twenty-five years earlier, but—and this was what he really needed to know—to confront her with the question which he had not dared to ask his grandmother in her lifetime: "Who was your father?" His mother's face had stiffened and turned white. All of a sudden, he said, she looked very old, and withdrew, only saying she had never asked her mother and knew nothing, anyway all this was long passed … and the nuns in the orphanage had been kind to her. Joe knew at this point that he had to bury his hope that one day the empty hole in the family history would be filled. What he did instead was to ask his mother to give him back the keys to his flat, to which, until that day, she had had free access whenever she wanted, with the pretext of cleaning his kitchen or ironing his shirts. This was an act of conscious emancipation, the refusal to collude further with the silenced truths of his family history.

Only gradually did the deep metaphoric meaning of the passage of ownership of those keys come fully to the fore. The autistic enclave with its central void, in which he had been locked since the beginning of his life, but of which he had, at the same time, colluding with the family secret, become the guardian, now had a door, which he was free to open and to close, and which connected and separated two spaces, the external and the internal world. At the intrapsychic level, the confrontation with his mother had revealed that he had become capable of observing and seeing her from outside, as it were, and to describe her reaction to his questioning her with great emotional precision. He had been both a participant in and a witness to their encounter. Observation needs three-dimensional mental space to become operative.

> A *third position* then comes into existence from which object relationships can be observed. This provides us with the capacity to see ourselves in interaction with others and for entertaining another point of view while retaining our own - for observing ourselves while being ourselves.
>
> (Britton, 1998, p. 42, original emphasis)

In search of the lost voice

From outside the tombstone of his autistic enclave, Joe had become capable of seeing and giving meaning to other human beings' mental states, as well as resonating empathically with their psycho-physical emotional realities. The description of his mother's mental state after grandmother's death, as well as her reactions during their conversation, bore witness to his new capacity to observe and take in emotional clues which allowed him to sense other people's internal worlds. He could now begin to observe himself as well, referring spontaneously to his former state of psycho-physical imprisonment, which he now described in bodily terms with keen precision. His wall,[4] he said, coincided with the trunk of his body, from the genitals to his shoulders. Joe added that "the wall was made of white armed concrete to the very core. It was one solid block with no space for internal organs". This is what occurs in *Malina*, when the prison and the imprisoned become one solid and undifferentiated wall. Both scenes, *Malina*'s wall and Joe's concrete block, show the dehumanising effect of the breakdown of the relationship between container and contained and the collapse of three-dimensional mental functioning (Maiello, 2017).

Joe made several hypotheses about what would happen if his wall was to crumble: his skin bag might collapse to the ground and he would need another plaster cast to keep him standing upright, or he would start spinning in circles, as he used to do, by asking insistent questions and forcing people to give him the answers which he already knew and only needed to hear again. He went through the whole inventory of his earlier protective manoeuvres which had been meant to keep at bay an uncontained and emotionally premature baby's fear of dying. Formerly unutterable anxieties could now come to the fore, in search of a container to receive them.

At the beginning of a session, the temptation to escape into immaterial lightness, which is only in appearance at the opposite end of the retreat into the concrete wall, dominated once more. (While the manifest content of this image may seem different, from the process perspective of autistic objects and their uses, it is a gesture that serves the

---

[4] It was Joe's description of his body as a "wall" that brought about my association with Ingeborg Bachmann's *Malina*.

same function as the retreat into the concrete wall.) Both are attempts to escape unbearable pain: Joe indulged once more in the idea of being a balloon, flying off and dispersing in the air. After what felt like a long, but not deadly silence, he added that there ought to be a ceiling. He himself introduced a boundary to the temptation to dissolve in limitless space and expressed the need for a container to keep him down in our limited, but real three-dimensional external and internal reality.

At this point, apparently out of the blue, Joe revealed a thought that had been haunting him for some time: he was obsessed by the idea that he might have a stroke and would no longer be able to ask for help. His daughter would hear him, although he was voiceless, but she was only fourteen, and he could not put this burden on her. His brother would be capable of noticing his distress, but he lived abroad. His mother would assist him day and night, but she was unable to hear. If anybody spoke to him, he would have no voice to reply and would die. In a state of deep existential anguish, he said: "Void, the fear of nothingness. There is nothing. I am nothing."

Joe's internal maternal object was similar to Malina, "who no longer hears", but now he deeply felt that he would die if nobody noticed his need to be vitalised. He was in touch for brief moments with his despair about his deaf internal maternal object. He was in desperate need for something that was missing when he said: "*Somebody* must interpret what I feel." He added that as a child he never cried and never had tantrums. He only whimpered and was told to shut up. Was his bodyless voice rooted in those experiences? At this point in Joe's analysis, the unconscious link with the preconception of primary connectedness was painfully awakening. Absence could be named without the terror of precipitating into the black hole or suffocating in the autistic prison. The meaning of the adolescent's isolation, locked in his room with his headphones, made sense at deep levels of experience. Canned music had to fill the void of mother's emotional silence. Joe was moved and moving the day he said: "I never heard a mother's song, *il canto della mamma*, through which the air around the child becomes fluid and vibrating." He could now not only feel what had been dramatically absent in the earliest experiences of his life, but translate it into sensitive poetic language.

Patients who become able, when they emerge from autistic ways of functioning, to bear witness to the void of their earlier state of *non-being*, are precious for our deeper understanding of the utter desolation, the "nowhere-ness" (Durban, 2017) of autistic states. Once Joe had accepted his need for a boundary and could face the terror of being trapped in an autistic enclave, he could not only describe the existential anguish connected with not being able to call, to cry out and be heard, but ask for help in the here and now of the transference relationship. It could now dawn on him that communication is a two-way process. A voice needed to be heard by receptive ears, and another voice needed to respond. Joe was beginning to trust that his call would be received, and he could not only *feel* the terrors of being buried in an autistic enclave, but find words for those nameless states of anguish by creating a narrative around formerly unutterable emotional states connected with the breakdown of all channels of communication.

During the thirteen years of his analysis, Joe's voice had become less toneless and more modulated, but the change had been so gradual that I took notice of it only once it had come to life and the patient had become capable of using it as a vehicle for the first emotional sparks which permeated his verbal communications. At one point he himself drew my attention to vocal aspects of the early communication between mothers and infants when he recalled how he hated his mother's voice when she woke him up in the morning, because he had to get up and go to school. Her voice, he said, was metallic. One day he told me, no longer with bitter feelings, but with deep regret, that he never heard his mother sing nursery rhymes or lullabies to him, which mothers, he said, usually do for their babies. In silence I wondered whether the absence of musicality in his own and his mother's voices might have been rooted in her own infancy and childhood in the orphanage, being brought up by nuns whose wombs had never borne a baby, had never given birth, raised and loved a child of their own.

Who's dream am I dreaming?

During the winter break of the last year of our analytic journey, Joe had a dream which he reported from his memory on his return:

> He was on the roof terrace of his childhood home with his mother and his brother. His mother leaned over the railing, and he was in terror that she would precipitate. His brother climbed over the railing too. Joe was helpless, paralysed. But then he noticed that there was a platform on the other side of the railing, and his brother managed to climb back onto the terrace.

At this point Joe consulted his dream notebook to check that he had not forgotten any detail. He discovered that one sequence had indeed escaped his memory:

> His mother was leaning over the railing, because a little girl had fallen from a window of the building in front, and people were screaming in despair down in the street.

Joe's precipitation anxiety had become thinkable and dreamable. In part, it concerned himself, his own terror of falling as an uncontained, abandoned (prematurely born?) infant, and, in the transference, the anticipation of the end of his analysis, with the inevitable return and reworking through of the earliest anxieties of abandonment. But at the same time, by forgetting *that* part of the dream, he seemed to have given back to his mother *her* trauma of being dropped at an orphanage at birth, of which he, her first-born child, had been the receptacle through maternal projective identification in reverse. His mother herself would have to deal with the despair of the little girl who, in the dream, had fallen from *another* building. The traumatic event of the forgotten part of the dream felt no longer like a split-off and unthinkable part of his own early trauma, but seemed to be related to his mother's biography, with which she would now have to deal herself. The fact that Joe had forgotten her part of his nightmare could be seen as part of his process of emancipation from the mutually controlling relationship with his internal maternal object.

In the dream, his brother, who had appeared late in the analytic process, had come to represent Joe's own growing feeling of agency: a protective platform had prevented his fall into the abyss, and he had come back safe and alive.

Moving on and coming to life

During the last part of his analysis, Joe had gone back to university and resumed his interrupted studies. He wrote his dissertation with genuine interest and commitment, supported by the professor whom he had abandoned years earlier and who now had become his mentor not only at an intellectual level. His graduation ceremony took place only a few months before the end of our analytic journey. It opened new perspectives not only for his professional career, but he was to be appointed as co-ordinator of a group of colleagues, which implied the capacity to relate and mediate also at a human level.

A brief flash-back onto the phases of Joe's relationships with women may be necessary before ending. Initially, his sexual life had been promiscuous and hyperactive. Feeling that his own life was unbearably grey, he needed to "feed", for sheer survival, on the colours of what he called the "female world". His sophisticated seductive strategies had allowed him to entertain a constantly changing harem of females. His lovers used to tell him their dreams, and he had relished becoming what he described as a "great ear", a narcissistic guru figure who interpreted their unconscious lives by penetrating their most secret internal spaces, both sexually and mentally, ready to drop them like empty shells once he had absorbed their life-giving colours.

Over the years, Joe's insights into the driving forces of the quality of his earlier relationships brought about meaningful changes. In the last years of his analysis, he had only one relationship at a time, and there had been an inversion in terms of who was the needy partner. Before, his many girlfriends had needed *him*. Now, he needed *them*, but his need was so intense that he tended to suffocate them with his breathless possessiveness, until they would break up the relationship and leave him once more in a state of devastating loneliness. However, he had become capable of observing himself and was increasingly aware of the reasons why he could not loosen his grip: he was in terror that the woman would turn her back on him and said: "Her eyes would disappear, and I would be extinguished." Frances Tustin refers to this very experience when she writes: "Encapsulation … is called upon to deal with a body that feels so vulnerable that it is threatened with extinction" (1990, p. 153). Pockets of autistic functioning still surfaced here and there, although Joe was by now in touch with the baby's vital need to be seen, heard, held, and illuminated by the light of mother's eyes. His new relationships awakened these overwhelming primary emotions and became the scenario on which his annihilation anxieties re-emerged. But it dawned on the more grown-up part of his personality that his urge to maintain control over the availability of his objects led to their loss. The last years of his analysis accompanied him towards the growing confidence that he could dare to expose himself to and gradually tolerate the intensity of those primary emotional states and anxieties, from which he had sought protection since his early childhood by locking himself in his autistic enclave.

Two years before the end of his analysis, Joe met the woman who was to become his wife. She was a musician, a singer. Their relation grew more intimate very gradually and with great caution on both sides. One year after concluding our analytic journey, I received a card announcing the birth of a baby daughter. Between the lines of Joe's few and sober accompanying words, I felt his happiness around his marriage and the second experience of fatherhood.

Conclusion

Autistic states, including autistic enclaves in patients who may otherwise be functioning in seemingly normal ways, seem to have laws and criteria of their own. They cannot always be caught to their full extent within a more traditional psychoanalytic frame of reference. This may be one of the reasons why Frances Tustin often resorted to poetry in her books on autism. She felt that the poets' creative intuitions went deeper and were closer to the unfathomable world of autism than traditional psychoanalytic language. Anxieties connected with absence can be described in prose, as long as presence remains in our minds as the other side of the coin. The autistic *void* is not only difficult but impossible to translate into plain and shareable verbal language. This may be the deep reason for calling up a poet's novel as a companion through the desert of no-life over the first years of Joe's analysis.

In transgenerational transmission, we know that the silenced traumatic events become more and more unthinkable and take on an autonomous deadening existence of their own. This is true not only for collective trauma connected with persecution and genocide (Gampel, 1986, 1997), but occurs equally, as shown in Joe's material, on the intimate scale of transgenerational transmission of silenced family histories.

In relation to autism, we have come to use expressions like no-body and no-thingness, to get as close as possible to those unfathomable states of non-existence. This was the no-where, from which Joe's mute voice originated. It did not call nor ask to be rescued by any live companion (Alvarez, 1992). There seemed to be no idea or hope in the patient of a lifeline, no experience of links, which might have been attacked and destroyed (Bion, 1959), but rather the passive breakdown of the very preconception of linking, as the result, in his case, of the absence of primary positive realisations (Maiello, 2000). The very preconception of container/contained with the ongoing emotionally intense negotiation around one-ness and separation is frozen. In his description, Joe's body had no inside space for internal organs. Container and contained were just one massive concrete block, with no in-between space for the basic unconscious processes of projective and introjective identification to develop, and no nutrition for primary dream-work (Bion, 1959, 1992).

When formerly autistic patients begin to dream, a dialectic relationship between container and contained is developing, and there is space for persecutory phantasies and anxieties to appear, like in Joe's Mafia dreams. The emotional dynamics of the paranoid–schizoid position have been set in train. This is a crucial development in the therapeutic history of formerly autistic patients. From that moment they are no longer ghost-like no-bodies in autistic no-whereness. Their potential imprisonment in an internal object may lead to claustrophobic anxieties (Meltzer, 1992), which will break forth on the scene of three-dimensional mental functioning and are accompanied by emotionally intense persecutory phantasies, but, at this stage, prisoner and jailor are no longer two parts of the same coin, and the transference relationship can begin to develop and display its multiple facets.

What remains to be explored further is the fathomless *no-whereness* of deep autism.

References

Alvarez, A. (1992). *Live Company*. London: Routledge.

Bachmann, I. (1971). *Malina*. Frankfurt a/Main: Verlag Suhrkamp.

Bion, W. R. (1959). Attacks on linking. *International Journal of Psycho-Analysis, 40*: 5–6.

Bion, W. R. (1962). *Learning from Experience*. London: Heinemann.

Bion, W. R. (1992). *Cogitations*. London: Karnac.

Britton, R. (1998). *Belief and Imagination: Explorations in Psychoanalysis*. London: Routledge.

Durban, J. (2017). Home, homelessness and nowhere-ness in early infancy. *Journal of Child Psychotherapy, 43*(2): 175–191.

Gampel, Y. (1986). La vie, la mort et le prénom d'un enfant. In: P. Fédida & J. Guyotat (Eds.), *Actualités transgénérationnelles en psychopathologie*. Paris: Editions G.R.E.U.P.P.

Gampel, Y. (1997). Penser la mémoire impensable de l'extermination. In: J. Gillibert & P. Wilgowicz (Eds.), *L'ange exterminateur*. Cerisy: Revue de l'Université de Bruxelles.

Houzel, D. (2005). Splitting of psychic bisexuality in autistic children. In: D. Houzel & M. Rhode (Eds.), *Invisible Boundaries: Psychosis and Autism in Children and Adolescents*. London: Karnac.

Houzel, D. (2007). Memories in feeling and autistic barriers in adult analysands. Paper read at IPA Congress Berlin 2007.

Maiello, S. (1995). The sound object—a hypothesis about prenatal auditory experience and memory. *Journal of Child Psychotherapy, 21*(1): 23–41.

Maiello, S. (2000). Broken links—Attack or breakdown?—Notes on the origin of violence. *Journal of Child Psychotherapy, 26*(1): 5–24.

Maiello, S. (2001). Prenatal trauma and autism. *Journal of Child Psychotherapy, 27*(2): 107–124. (Reprinted in: J. Mitrani & T. Mitrani (Eds.), *Frances Tustin Today*. London: Routledge, 2015.)

Maiello, S. (2017). Point—Line—Surface—Space—On Donald Meltzer's concept of one and two-dimensional mental functioning in autistic states. In: M. Cohen & A. Hahn (Eds.), *Doing Things Differently: The Influence of Donald Meltzer on Psychoanalytic Theory and Practice*. London: Karnac.

Meltzer, D. (1965). The relation of anal masturbation to projective identification. *International Journal of Psycho-Analysis, 47*: 2–3.

Meltzer, D. (1975). *Explorations in Autism: A Psycho-analytical Study* (with J. Bremner, S. Hoxter, D. Weddell, & I. Wittenberg). London: The Roland Harris Educational Trust.
Meltzer, D. (1988). *The Apprehension of Beauty*. London: The Roland Harris Educational Trust.
Meltzer, D. (1992). *The Claustrum: An Investigation of Claustrophobic Phenomena*. London: The Roland Harris Educational Trust.
Resnik, S. (2004). Spazio-tempo nell'autismo e nella schizofrenia. In: S. Resnik, E. Levis, S. Nissim & M. Pagliarani (Eds.), *Abitare l'assenza—Scritti sullo spazio-tempo nelle psicosi e nell'autismo infantile*. Milano: Franco Angeli.
Resnik, S. (2006). Riflessioni su autismo e psicosi—Omaggio a Frances Tustin. Presented at the third International Frances Tustin Conference (Frances Tustin Memorial Trust). Venice, 2006.
Segal, H. (1972). A delusional system as a defence against the re-emergence of a catastrophic situation. *International Journal of Psychoanalysis*, 53: 393–401.
Spitz, R. A. (1945). Hospitalism: An enquiry into the genesis of psychiatric conditions in early childhood. *Psychoanalytic Study of the Child*, 1: 53–74.
Steiner, J. (1988). The interplay between pathological organisations and the paranoid–schizoid and depressive position. In: E. Bott Spillius (Ed.), *Melanie Klein Today: Developments in Theory and Practice, Vol. 1*. London: Routledge.
Steiner, J. (1993). *Psychic Retreats: Pathological Organisations in Psychotic, Neurotic and Borderline Patients*. London: Routledge.
Tustin, F. (1972). *Autism and Childhood Psychosis*. London: Hogarth.
Tustin, F. (1986). *Autistic Barriers in Neurotic Patients*. London: Karnac.
Tustin, F. (1990). *The Protective Shell in Children and Adults*. London: Karnac.
Winnicott, D. W. (1974). Fear of breakdown. *International Review of Psychoanalysis*, 1: 103–107.

CHAPTER ELEVEN

From nothing to being? Technical considerations for dealing with unrepresented states

Bernd Nissen

The term "unrepresented" has now become established as an umbrella term for a variety of phenomena, including autistic/autistoid phenomena, nameless, and early traumatic states, and those of breakdown. This subset of unrepresented/not-yet-psyche states is characterised by two fundamental features: the states have not been transformed into the psychic and the hope for a containing object has been abandoned. These two features, together with a failure of projective identification, are found, in my view, in autistic and autistoid dynamics, which—unlike, for example, theory of mind of autism research—I conceive of as an object relations disorder (see Nissen, 2008, 2014; Rhode, 2018).

With this rough identification of the subset of unrepresented states, a variety of questions immediately arise: How can the "unrepresented" be treated? Can it be interpreted at all? How should that which is not yet psychic become psychic, be qualified in an interpretation? How can the analyst emerge as a psychic object? Even become the containing one? Does the unrepresented become the represented? Or do we create something that enables a relation to the unrepresented? I prefer to stop my questioning at this point …

In the following, I would like to examine a few treatment-/technical-related aspects in detail,[1] limiting myself to the dynamics in which the unrepresented shows itself sensually, can be sublated into the psychic, and is finally structurally available to the psychic apparatus.

Marking the unrepresented: the revealing of the pre-psychic

How can we discover the unrepresented, how can we deal with it technically? I would like to illustrate this with a small example.

When entering the treatment room, a patient noticed in a flash that a book with a glowing orange cover was missing from bookshelf. On the couch, her gaze kept going to this spot.

This observation by the psychoanalyst has a certain empirical objectivity, but is already an interpretation (e.g., qualifying the grasping as lightning-quick) grounded in a kind of atmospheric, sensual, somatoform countertransference. But what does it say about the patient's psyche and about the interpsychic, the transference? Little, at best. The object of psychoanalysis cannot be grasped with the senses (see Freud, 1900a, p. 613; Bion, 1970, pp. 6f), even if we would be blind without sensory sensations and impressions. But the "communications of our sense organs" ("*Angaben unserer Sinnesorgane*") (Freud, 1900a, p. 613, p. 618) do not provide us with psychic qualities. At the same time, we cannot order the interplay of our sensory sensations and impressions without a conceptual/theoretical pre-understanding, which, however, must not be overpoweringly predetermining and must be suspended in the treatment situation.

---

[1] In my experience—despite all the rough verse simplification—some typical course characteristics could be described in the treatment of unrepresented states: it begins with a long phase of holding (Winnicott), in which the unrepresented states emerge dimly and a hope develops in which the analyst can appear as a psychic object. Then the unrepresented emerges (presence moment), often followed by a paranoid–schizoid phase of massive uncertainty, which can be accompanied by suicidal, reactive-psychotic or psychosomatic phenomena. In this phase, the conception that emerges at the moment of presence becomes a thought. The subsequent working through secures this thought and differentiates more complex objectal dimensions so that sustainable psychic structures appear (see clinical case studies of such progressions, e.g., Nissen, 2008, 2013).

I would like to briefly outline the following metapsychological model: a drive, for example, hunger, passes from the somatic into the psychic and expresses itself as sensual sensations. I do not conceive of this experience as phantasy like Isaacs, but, with Freud and Bion, as raw, pre-psychic material, emerging from the somatic. In parallel, a pre-conception is activated, the expectation of the breast. This expectation permeates sensual experience. The cry, which an observer can describe as an attempt to expel, becomes a call for the mother. The mother also has a preconception[2] breast (the expectation of her child) and an α-function, that is, the capacity to qualify raw data. With the unconscious and preconscious orientation to her child and the faculty of the α-function, she is able to give order to her child's sensual experience, that is, to recognise it as hunger with a specific quality (e.g., nagging, anxious, greedy hunger). Does this create psychic elements? I think not. I will come back to this.

Let's go back to observation. Often, we are in a similar situation to the mother. We perceive sensory material (grasping the missing book in a flash; returning gaze) and will perhaps have an inkling of the patient's inner world and the relational situation, so that the circularity between the sensory and the preconceptual can be broken and set in motion. Let us assume, for example, that the analyst begins to sense[3] that the patient experiences the world in an autistoid way and has concretely made the walls of the treatment room with its wallpaper, parquet, curtains, picture, and bookshelf into her second skin (Bick; Tustin; Anzieu). This constellates[4] the various sensual impressions: the gaze, the empty space, etc., and atmospheric sensations: grasping in a flash, the returning gaze. With the idea of the second skin (corresponding to the mother's hunger

---

[2] Grotstein (2007) points out that Bion speaks of pre-conception (hyphenated) in the case when a pre-conception has not yet met its realisation, of preconception (unhyphenated) when a conception becomes a preconception again. Even though I cannot find it consistently in Bion, this distinction makes sense in individual cases.

[3] We have to trust our free-floating attention, our intuition (Bion) here. So we intuit a specific quality, which will have yet to become psychic, in the material, but must remain open to other, sometimes unexpected perspectives. For example, the blank space in the bookshelf would feel quite different in an anal dynamic to control and dominate, or an early oedipal dynamic.

[4] On the concept of constellation, see Bion (1970, p. 33).

hypothesis), the sensual sensations receive a qualitative pre-colouration; for the missing book could be experienced as a tear in the second skin. Such a tear can be experienced as an existential threat. Specific states would then be triggered that a trained observer could qualify as fear, threat and others.

It seems important to me to understand the deeper dimension: the second skin is a final rescue measure of a rudimentary, barely viable self that feels existentially threatened by "nameless" states *and* (sic!) has given up hope of a holding object (pre-conception "breast"). Survival is possible in a second skin, a rupture can lead to a verbally hardly graspable state, which we could paraphrase as "leakage", "spreading of nothingness" or the like. That is, we are dealing with (a) an existential threat, where (b) no object that secures existence can bethought of anymore.

The problem in such phases of treatment is that it is not possible *to understand* this depth dimension *psychically*. If the second-skin hypothesis is correct, the analyst is not present as a psychic object in the room. He becomes an autistic/autistoid object. He should be indistinguishable from a piece of furniture, as M. Klein observed as early as 1930. With the crack in that second skin, the existential self threatens to leak out—and the autistic/autistoid object psychoanalyst can then no longer hold anything. Bion wrote that people exist who "feel the pain but will not suffer it and so cannot be said to discover it" (1970, p. 9; an aspect to which Freud referred in countless places, e.g., 1912b; 1914g; 1915e; 1926e). What the patient does not suffer cannot be discovered, nor can it come into the communication from unconscious to unconscious. We can perhaps infer it empathically, but not discover it interpsychically and understand it directly.

An interpretation here can only prepare a future psychisation. In my opinion, it should, starting from a sensual level, cautiously guide towards the formation of the second skin as a defence against a state in which the self is threatened by dissolution. By interpreting this constellation of defensive states, we bring ourselves in as a being that can perceive the patient and her experience. We interpret a constellation (her gazing—the empty space—her restlessness) and we become potentially *sensually* perceptible as an object through interpretation—a nucleus from which a psychic object and a containing hope can develop.

This transference dimension to be formed out of the sensual is likely to be endurable for patients in an autistic threat situation.

For example, it could be said: "You are looking at the empty space that seems to be troubling you." The crack in the second skin (empty space) as well as a non-fixing sensual quality (troubling) are named—by a being who is able to perceive these dimensions, that is, probably is not a piece of furniture.

This means that the interpretation remains very close to the sensual experience as the observer/analyst can perceive it. To me, this attitude, which remains close to what is clinically observable and takes into account the analyst's own atmospheric, sensual, and physical experience, seems important. Only in this way can an approach to experience take place and the object carefully mutate from an inanimate object to a sensually perceiving being. That which is not yet must be allowed to develop—and to develop in the relationship. The unrepresented must be allowed to unfold slowly and the object to emerge slowly, otherwise patients quickly feel overwhelmed, react aversively to premature determinations. The remaining object-hoping parts in the patient will then tend to withdraw.

Becoming infected with the unrepresented: harbingers of the unspeakable

In the above example, the analyst is not directly affected much—the idea of an autistoid organisation slowly emerges. In my experience, situations then arise in which the analyst becomes more involved. The following material shows how the analyst is pulled into a psychic dissolution. In my opinion, the patient has developed an autistoid defence formation with which she tries to keep this danger of dissolution at bay. It concerns a grasping of inner states in oneself and in others. This grasping is of an unbelievable clarity. I spoke elsewhere (Nissen, 2021) of how she has X-ray eyes to the inner world of others and is able to see inside others as X-rays see inside the body. When, for example, in a flat-sharing community where she was a guest, there were serious arguments with a mentally ill flatmate, she recognised his situation immediately ("I knew exactly what it looked like inside him") and was not only able to de-escalate the situation, but also to reduce the young man's tension in the long term. This ability, probably the result of her own struggle for survival, also becomes a burden: although psychic material is recognised, for her it remains pre-psychic material that threatens to flood her again and again.

This capacity becomes even clearer when she describes her eating disorder: "When I unexpectedly get frustrating or threatening news, I immediately have to eat something, anything, bread crust, snack, it doesn't matter. I eat it, gulp it down. Then something dead is in my stomach, I vomit, violently. Relief, relief flows through me. Then I'm alive again, completely!"

What caught my attention at some point is that such descriptions are of an incredible precision, as if she could describe the unconscious without any refraction. I soon felt reminded of another (male) patient (see Nissen, 2008) who had a similar ability, but it was not directed inwards but outwards. This patient told stories (observations of everyday events as well as things he had experienced himself) in a form in which the narrative was dominated by a linguistic brilliance and visual complexity that was so astonishing that speaker and listener almost vanished. They were hyperrealistic and hypersensual. For example, he described elderly women on the underground so precisely that one could see their shape, hear their noises, and smell their smell. Yet it was striking that in a really unnarcissistic fashion he did not lie in wait for the reaction of the object. Telling stories was not interaction, not an interpersonal exchange. There was only the story-subject; object, speaker, listener, relationship did not exist. He also told himself such stories or lived in them. Telling stories as a second skin!

My recent patient has experienced severe and continuous traumatisation. I suspect that in traumatic events she developed a dissociative ability—as if observing in a split-off, uninvolved way—to perceive processes in others and to apply this ability to herself in "frustrating or threatening" situations—in order to secure and save her self. With this idea, the atmosphere that arose when she narrated such scenes became more understandable to me: if we remove the retrospective processing in which she presents herself as consciously (in the systemic sense!), reflexively, experiencing and chooses the "I" form of narration, traumatic material suddenly emerges that is not conscious and not unconscious, but actual. Hence the precision and the feeling that she can look into the unconscious. The dissociative observation of the traumatic experience could thus have been transformed into a form with which the fear of dissolution can be warded off.

But what is being warded off? The patient herself describes what is being warded off as "states of dissolution". When they appear, she feels extremely threatened: "I only endure them in the hope of surviving—I mean it, surviving, physically surviving."

In one session I had to experience this state of dissolution in which all orders perished: no orientation in temporal categories, timelessness and spacelessness, no distinction between objects, part and whole, infinite spaces, no logical structure, diffusion of life and things, etc. It could be conceived as a divestment of the primary process through all the unconscious spheres of depth, but, it seemed, there was almost no secondary process left.

I try to reproduce some moments of this dissolution (see also Nissen, 2021). They are fragments, reduced by me to a few sentences, much more confused in the situation, encompassing many minutes.

"I was with Max, suddenly he was standing in the room, we were wearing clothes, the child had, I had something with him once, sex, was it sex? Fifteen years ago, all full of rubbish. How did Ludwig get into the room? Crazy, huh? Sarah never came, not even in the evening. It was a party, really loud. There was nothing going on with Sarah, but she wants to give me her jacket. It's damaged, in the bin. W. [first name of an internationally known artist] was drunk, I've known him forever, with bottle. Sarah's in bed, at her party, can you imagine? Probably with Keith …"

While the patient—much more confused and disoriented in the scene—is talking, she lies as if in shock, with a slight head tremor, while making defensive movements with one hand.

I will now first write what I knew about the material at this point.

Max is an older man with whom she fell a little in love. Ludwig was probably standing in the room where she was lying with Max, still dressed. Did Ludwig have a child in his arms? Ludwig is seventy-five years old, did she have sex with him fifteen years ago? She wasn't even ten years old then! Sarah, depressive acquaintance of her mother's age, probably had a party, was lying in bed (or is she still lying in bed?).

Sarah once gave the patient a jacket, which she threw away, always afraid it would be discovered. The patient's father worked with W. at times. Keith's been dead for five years.

But I no longer had this knowledge at my disposal. For I was infected by the dissolution of thinking. A panic arose in me, I would go crazy, psychotic, if I continued to listen. This is not a paraphrase of a feeling or a countertransference, but a real fear, panic, from which I wanted to flee inwardly. I wanted to get out of my body, felt helpless, at the mercy, panicked that this was not possible. I know all kinds of reactions to similar material (depersonalising, distancing, e.g., taking refuge in rationalising, etc.). But in this scene the threat was different: a being at the mercy of something and a panic threat, that it would really happen, happen unavoidable.

I think it is very important that this "becoming infected" (elsewhere I have described it as an inductive process; see Nissen, 2014) is not a projective identification. *It is a becoming involved*, not an identification, not a symbiosis and not a delusion—as Moser (2021) points out. Benedetti (1983) speaks of osmosis between patient and therapist, Moser (2021) of permeability.

For the patient, it is also no message to the analyst, no communication, *a fortiori* no psychic communication—and yet this event is of extraordinary importance. With this being infected, I know about the dissolution, I have felt myself being pulled into the maelstrom of dissolution in my own body, felt the hopeless horror. Has this created psychic quality?

No. A psychic element, or the psychic, must be qualified in an object relationship. If there is a fundamental law in the psychic, it is that the psychic can only arise in a relationship. It is not possible on its own. In the situation described, I was infected by her traumatic experience, traumatic helplessness and fear appeared (and have remained in a mild form until today). Traumatic experience is objectless experience! It remains in the actual. The breakdown in going on being appears, but an object is not there. Such traumatic (e.g., transgenerational) transmission does not alleviate, does not abolish, but only perpetuates.

Nevertheless, the event was of fundamental importance. If I spoke of dissolution in the future, she heard that I "knew something". This is doubly important, namely for the qualification and for the relationship.

A first, cautious relation to the actual becomes possible, the term "dissolution" moves in the direction of "name". If the patient only has splitting off and retraumatic closeness available to her in dealing with this state, a relational context (a relationing?) now becomes possible, since an object knows about the state and can address it in the relationship. The object transforms from a sensual to a holding being that can retain states within itself. The pre-conception of a containing object emerges, object hope appears.

Incidentally, in the situation in which the states of dissolution spread through me, I was unable to give any interpretation; such thinking, psychoanalytical faculty had been torn away. I was saved by a hint of reality. I said, "Keith is dead after all, died of drugs." She was silent, but somehow more grounded. Then I said, "Something is pressing on you, threatening you, making you lose yourself." Long pause, then she said "It's been like that here for some time."

I evaded the vortex of dissolution with a reference to reality, a form of distancing myself from what was happening. The patient seems to have used dissociative detached observation to survive.

The being-there of the unrepresented: presence in relationship

Such being infected paves the further way into psychic understanding, which will only be possible in the relationship (see Freud's concept of transference resistance; Klein's transference as total situation; Bion's T→O; Winnicott's event of breakdown in transference; Stern's present moment; my concept of the moment of presence, etc.). If the dissolution described above had occurred in the relationship, if the analytic couple had been ready for this realisation, then a joint discovery could have taken place. But this *kairos*[5] had not yet occurred.

In another patient, this *kairos* occurred unexpectedly. The patient (born in the German Democratic Republic (GDR)) was a premature baby, long in the incubator, as was customary at the time, with only medical care. The very young mother, a single parent, was overwhelmed.

---

[5] The term *kairos* refers to the right/most favourable time. It stands in contrast to *chronos*, as passing, continuous time.

He is said to have spent the first two to three months at home, only crying, which put the mother under massive stress: she did not know "what the child had", she was afraid of the neighbours, of state authorities (not unfounded in the GDR! Children were sometimes forcibly sent to the weekly crèche or taken away from their parents). She soon felt completely exhausted. Then the child was "suddenly quiet, totally low-maintenance".

The treatment was uncomplicated. I soon "forgot" the fact that the patient had been in the incubator for weeks. He was smart, funny, a bit crazy, which I like, engaged me in clever conversations. I didn't notice for a long time, although it was pointed out to me in supervision, that the analysis had become a completely conflict-free space, without "rough edges".

Then the crying became an issue. He had internalised the mother's narratives very much, kept coming back to this topic; the oppressive, exhausted atmosphere became very palpable. Although he remained very calm and polite, I felt "something" inside him screaming even in the treatment. Then he mentioned the incubator in a side sentence. I was struck by it, full of feelings of guilt and shame for having "forgotten". Out of this consternation, I said, "It was the unscreamed cries from the incubator ..." The patient immediately understood the incomplete interpretation; never had such a connection been made.

In my opinion, this situation is a moment of presence in which the unheard crying and the silent terror of the incubator became psychic for the analytic couple. In the transference relationship, in which the early situation was repeated in a different form, "unrepresentations" were given a psychic qualification. In the presence moment (T→O) something has been discovered; at the same time it has been created beyond the sovereignty of the participants. In the presence moment, a reality shows itself in an undeniability and clarity that unfolds its own efficacy and subjugates the actors. In the moment of presence, reflexive consciousness is absent, it is a pure consciousness of perception (see Freud, but especially the further development by Bion, 1962b). In this way, the reality that has occurred can be experienced and named and discovered in the transformation into the presentative (see Langer's concept of the presentative, 1942). A psychically qualified conception (O→K) has arisen in the analyst's witnessing, which must then become thought in further working through (see Bion's theory of thinking, 1962a, 1962b, 1963, 1965).

What has become real here for the analysand as well as the analyst in a highly condensed way? In the relationship, the facticity of the incubator and the crying with its horror and threateningness has become real with further qualities of denial, feelings of guilt and shame. The analyst has become the understanding object, even though the object that was absent and did not understand is already present as a shadow (see my shock at "forgetting"). This complex occurred in the moment of presence and has experienced its sublation into the presentative. The presentative terms, for example, the silent survival in the incubator, the unheard cry in the relationship, "contain" the content of the moment of presence, even if they are subjectively weighted differently. Through this, a unique relationship with specific psychical qualities has been constituted. The relationship is there, the patient is there, the analyst is there, united in the discovery that is their creation, at the same time subjugating the actors. The conception contains the psychic elements, the elements stabilise the conception.

The sublation of the unrepresented: the unrepresented in the represented

In this description, the singularity of a conception becomes visible. It is only secured, especially for the patient, if the object preserves it. The oppressions of the traumatic are too great for the patient to protect the conception against the dissolving dynamics. We say that the conception must become the thought, that is, "survive" the absence of the object. No breast is the first thought; we can paraphrase Bion. But what does this mean? Freud operates with the concept of the memory trace, which can be cathected hallucinatorily, then fails because of the exigencies of life. Is, as Winnicott (1971) thinks, the experience of the breast coming back, so that it has survived the attacks, enough for it to be thought "someday"?

I would like to deepen these considerations a little with clinical experiences. In the psychic, reality (truth) is a complex of opposites.[6] In the above moment of presence, the analyst ostensibly appears as an

---

[6] In particular, the central propositions of logic (see also Matte Blanco, 1998), that is, the proposition of identity, the proposition of contradiction, and the proposition of the excluded middle (see also Heinrich, 1987) do not apply in the psychic.

understanding object that establishes a connection and meaning with the interpretation. At the same time, the analyst was also the object that had forgotten the incubator and did not sufficiently perceive the crying that was hidden in the pleasantries—just as the mother, for whatever reason, had not made the connection to the incubator and probably experienced the crying as stress.

Even these few details make it clear that the patient, who still feels oppressed by the unrepresentative, cannot hold and think the presentative alone. How is he supposed to understand the analyst as an understanding object if the same object is also the traumatising one. The presentative as a conception is thus endangered not only as a singularity, but also because it is unthinkable—does the breast now give milk (love) or poison (decomposition)?

In my opinion, the solution to this requirement can only lie in further differentiation. Both existing conceptions must further differentiate and further conceptions must be created so that a structure emerges that is so stable that the necessary PS-mechanisms are not destructive but developmental.

In my experience, these processes occur regularly in a holding transference relationship. In this treatment, the patient began to react very irritably to small deviations quite soon after the above scene. A word that was perhaps not quite appropriate outraged him, I remained silent longer, he was convinced I had fallen asleep, etc. The patient no longer began to greet me, nor did he look at me when I greeted him. I continued to say, "Good afternoon, please come in." Once I just said in a friendly way, "Please come in." Twenty minutes of tense silence. I suspected the reason for the silence, but still asked what was wrong. It burst out of him: I had not welcomed him, I was tired of him, I was no longer interested, I should finally say it, that I would rather use the time differently, etc.

I told him that he experienced me like his mother, who was never really with him during stress, always listening to the neighbours, thinking about the government office. He confirmed, said that there were many situations in which he could not stand it when others were "somewhere else". I said that his crying was also a cry for primary maternal attention, not just the result of the incubator. Again, a small moment of presence.

As a result, it could be deepened that the crying was a desperation, that the pre-conception breast, which for inexplicable reasons had apparently "somehow" survived the incubator, did not meet the desired realisation in which the longed-for two-unity with the mother would have been established. This mis-realisation was also experienced traumatically, but differently from the incubator. In the incubator, it seems, there was no object, only survival.[7] In the crying there was an object, but it seemed unattainable—a difference that could be important for working on the unrepresented.

But back to the scene where we had understood that the screaming was a desire for realisation of the pre-conception; the lack of it was agonisingly tearing for him. I confronted him in the same session that I could not imagine that he did not feel welcome, even if the "good day" was missing. He reacted as if very affected and said very touchingly: "I know that, and somehow I also know that my mother loved me. She was so young and so overwhelmed, she told me that once, I felt that was true."

I will stop the clinical illustration now, as I am concerned with the development of thoughts. Bion writes on thinking and thoughts: "Nevertheless there are grounds for supposing that a primitive 'thinking,' active in the development of thought, should be distinguished from the thinking that is required for the use of thoughts" (1963, p. 35). "I proposed that thoughts should be regarded as prior to the apparatus for using thoughts" (p. 44). In the clinical material presented, we can trace the emergence of four conceptions that are related to each other: the belated, unheard crying from the incubator; the crying for a realisation of the pre-conception breast,[8] that is, a sufficiently good mother–child relationship; incubator as trauma in which the pre-conception could rest and endure (for whatever reasons); the love and dignified sincerity of the mother. There are four conceptions, three of them created through presence events directly in the relationship, one (incubator as trauma) with relative evidence. The following consideration now seems

---

[7] An interesting phenomenon! The psyche sometimes seems to be able to "switch off" completely, to let the threat rush over it. Mächtlinger (2012) describes children who survived concentration camps as infants and developed incredible abilities as a group, but also in their own resilience.
[8] I always understand the pre-conception breast as an expectation of a mother–child relationship, never as a partial object or the like.

important to me: emerging conceptions further differentiate the other existing ones: the subsequent crying out of the incubator, for example, remains a psychological fact, even if it is to be considered in a newly differentiated way with the crying out of realisation. The conceptions are thus subjected to "thinking". But the four conceptions, which with "thinking" are transformed from the presentative into the representative, that is, into thoughts, relate to each other. They are hardly "thinkable" individually. This relationing becomes a psychic structure within the relationship, even if it emancipates itself from this relationship further on. I therefore think that it is not so much a thought that survives the absence of the object, but a psychic structure that is available to the psychic apparatus and enables understanding, forgiveness, pardon, reparation, in short, the depressive position as described by the Kleinians.

Outlook

Can the unrepresented now be represented, that is, become the represented? In my opinion, there is no simple answer to this. The mother's ability, together with the understanding in the analysis, has perhaps made it possible, for the patient, that the misconception of the breast has lost something of the traumatic and could become more of a psychic conflict. The incubator remains the incubator, remains trauma, remains unrepresented. But perspectives have emerged on how it could work in relationships; and a specific stress from which the patient suffers has become identifiable.

It seems important to me to "pick up" patients who are struggling with unrepresented states from the still sensual, somatoform world and very gently name the features and defences that emerge. In this holding, hopes for an understanding object emerge alongside sensual qualities. Then psychic worlds can be created.

In this process, we asymmetrically *discover* states, that is, structures and dynamics, in the analysand, but at the same time what is discovered is a *creation* of the analytic couple (see Freud's concept of "deed"/"fact" ("*Tat*"), e.g., 1926e, and construction, 1937d; Bion's (esp., 1970) concept of becoming, realisation, and truth). The discovered shows up in the present moment, and yet will have been created by the couple.

With the sublation into the presentative, the created discovered is then determined, whereby this determination is *beyond the sovereignty* of the participants, and *subjugates* them. Nevertheless, it must be empirically valid, that is, it must be connectable. The participants finally believe that they empirically share the same thing. The presentational symbolism with its vagueness makes a lot possible here, but strictly speaking it remains an erroneous belief—a reassuring erroneous belief.

I have been working with "such" patients for a long time now. If holding succeeds above all, very sustainable relationships and touching moments often arise. Even when processes have not gone well enough (see my treatment of 2008), these patients benefit. Transformative processes are possible, sometimes even mutative.

References

Benedetti, G. (1983). *Todeslandschaften der Seele*. Göttingen. Vandenhoeck & Ruprecht.

Bion, W. R. (1962a). *Learning from Experience*. London: William Heinemann. (Reprinted London: Karnac). Reprinted in *Seven Servants* (1977).

Bion, W. R. (1962b). The psycho-analytic study of thinking. *International Journal of Psycho-Analysis*, 43: 306–310.

Bion, W. R. (1963). *Elements of Psychoanalysis*. London: William Heinemann. (Reprinted London: Karnac). Reprinted in *Seven Servants* (1977).

Bion, W. R. (1965). *Transformations*. London: William Heinemann. (Reprinted London: Karnac). Reprinted in *Seven Servants* (1977).

Bion, W. R. (1970). *Attention and Interpretation*. London: Tavistock Publications. (Reprinted London: Karnac). Reprinted in *Seven Servants* (1977).

Freud, S. (1900a). *The Interpretation of Dreams. S. E.*, 4. London: Hogarth.

Freud, S. (1912b): The dynamics of transference. *S. E.*, 12. London: Hogarth.

Freud, S. (1914g). Remembering, repeating and working-through. *S. E.*, 12. London: Hogarth.

Freud, S. (1915e). The unconscious. *S. E.*, 14. London: Hogarth.

Freud, S. (1926e). *The Question of Lay Analysis. S. E.*, 20. London: Hogarth.

Freud, S. (1937d). Constructions in analysis. *S. E.*, 23. London: Hogarth.

Grotstein, J. S. (2007). *A Beam of Intense Darkness: Wilfred Bion's Legacy to Psychoanalysis*. London: Karnac.

Heinrich, K. (1987). *Tertium datur. Eine religionsphilosophische Einführung in die Logik*. Basel: Stroemfeld/Roter Stern.

Klein, M. (1930/1989). Die Bedeutung der Symbolbildung für die Ichentwicklung. In: *Das Seelenleben des Kleinkindes*. Stuttgart: Klett-Cotta.

Langer, S. K. (1942). *Philosophy in a New Key*. Cambridge, MA: Harvard University Press.

Mächtlinger, V. (2012). Resilienz. Psychoanalytische Überlegungen zur späteren Entwicklung der sechs Kinder, die als Kleinkinder Theresienstadt überlebt haben (Die Kinder von Bulldogs Bank). In: B. Nissen (Ed.), *Wendepunkte. Zur Theorie und Klinik psychoanalytischer Veränderungsprozesse* (pp. 25–52). Giessen: Psycho-Sozial-Verlag.

Matte Blanco, I. (1998). *Thinking, Feeling and Being: Clinical Reflections on the Fundamental Antinomy of Human Beings and World*. London: Routledge.

Moser, U. (2021): Kommentar zu Nissen: Das Erleben von Auflösung. In: *Jahrbuch der Psychoanalyse, 84*.

Nissen, B. (2008). On the determination of autistoid organisations in non-autistic adults. *International Journal of Psycho-Analysis, 89*: 261–277.

Nissen, B. (2013). On mental elements. Based on the example of an autistoid perversion. *International Journal of Psycho-Analysis, 94*: 239–256.

Nissen, B. (2014). Autistoide Organisationen. In: *Jahrbuch der Psychoanalyse, 68*.

Nissen, B. (2021). Das Erleben von Auflösung. In: *Jahrbuch der Psychoanalyse, 84*.

Rhode, M. (2018). Object relations approaches to autism. *International Journal of Psycho-Analysis, 99*(3): 702–724.

Winnicott, D. W. (1971). *Playing and Reality*. London: Tavistock.

Index

ABA *see* Applied Behavioural Analysis
Abraham, N., 97
Abram, J., 164
absence of dream life, 198–200
Acquarone, S., 133
adhesive identification, 43, 45, 53, 121, 130, 142
afterwardness theory, 99, 102
agonies *see also* anxieties
    felt-self, 170
    primitive, 164
Aitkin, K. J., 24, 33, 95
Allen, J., 28
alliance, unconscious, 39, 42–43, 109–110 *see also* anxieties
alpha (α) function, 3, 4, 16, 33, 221
    see also Bion, W. R
Alvarez, A., 3, 8, 10, 13, 16, 21, 26, 27, 33, 34, 41, 42, 68, 75, 85, 86, 131, 135, 215
    anxiety and modes of interpretations, 43, 47–48
    early developmental disturbances, 7–8

explanatory interpretations, 54
levels of interpretation, 164–165
levels of intervention, 11, 68, 83–84
live company, 81
psychoanalytic theory, 68
sense of efficacy, 153
unrepresented, the, 3
Amir, D., 47
Anderson, S., 24
anger, 80
anxieties, 39, 60–61, 151
    analytic object implant, 48
    autistic and psychotic, 40
    autisto-psychotic spectrum, 40–46, 60, 158
    awareness of existential circumstances, 157
    based on projective mechanisms vs. primitive one, 47
    borderline autistic, 45, 60
    case vignette, 48, 161–165
    child analysis, 44–45
    crossing over, 58–59
    early self-experience, 154–155

emotional catastrophe, 152, 156, 157–164
emotional experience, 153–157
explanatory interpretations, 54
interaction between, 42
intracorporal identifications, 56
invocatory drive, 56
levels of interpretation, 164–165
linking, 57
mantling, 41, 42, 45, 57
modes of interpretations, 43, 47–48, 57–58
object of annihilating forces, 158–159
paranoid and depressive, 42
parent–child vicious circles, 41
pathological momentum, 156
precipitation, 117
pre-object relatedness, 152–153
primitive agonies, 164
psychotic, 47
self as object, 155, 159–160
sensation, 155
sound-object, 154–155, 156
splitting and projective identification, 45
survival defences, 152
symbolic play, 48
technical considerations, 46–48
thinking on a single track, 164
unconscious, 39, 42–43
anxieties-of-being, 42, 46, 76
emergence of primitive, 54–58
Anzieu, D., 95, 131, 143, 153
Applied Behavioural Analysis (ABA), 144
ASD *see* Autistic Spectrum Disorders
Atlantis, 93
attractor, 117, 122
Aulagnier, P., 14
autism, 133 *see also* anxieties; infantile autism
anxieties, 40
autistic shapes, 9–10, 123
autistoid object, 222
autisto-psychotic spectrum, 40–46, 60, 158

differentiation between childhood schizophrenia, autism, and psychosis, 44
escaping, 135
grown-up, 138
Houzel on, 72
manoeuvres and defences, 8–10, 84
pathological organisation, 40
psychic retreat, 40–42
psychic states, 198
spared function in, 23, 27
autistic enclaves, 189, 193–194, 214–215
autistic states, 190–194
case vignette, 194
container/contained, 215
preconception of linking, 189
prisoner in, 194
autistic objects, 9–10 *see also* object(s)
hard and soft, 73–74
use of mermaids as, 72
Autistic Spectrum Disorders (ASD), 3, 40
diagnosed in Israel, 45
ego capacity, 11
psychoanalyses of, 41
subtype linked to comorbid psychosis, 46
autistic states, 190, 214 *see also* autistic enclaves
birth, 190
communication between external and internal world, 191–192
container and contained, 193
nothingness, 193, 197
post- and prenatal, 191
primary messenger of otherness, 191
psycho-physical, 190–191, 192–193
three-dimensional space, 192
two-dimensional world, 192
auto-sensual activity, 8, 14, 169, 170, 171, 172, 177, 178 *see also* sensual; sensuousness
awareness
of existential circumstances, 157
premature, 132

INDEX 237

Bachmann, I., 189–190, 192
background of emotional catastrophe (BEC), 156
Balint, M., 100
Baron-Cohen, S., 28, 46
Barrows, P., 33
BEC *see* background of emotional catastrophe
Beebe, B., 24
being alive, 79
Benedetti, G., 226
Bergeret, J., 96
Bergstein, A., 15, 71, 133
beta elements, 3, 4, 176–177, 187 *see also* Bion, W. R.
Bick, E., 71, 118
   adhesive identification, 130
   adhesiveness and two-dimensionality, 121
   feeling of skin/sack, 130
Bion, W. R., 3, 23, 24, 33, 60, 67, 76, 78, 95, 103, 133, 159, 199, 202, 215, 220, 221, 228, 232
   alpha function, 3, 4, 16, 33
   beta elements, 3, 4, 176–177, 187
   beta to alpha elements, 4
   caesura, 116
   container/contained, 3, 16, 193
   dream-work-alpha, 81
   feeling of reciprocity, 117–118
   ignorance and non-knowledge, 15–16
   mother's capacity for reverie, 119
   projective identifications, 84
   proto-representation, 103–104
   psychic digestion system model, 129
   psychic growth facilitation, 4
   psycho-analytic experience, 14–15
   psychotic and non-psychotic parts of personality, 39–40
   on thinking and thoughts, 231
bisexuality
   infant's, 73
   psychic, 68, 72, 83, 115–116, 119, 127
     and container, 121–124, 202
     clinical illustration, 124–127

Bleger, J., 41
   framework of psychoanalysis, 97–98
   ghost world, 98
Blin, D., 94
Bollas, C., 153
borderline autistic, 45, 60
Bowlby, J., 23, 100
Brazelton, T. B., 28
Bremner, J., 130
Brenman Pick, I., 41, 42
Bretherton, I., 105, 106
Britton, R., 42, 134, 208
Bruner, J. S., 26, 131
   capacity for gaze monitoring, 25
   language, 26
Brusset, B., 99, 108
Burhouse, A., 25
Bursztejn, C., 40
Bydlowski, M., 108

child analysis, 44–45
childhood schizophrenia, 44, 49
chronos, 227
Clements, R., 67
communication
   emotional, 24
   external and internal world, 191–192
   face-to-face interpersonal, 24
   interplay and, 81–82
   relationship and, 117
communication with autistic children, 21
   alpha function, 33
   capacity for gaze monitoring, 25
   case vignette, 28–34
   early two-person relationships, 26
   emotional, 24
   eyes, 25
   face-to-face interpersonal, 24
   internal objects, 23
   language and triadic skills, 25–26
   listening, 21–22
   normal development, vision and proto-language, 24–25
   pointing and expressive sounds, 26
   projective identification, 24

psychotherapy, 27–28
representational models, 23
spared function, 23, 27
theory of mind, 24
therapeutic approach, 27–28
therapeutic implications of impairments, 26–28
transference and countertransference, 26, 30
triad of symptoms, 22
two-person psychology, 22
vision, 24–25
conceptual levels of intervention, 11, 68, 83–84
considerations of representability, 119
container/contained, 3, 16, 193, 215 *see also* autistic enclaves; Bion, W. R.
containing function, 95
containing object
    bisexuality of, 121
    pre-conception of, 227
    presence of paternal elements in, 122
containment, 4, 5, 33, 121, 134, 191, 192, 201, 202, 204
    external, 132–133
    partner-in-, 11
Coraline, 76
countertransference, xviii, 13, 16, 26, 27, 30, 48, 73, 84, 98, 111, 112, 127, 144, 179, 193, 198, 220 *see also* transference
Crown, C., 24

Dawson, G., 28
dealing, 8
deficit theories, 6–7
Dejours, Ch., 99, 109
De Masi, F., 14
Demos, V., 24, 26
de M'Uzan, M., 6
depressive anxieties, 42 *see also* anxieties
development of I-ness, 167, 168–171, 187–188
    auto-sensual activity, 170
    beta elements, 176–177, 187
    case vignette, 172–187

    child's unconscious, 187
    fate of sensation, 171, 178
    felt-self, 167, 168, 169, 187, 170
    intrusive projective identification, 177
    Obstructive Object, 178
    psychic reality, 171
    sensation, 168, 170
    sense of orientation, 168
    sensory superego, 178
    sensuousness vs. auto-sensuousness, 169
    symbolising background catastrophe, 185
    too muchness, 177
    unconscious phantasy, 177
development, symbolic, 133, 134
Diatkine, R., 99
Die Wand, 189
dismantling, 131
disobjectification, 102
dissolution, 222, 223, 225, 226, 227
dream life, absence of, 198–200
dreams as complex amalgams, 76–77
dream-work-alpha, 81
drive(s), 2–3, 4, 16, 101–102, 119, 221
    death, 43, 119
    derivatives, 4, 16
    invocatory, 56
Durban, J., 41, 42, 45, 48, 50, 51, 68, 77, 86, 157, 211
    analyst as developmental reparational object, 84
    anxieties, 157
    anxieties-of-being, 76
    autisto-psychotic spectrum, 158
    work of, 151, 152, 165
dynamic systems theory, 122

early developmental disturbances, 7–8
early self-experience, 154–155 *see also* anxieties
Eaton, J. L., 8
    Obstructive Object, 178
    unconscious floor for emotional experience, 168, 169

ego capacity, 11–12
Eigen, M., 153
Emde, R., 117
emotional catastrophe, 152, 157 see also anxieties
    autisto-psychotic spectrum, 158
    awareness of existential circumstances, 157
    case vignette, 161–165
    object of annihilating forces, 158–159
    primitive agonies, 164
    self as object, 159–160
emotional communication, 24
emotional experience, 153–157 see also anxieties
enclave, 198 see also autistic enclaves
Erikson, E., 155
Evans, C. D. S., 94
experience
    of dirtiness, 78
    emotional, 153–157
    traumatic, 226
explanatory interpretations, 26, 47, 54, 83, 85, 164
eyes, 25

FEE see floor for emotional experience
Feldstein, S., 24
felt-self, 167, 168, 187 see also development of I-ness
    in agony, 170
    experiences, 169
Ferro, A., 11
floor for emotional experience (FEE), 156, 168, 169
Fogel, A., 24, 25
fragmentation, 41, 43, 45, 54, 60, 68, 76, 87, 156
Freud, S., 1, 60, 220, 228, 232
    anxiety, 157
    considerations of representability, 119
    difference between sexes, 115
    drive derivatives, 4
    intrauterine life, 96

killing of death, 97
    Mourning and melancholia, 93, 97
    neuro-psychoses of defence, 2
    Beyond the Pleasure Principle, 2, 120
    Topographic Theory, 2
    topographies proposed by, 99
    unconscious meanings and psychic conflicts, 1
Frith, U., 133

Gampel, Y., 215
gaze monitoring, 25
GDR see German Democratic Republic
German Democratic Republic (GDR), 227
ghost world, 98
Gillberg, C., 28
Golse, B., 93, 99, 105
Green, A., 2
    disobjectification, 102
    psychic voids, 3
    work of representation, 118–119
Grotstein, J. S., 56, 153, 155
    pre-conception, 221
    safety from object of primary identification, 56, 83

Haag, G., 40, 44, 45, 56, 111, 118
    rhythmic portrait, 107
    same/not same, 106
Harris Williams, M., 131
Haushofer, M., 189
Heinrich, K., 229
Hobson, R. P., 23, 24
Holland, A. J., 46
Hopper, E., 94
Houser, M., 96
Houzel, D., 27, 40, 44, 45–46, 68, 202
    autism, 72
    precipitation anxiety, 117
    psychic bisexuality, 83, 202
Hoxter, S., 130
Hubley, P., 26, 28
Hugues, P., 94
Hunt, J. M. V., 25

identification
  intracorporal, 56
  intrusive projective, 177
  projective, 24, 84
infanticide, 96
infantile autism, 115, 127
  clinical illustration, 124–127
  splitting of containing object and psychic bisexuality, 115–124
internalisation
  the function of external object, 130
  object, 130
  and projection processes, 129
internal objects, 23, 101
  maternal, 210
intersubjective topography, 101, 109
intersubjectivity, primary, 95
intracorporal identifications, 56
intrauterine virtual object-relation, 93, 95–96
invocatory drive, 56
Isaacs, S., 135

Jaffe, J., 24
Jeannerod, M., 107
Jones, P. B., 46
Joseph, B., 27, 42
judgement of existence, 116

Kaës, R., 99, 108
  third topography, 109
  unconscious alliance, 109–110
kairos, 227
Kanner, L., 27
  immutability, 121
  sameness, 120, 123
Keinan, N., 143
Klein, M., 23, 24, 39, 68
  absorption, 61
  differentiation between childhood schizophrenia, autism, and psychosis, 44
  early two-person relationships, 26
  interaction between different anxieties, 42
  internalisation and projection processes, 129

  objects, 115–116
  symbolic development, 133
  transference, 227
Klein, S., 14
Koslowski B., 28
Koulomzin, M., 24
Kumin, I., 152

Lacan, J., 40, 56
Lai, M.-C., 46
La Llorona, 76
Langer, S. K., 228
language and triadic skills, 25–26
Laplanche, J., 6, 97, 103
Larson, F. V., 46
Laznik, M. C., 40
  invocatory drive, 56
Lebovici, S., 102
Lechevalier, B., 40
Lee, A., 23
Leslie, A. M., 23, 24
levels of interpretation, 164–165
  see also anxieties
Levine, H. B., 2, 3, 6, 10, 11, 14, 16
  anxieties, 39
  beyond neurosis, 68
  psychoanalytic theory, 68–69
Lewy, A., 28
linking, 57 *see also* anxieties
listening, 21–22
live company *see* Alvarez, A.

Mächtlinger, V., 231
Maiello, S., 124, 151, 191, 193, 209, 215
  rhythmic prenatal "song-and-dance" experience, 155
  sound-object, 154–155, 156
Main, M., 28
Malina, 189–190, 192 *see also* autistic enclaves
Mandelbrot, B., 122
mantling, 41, 42, 45, 57 *see also* anxieties
Marty, P., 6
Matte Blanco, I., 229
Maurer, D., 25

Meltzer, D., 26, 41, 68, 73, 82, 117, 137, 193, 196, 200, 215
    adhesiveness and two-dimensionality, 121
    anxieties, 39
    autistic psychic states, 198
    dismantling, 131
    intrusive projective identification, 177
    object internalisation, 130
    psychic skin, 130
    relationship of intimacy, 123
Mentalization Based Treatment, 141
metapsychology, 101
    of the bond, 108–109
    model, 221
    perinatal, 99, 103, 111–112
Miller, L., 27
Miller, P., 14
Misès, R., 40
Missonnier, S., 93, 104
Mitrani, J., 177
Mitrani, J. L., 14, 69
Molinari, E., 85
Moser, U., 226
motherese, 28, 32
mourning the hidden child, 93–94
Murray, L., 28
Musker, J., 67

narcissistic/objectal balance, 102
neonatal intensive care unit (NICU), 161
neurosis, 1–2, 6, 11, 67, 68
Newson, J., 24
NICU *see* neonatal intensive care unit
night terrors, 89–93, 96
Nissen, B., 219, 220, 223, 224, 225, 226
non-neurotic states of mind, 13
no object, 8
normal infant development, 24–25
nothingness, 193, 197 *see also* autistic states

object(s), 12, 95, 115–116 *see also* anxieties; autistic objects
    analyst as, 84
    of annihilating forces, 158–159
    bisexuality of containing, 121
    contact with as, 74
    disobjectification, 102
    of identification, 56, 83
    internal, 101
    internalisation, 130
    intrauterine virtual object-relation, 93
    invested before being perceived, 102–103
    partial to total object-relation, 95
    related contact, 74
    relationship, 95
    rhythmical, 154
    self and, 116
    uterine virtual object-relation, 95, 96
object representation, 103, 107–108
    with bonds, 104–107
    generalised representations of interaction, 105, 106
    internal working models, 105, 106
    investment of interactions, 104–105
    place of the object, 103–104
    strange situation, 105
Obstructive Object, 178
Ogden, T. H., 48, 80 131, 153
one-person psychology, 22
Other, 115
otherness, 42, 72, 115, 116, 127, 191, 192
    clinical illustration, 124–127
    integration of, 121
    pathology of, 115, 127

Papousek, H., 25, 28
Papousek, M., 25, 28
Pessoa, F., 22
Piontelli, A., 144
Pollak, T., 48, 57
Power, D. G., 9, 13–14, 68
    anxieties, 39
pre-conception breast, 221, 231–232
preconception of linking, 189 *see also* autistic enclaves
    postnatal realisation of, 191
premature awareness, 132
pre-object relatedness, 152–153 *see also* anxieties

pre-psychic, 220–223
primary intersubjectivity, 95
primitive agonies, 160, 164 *see also* anxieties
primitive anxieties-of-being, 54–58 *see also* anxieties
projective identification, 24, 84
    intrusive, 177
proto-language, 24–25
    and triadic skills, 25–26
proto-mental, 133
proto-representative sensory traces, 92
psyche, 4, 15, 41, 68, 99, 101, 106, 220, 231
psychic, 226
    conflicts, 1
    growth, 4
    pre-psychic, 220–223
    reality, 171, 229–230
    retreat, 8
    skin, 56, 130
    stability, 119–121, 123
    voids, 3
psychic bisexuality, 83, 115–124
    and container, 121–124
psychoanalysis framework, 97–98
psycho-analytic experience, 14–15
psychoanalytic theory, 68–69, 193
psychoanalytic thinking, 143
psycho-physical *see also* autistic states
    life, 192–193
    survival, 190–191
psychosis
    childhood schizophrenia, autism, and, 44
    comorbid, 46
psychotherapy
    aspects of symbolising through, 167
    joint, 111
psychotic anxieties, 40, 47 *see also* anxieties

reciprocity, 117–118
reclamation, 11, 16, 83–84, 132
Reed, G. S., 3, 14, 69
Reid, S., 26, 27, 33
relationship and communication, 117
representation(s), 2, 5, 6, 10, 13, 16, 17, 61, 69, 79, 96, 109, 110, 119, 120–121 *see also* representing bond before representing object; unrepresented states
    felt-self, 171, 174–176, 182, 186
    models, 23
    work of, 118
representing bond before representing object, 101
    debate between Stolorow and Friedman, 101–102
    disobjectification of the object, 102
    internal objects, 101
    narcissistic/objectal balance, 102
    object is invested in before being perceived, 102–103
    three levels of object representation, 103–108
Resnik, S., 196–197
Rhode, M., 27, 40, 41, 42, 44, 45, 47, 219
rhythm(ical)
    experience, 191, 193
    of exploration, 175
    object, 154
    pre-and postnatal, 155, 190, 197
    of union, 169
Robson, K., 25
Rochat, P., 26
Rosenfeld, D., 143
Rosenfeld, H., 131
rotatory thinking and language, 196–198, 205
Roussillon, R., 14, 69, 153
Rustin, Margaret, 27
Rustin, Michael, 27

SAA *see* self as agent
Salapatak, P., 25
sameness and otherness, 115
Santamaría, A., xiv, xviii
Santamaría, J., 67
SAO *see* self as object
Scaife, M., 25
scale invariance, 122, 123

Scarfone, D., 3, 14, 69
Schore, A., 25
Sechehaye, M. A., 48
second skin, 221, 222, 223
Segal, H., 41, 131, 206
Self, 115, 116
self as agent (SAA), 155
self as object (SAO), 155, 159–160
    see also anxieties
sensation, 155, 168, 170 *see also*
    anxieties; development of
    I-ness
  fate of, 171
  as object, 72, 73
sense of efficacy, 153 *see also* anxieties
sense of orientation, 168
sensory regulation, 131
sensual, 73, 83, 220, 221–223, 227, 232
    see also auto-sensual activity;
    sensuousness
  hyper-, 224
sensuousness, 169–170 *see also* auto-
    sensual activity; sensual
separateness, 43, 55, 193
  awareness of, 169, 197
  defence against, 41
  physical, 9
Shuttleworth, J., 27
skin, missing, 46, 56, 134, 158, 195, 209
    see also second skin; skin ego
skin ego, 131, 153 *see also* psychic, skin
sleep disorder, 89–93
somato-psychic, 9, 122
Soubieux, M. J., 94
sound-object, 154–155, 156 *see also*
    anxieties
spared function in autism, 23, 27
Spitz, R. A., 195
splitting and projective identification, 45
splitting of containing object, 115–124
stability, 119
  periodic, 120
  simple, 119–120, 123
  structural, 120–121
Steiner, J., 40, 42, 205
Stern, D. N., 24, 33, 106, 117

representations of interaction, 105, 110
Striano, T., 26
superego, 99, 157
  deadly, 52
  development of, 133
  sensory, 178
survival defences, 152 *see also* anxieties
symbolic development, 133, 134
symbolic thinking, 142
symbolisation, 131 *see also* development
    of I-ness
  catastrophe, 185
  development of, 172
  through psychotherapy, 167
Symington, J., 130, 152, 177

Tantam, D., 46
thinking, symbolic, 142
three-dimensional space, 192 *see also*
    autistic states
three-dimensional state, 134
too muchness, 175, 177, 187
topography
  case vignette, 89
  intersubjective, 101
  third, 109
  Theory, 2
Torok, M., 97
transference, xviii, 6, 26, 27, 54, 61, 70,
    73, 75, 80, 81, 90, 98, 110, 144,
    176, 196, 204, 211, 212, 215,
    220, 223, 227, 228 *see also*
    countertransference
transgenerational transmission, 205,
    214–215, 226 *see also* autistic
    enclaves
trauma and sublimation theories, 4
Trevarthen, C., 24, 28, 33, 95, 117
  early two-person relationships, 26
triad of symptoms, 22
triangular perception, 134
Turton, P., 94
Tustin, F., 7, 14, 26, 27, 41, 68, 83, 117,
    120, 124, 127, 134, 167, 168,
    177, 195, 196, 197, 201 *see also*
    development of I-ness

anxieties, 39
  on autistic children, 72
  on autistic defences, 84
  autistic objects and autistic shapes, 9–10
  autistic sensation shapes, 123
  container and contained, 193
  encapsulation, 213
  felt-self, 169, 170, 187
  objects in autistic states, 73–74
  premature awareness of separation, 132
  two-dimensional child, 131
two-dimensional *see also* autistic states
  child, 131
  thinking, 134
  world, 192
two-person psychology, 22

unconscious, 1, 15, 85, 168, 202, 222, 224–225
  alliance, 39, 42–43, 109–110
  amential, 109
  anxiety, 39, 42–43, 45, 54, 60
  child's, 187
  conflict, 2
  creativity, 175, 176
  dream-work, 198, 199
  felt-self, 186–187
  guilt, 2
  meaning, 6
  parental dynamic, 102
  phantasy, 8, 40, 41, 42, 44, 47, 57, 59, 135, 144, 158, 177
  unstructured, 4

undrawn patients, 12
unrepresented states, 3–4, 6, 8, 10, 219–220, 223, 228, 232 *see also* representation
  sublimation of, 229–232
Urwin, C., 25
uterine virtual object-relation, 95, 96
Uzgiris, I. C., 25

vision, 24–26
vitalisation, 5, 11, 13, 47, 69, 102, 165, 210
void, 8, 210
  autistic, 198, 205, 208, 214
  psychic, 3, 13, 69

Wagner, A. P., 46
Weddell, D., 130
Weinberg, S., 116
Widlöcher, D., 100
Winnicott, D. W., 5, 75, 220, 229
  anxieties, 39
  early two-person relationships, 26
  fear of breakdown, 6
  primitive agonies, 164
  psychic growth facilitation, 4
  Squiggle Game, 11
withdraw from object, 8
Wittenberg, I., 130
work of representation, 118–119